100 THINGS
PACKERS FANS
SHOULD KNOW & DO
BEFORE THEY DIE

Rob Reischel

TRIUMPH
BOOKS

This book was previously catalogued by the Library of Congress as:
Reischel, Rob, 1969–
    100 things Packers fans should know & do before they die / Rob Reischel.
    p. cm.
    One hundred things Packers fans should know and do before they die
    ISBN 978-1-60078-398-2
    1. Green Bay Packers (Football team)—History. 2. Green Bay Packers (Football team)—Miscellanea. I. Title.
GV956.G7.R44 2010
796.332'640977561—dc22
2010010588

This book is available in quantity at special discounts for your group or organization. For further information, contact:
    Triumph Books LLC
    814 North Franklin Street
    Chicago, Illinois 60610
    (312) 337-0747
    www.triumphbooks.com

Printed in U.S.A.
ISBN: 978-1-60078-870-3
Design by Patricia Frey
Photos courtesy of AP Images unless otherwise indicated

To my daughters, Madison and Mia.
You've brought me more laughter and happiness
than I could have ever imagined.

And to my parents, Bob and Sherry,
who showed me what hard work truly is.

Contents

1 Brett Favre

Brett Favre is the greatest Green Bay Packer of all time.

Chew on that for a second and see how it tastes.

Don Hutson certainly merits consideration. So does Bart Starr. But when the accomplishments of every Packers great are placed under the microscope, it's Favre by a whisker.

Favre set virtually every NFL passing record during his 16 seasons in Green Bay. He was the NFL's first player to win three MVPs. Favre is the game's all-time leader in wins with 186 and 160 of those came with the Packers. Favre never missed a start with Green Bay, and he played in more games (255) than any other Packer. Favre also led the rebirth of an organization that had gone through more than two decades of despair.

Perhaps what separates Favre more than anything is he thrived during an era when football has never been more sophisticated. Hutson (1935–1945) played at a time when football was a weekend event and many of the league's greats still left for war. Starr (1956–1971) played with 225-pound linemen at a time many players got off-season jobs. Today, players get bigger, faster, and stronger by the year. And, remarkably, Favre maintained his greatness and never left the lineup.

Favre's popularity among Packers fans took a hit when he chose to play for the Minnesota Vikings in 2009. Still, what he did in Green Bay may never be equaled. So by the narrowest of margins, Favre gets the nod.

"One thing, I think it's by era," said Ron Wolf, the Packers' former general manager and the man who traded for Favre in February 1992. "I don't think you can pinpoint, but I think certainly in his era he'd be in the top five. When you think of somebody now, you think of the great tradition you guys [have] up there, you're part of that great tradition of the Green Bay Packers. So for Brett Favre to be now said to be the greatest player ever to play for the Green Bay Packers, that's rare air."

Wolf had the courage to trade a first-round draft choice to Atlanta for Favre, who was a second-rounder himself the previous year. But Wolf's deal will go down as one of the most lopsided in league history.

Favre replaced an injured Don Majkowski in Week 3 of the 1992 season and made his first NFL start the following week. Between then and his final start in the 2007 NFC Championship Game, Favre never missed a game—a remarkable run of 275 games, including playoffs. If ever the term "Iron Man" was invented for a player, it was Favre.

"I was fortunate I got to play with Brett Favre for nine years," said former Packers guard Marco Rivera. "His presence in the huddle, his leadership, it forced everybody to play better. You had to bring your 'A' game when you were going to be in Brett Favre's huddle."

Favre certainly brought his "A" game most weeks.

Favre and Mike Holmgren—who coached him from 1992 to 1998—butted heads early as the stubborn coach tried taming the young gunslinger. But as Favre matured, the Packers took off. Favre led the Packers to their first postseason win in 11 years in 1993, and another the following season.

His game then reached new heights from 1995 to 1997. Each of those three seasons, Favre was named the Associated Press' MVP. In that time, Favre threw an NFL-best 112 touchdown passes against just 42 interceptions. The Packers were 37–11 in that stretch, including a remarkable 23–1 at home. And Green Bay went 7–2 in the postseason, highlighted by a win in Super Bowl XXXI and a trip to Super Bowl XXXII.

Brett Favre celebrates a two-point conversion during the Packers' 35–21 victory over the Patriots in Super Bowl XXXI. Favre won three MVPs and set numerous team and NFL records during his 16 years as the Packers' quarterback.

"He truly was as gifted a player as I have ever seen," Holmgren said.

Favre accomplished this all despite developing an addiction to Vicodin, one that led to a 46-day stay in a rehabilitation facility before the 1996 season. But he came back stronger than ever and led the Packers to their first Super Bowl win in 29 years.

"I learned a lot through the '90s of [Favre's] ability to take a receiver who's not even open and putting the ball in a spot where that guy can catch the football," former 49ers quarterback Steve Young said of Favre. "Instead of kicking field goals, Brett Favre was throwing touchdowns when most weren't."

When Holmgren left after the 1998 season, there was an enormous adjustment period for Favre. But he had the Packers back in the postseason by 2001 and led Green Bay to NFC North championships from 2002 to 2004.

Aside from the Super Bowl loss in 1997, Favre's most devastating moment probably came in the 2007 NFC Championship Game. There, he threw an interception on the second play of overtime, which helped the Giants topple the Packers 23–20.

Six weeks later, Favre announced his retirement. He later changed his mind, which led to his controversial trade to the New York Jets on August 6, 2008. Many fans were livid with general manager Ted Thompson for trading Favre—despite the fact Favre began hinting at retirement as early as 2002 and almost seemed to make it an off-season game. But public sentiment swung back in Thompson's direction the following year, when Favre was released by the Jets and signed with archrival Minnesota.

Still, an entire generation of Packers fans grew up on Favre and was spoiled more than they'll ever know.

"He's a tremendous player. He was a joy to coach, day in and day out," said Mike McCarthy, who was Favre's head coach in 2006 and 2007 and his position coach in 1999. "[He has a] unique personality, the way he could affect people, the way he can walk into a room, the effect he had on the room, regardless of the age or the type of people in that room. Clearly one of the most unique individuals I've had the opportunity to work with."

Green Bay played in three postseason games between 1968 and 1991, then played in 22 during Favre's brilliant career, going 12–10 in those contests. Favre led the Packers to seven division titles, and

Green Bay had just one losing season during his stint. Favre was named to nine Pro Bowls as a Packer and was a first- or second-team All-Pro selection six times. He was also the NFC's Player of the Year five times and named the quarterback on the 1990s All-Decade team.

Favre holds virtually every Packers passing record, highlighted by touchdown passes (442), completions (5,377), and yards (61,655). Favre also holds the team record for interceptions (286), but he also threw nearly three times more passes (8,754) than any Packer ever. Perhaps what stands out most, though, is the Packers had a 160–93 regular-season record under Favre (.632), and went 172–103, including the playoffs (.625).

"Brett Favre is one of the greatest quarterbacks in the history of professional football," said Mike Shanahan, who coached the Broncos past Green Bay in Super Bowl XXXII. "You're judged by winning, and he's won more games than any other quarterback who has ever played. He was the face of the Packers and a great credit to our game."

On top of that, Favre was a Hall of Fame teammate, as well. Those that played with Favre marveled at his ability to bring people together, no matter their walk of life.

"Here's why they'll never be another Brett Favre," former Packers safety LeRoy Butler said. "When Brett Favre got there, you had black guys playing a game of spades, white guys playing back-gammon, the younger guys playing video games, the older guys playing hearts. And Brett fit in with every culture.

"He'd go over to the brothers and listen to hip-hop. He'd go over to the white guys and listen to country. He'd go hang out with the hunters, he'd go hang with the young guys. There was no guy that ever did that. Hell, I never did that.

"When he came in the locker room, he didn't wait for people to come over to him. He went over to people. And that wasn't publicized. He didn't want the publicity of that. But he was an unbelievable teammate. I'm telling you, no quarterback has ever done that, to realize there are so many different cultures in the locker room and he could fit in with all of them."

And he fit perfectly in Green Bay.

That's why No. 4 is No. 1 on this list.

2 Vince Lombardi

The greatest coach in the history of the National Football League has been gone for more than four decades now. But good luck going more than a few minutes before the name Vince Lombardi comes up in any discussion regarding the Green Bay Packers.

Take a trip to Lambeau Field, and you'll see a 14-foot statute of Lombardi. The Super Bowl trophy itself has Lombardi's name attached. There's even a man named Saint Vince that roams the parking lot and the stadium on game days. After winning five NFL championships in seven years, it's easy to see why Lombardi will always be revered in the NFL's smallest city.

"He was the best coach ever, and I think few would question or argue that," said Jerry Kramer, a Packers guard from 1958 to 1968. "He always had you ready to go, mentally and physically. All you had to do was watch him and emulate him, and you'd be ready to play. Plus, he was just a tremendous teacher, very thorough. It was an honor to play for him."

Lombardi was beginning to wonder if a head coaching job would ever come his way back in 1959. The Brooklyn native had been a standout guard at Fordham University, part of that school's legendary "Seven Blocks of Granite" offensive line. And when Lombardi's playing days ended, he was an assistant coach at Army

Vince Lombardi paces the sideline during the NFL Championship Game on January 2, 1967. The Packers beat the Dallas Cowboys 34–27 to earn a spot in Super Bowl I against the AFL-champion Kansas City Chiefs, one of five NFL and two Super Bowl championships Lombardi won in Green Bay.

and then with the New York Giants. He had built a reputation as one of the top assistants in football and was seen as a potential successor to Jim Lee Howell when the Giants' coach retired. But in January 1959 all Lombardi knew was he was beginning his off-season job at Federation Bank and Trust, and deep down, he feared he was destined to remain a lifelong assistant coach.

Green Bay was in the market for a head coach, though, and Jack Vainisi, the team's personnel manager, soon came calling. It didn't take long for the two sides to work out a deal that paid Lombardi $36,000 per year for five seasons.

"I want it understood that I am in complete command here," Lombardi told the team's executive committee upon his arrival on February 2, 1959.

Technically, he wasn't, but two days after accepting the head coaching job, Lombardi was also given the vacant general manager position.

"He had prepared for that job for a long time," former Green Bay tackle Norm Masters said of Lombardi. "He came in and he had a plan, and we used his criteria as a leader. He demanded that people respond to his program, and he convinced us that we'd be successful if we listened to him. And we were."

That's for sure.

Lombardi did all he could to reverse the losing culture established under Scooter McLean (1958) and Lisle Blackbourn (1954–1957). His system was predicated on organization and structure, and he demanded perfection. That didn't come easily, of course. But by late in the 1959 season, there were signs of progress as the Packers won their final four games and finished 7–5 for their first winning season in 12 years.

By 1960 Lombardi had guided Green Bay to the NFL Championship Game, where the team fell to Philadelphia 17–13. But the Packers made amends the following year, defeating Lombardi's old New York Giants team 37–0 for the title. In 1962 the Packers not only repeated as world champions, they produced one of the best years in NFL history. Green Bay went 13–1 that season, then toppled the Giants 16–7 for the title.

"His philosophies weren't just those of a football coach," former tackle Bob Skoronski said. "He was like a father and a teacher. We were all part of something special and didn't even know it was happening."

After a two-year drought, Lombardi's Packers defeated Cleveland 23–12 for the 1965 NFL championship. The Packers repeated in 1966, defeating Dallas 34–27 for the NFL championship, then hammering Kansas City 35–10 in Super Bowl I.

"Coach Lombardi was so special, and the biggest reason why was his ability to always motivate people," said Boyd Dowler, a Packers wide receiver from 1959 to 1969. "He motivated the same people over a nine-year period, and the nucleus was almost always the same…you never saw a real letdown."

Lombardi knew his aging team could easily let down in 1967. So, before that season, he had a message for that group.

"The one thing that really stands out is when we were going for three straight championships, that was something that had never been done before," said Tom Brown, a Packers cornerback from 1964 to 1968. "He told us we wouldn't appreciate it until we were 50 years old. And the Old Man—we always used to call him 'the Old Man'—was right."

Winning that third straight championship was a challenge like no other. The Packers appeared to have tired legs when they lost their final two regular-season games that year. But they defeated Dallas 21–17 in arguably the greatest game ever played—one known simply as the Ice Bowl. That gave Green Bay its third straight NFL championship, and two weeks later, the Packers defeated Oakland 33–14 in Super Bowl II.

"We were a group of men who were always together," said former wideout Carroll Dale. "The offense was not geared toward one individual. We took what the defense gave us, and that helped us rise to another level."

"He created a profile for high performance and leadership," added former cornerback Doug Hart. "He told you to figure out your target, then commit yourself to that. His role was to be a highly demanding leader, and he knew how to play his role."

At the end of the 1967 season, Lombardi resigned as head coach but stayed on as general manager. Needing a new challenge, Lombardi accepted the head coaching job in Washington in 1969 and took over a team that hadn't had a winning season in 14 years. To the surprise of no one, Lombardi's first Redskins team went 7–5–2.

It proved to be Lombardi's only team in Washington, as he died of cancer in September 1970.

"He altered my life dramatically and for the better," said Bob Long, a Packers wide receiver from 1964 to 1967. "He changed my football life and my business life, and I learned a lot from him. I learned to be mentally disciplined. I learned that, in business, everything needs to be done correctly. I learned that when I had a meeting, you get there 20 minutes early. I learned to set goals. I learned so much from Lombardi, it's incredible."

Lombardi finished his Green Bay career with a 98–30–4 record (.766), including a remarkable 9–1 mark in the playoffs. And in 1971 he was inducted into the Pro Football Hall of Fame.

"Lombardi always preached that whole team concept," Masters said. "He was the kind of guy who pushed you hard, and you didn't realize it until afterward, but he made you better than you thought you could be."

"He was easy to work for as long as you did your job," added former linebacker Dan Currie. "He was a guy you couldn't BS. He was exactly what he was. He was an educator and he was very smart."

On June 11, 2013, Lombardi would have celebrated his 100th birthday. And even though he'd been gone from Green Bay for more than 45 years, today's Packers spoke of Lombardi like he'd been in the building last week.

"Everybody's inspired by Coach Lombardi," Packers coach Mike McCarthy said. "It's important to always recognize that, particularly here in Green Bay. I think he's not only impressed upon us a sense of direction, but also the coaching profession and really society.

"It's amazing how many times his name comes up in every type of conversation, whether you're sitting at the table with a bunch of businessmen or on a golf course playing in a charity tournament, and how many things point back to coach Lombardi's time here. You talk about a major contribution not only to the Green Bay Packers...but what we stand for as a society today."

Packers quarterback Aaron Rodgers agreed.

"You see his face all over this place," Rodgers said. "And this is a special place to play because we've had so many names that are synonymous with the beginning of football and the emergence of football and the greatness of this franchise."

Lombardi is a huge reason for that greatness. And it's why he's still celebrated as the greatest coach in NFL history.

3 Curly Lambeau

Who would have thought tonsillitis was a good thing?

Back in 1919 Earl L. "Curly" Lambeau was forced to miss his spring semester at Notre Dame when he developed severe tonsillitis. The Green Bay native returned home, and along with former *Green Bay Press-Gazette* sports editor George Calhoun, helped form the Green Bay Packers.

Over the next 31 years, Lambeau would serve as the Packers' head coach, vice president, and a player for the team. No matter what he was doing, things were never dull.

"He was very interesting," said Bob Kahler, who played under Lambeau from 1942 to 1944. "He had a great personality, very outgoing and friendly, and really a players' coach. He was a very flamboyant guy. He was a flashy dresser and he drove a Lincoln Zephyr. But he expected you to do a job and made sure you did it. He was really a great coach."

Lambeau was a player/coach for the first Packers team in 1919 and enjoyed immediate success. That group went 10–1 playing non-league games against teams throughout Wisconsin and upper Michigan.

By 1921 the Packers were doing incredibly well, and Lambeau led a charge to apply for membership in the American Professional Football Association, which later became the NFL. Green Bay became a league powerhouse under Lambeau by the late 1920s. Between 1929 and 1931, the Packers compiled a 34–5–2 record and won three straight championships, which were decided at that time by regular season standings, not postseason games. The 1929 team was 12–0–1, then the Packers went 10–3–1 in 1930 and 12–2 in 1931. And those three teams outscored their foes by a combined score of 723–220.

"Curly was fairly strict with his players," said Hal Van Every, who played for Lambeau from 1940 to 1941. "He was pretty tough on the guys, but that's the way we wanted it back then. We thought that was the best way to win."

Green Bay's first postseason game came in 1936, when the Packers defeated the Boston Redskins 21–6 for the NFL title at the New York Polo Grounds. After the Packers lost the championship to the New York Giants in 1938, they gained revenge the following season and defeated New York 27–0 for the championship in a game played at Milwaukee's State Fair Park.

Lambeau guided the Packers to another title in 1944, when they topped the Giants 14–7 at the Polo Grounds. He left for the Chicago Cardinals after the 1949 season, when he tried to take over the team but lost an internal power struggle with the executive committee. Lambeau had some amazing accomplishments while in Green Bay, though, none bigger than winning back the Packers from the NFL in 1923 after a conspiracy involving George Halas and the Chicago Bears. Afterward, Lambeau became one of just six coaches to earn at least 200 career wins. He coached seven Packers who reached the Hall of Fame. He started daily practices in the 1920s and began flying to road games in 1938. He was seen as one of the pioneers of the passing game. And, of course, one of the most hallowed stadiums in all of sports was later named after him.

Because the Packers didn't play their first league game until 1921, Lambeau's official career statistics don't begin until that time. But over the next 29 years, Lambeau compiled a remarkable 212–106–21 record (.667), including playoffs, and led Green Bay to six NFL championships. He also enjoyed a nine-year playing career, in which he threw 24 touchdown passes and had 110 career points.

While Lambeau was embraced nationally, his outgoing life-style—which included three marriages and three divorces—wasn't a hit in conservative Green Bay. And it wasn't until later in life that Lambeau was welcomed back as the head of the Packers.

Today, his name remains gold in Green Bay.

4 Don Hutson

Back in 1935, there was no such thing as a sophisticated passing attack. Heck, receivers didn't even run pass routes in those days.

Then along came Don Hutson, who revolutionized the wide receiver position and set 18 records during a brilliant 11-year career.

Hutson so dominated his position that *Sports Illustrated*'s Peter King concluded that Hutson was the greatest player in pro football history. Former Packers historian Lee Remmel listed Hutson as the No. 1 player in team history when he put together a top 50 list for Triumph Books in 2005.

"I think he's the best [player] ever," said Bob Kahler, a halfback with the Packers from 1942 to 1944. "I really do. I've never seen anybody come around who was any better than he was."

"If you missed Hutson, you missed one of the greatest ever," said Hal Van Every, who played with Hutson in 1940 and 1941. "He had that speed and he had some pretty good passers back then. But they could just lay the ball out there, and he'd run under it. There was nothing better than old Don Hutson. He was just an amazing player."

The Packers came perilously close to never having Hutson suit up for them, though. A star at Alabama, Hutson signed deals with both Green Bay and the Brooklyn (football) Dodgers. But Joe Carr, the league's president, ruled that the Packers' contract with Hutson was postmarked 17 minutes earlier than Brooklyn's, and so Hutson became a Packer. It was one of the best things that ever happened to the franchise.

In 116 games, Hutson caught 99 touchdown passes, an average of 0.85 per game. Comparatively, Jerry Rice—the other player usually discussed as the best receiver ever—averaged 0.65 TDs per game during a time the NFL became a pass-happy league.

"Different era, different time, but the numbers he put up in a time when they didn't throw as many passes were unbelievable," said Mike Holmgren, who coached the Packers from 1992 to 1998, in an interview with ESPN. "He was better than everybody he was playing against, clearly."

That's for sure.

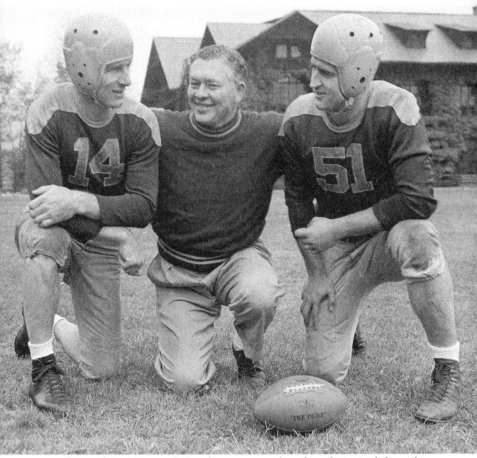

Packers end Don Hutson (14), who set 18 records and revolutionized the wide receiver position, poses with head coach Curly Lambeau and tailback Irv Comp (51) during training at Bear Mountain, New York, in November 1944.

Hutson led the NFL in receptions eight times and had the most consecutive seasons leading the league in overall TDs (four in a row, on two occasions). He led the league in receiving touchdowns nine times and receiving yards seven times. Hutson was a nine-time All-Pro and received the NFL's Joe F. Carr Trophy as the league's most outstanding player in 1941 and 1942. He held 18 records when he retired, 10 of which were still standing when he died in

1997. Among the records Hutson still holds today are scoring 29 points in a quarter, leading the NFL in scoring five times, and leading the league in overall TDs eight times.

Hutson was also credited with creating routes such as Z-outs, buttonhooks, and hook-and-gos. His 9.5-second speed in the 100-yard dash helped change the way the passing game was viewed. And several experts have named him the greatest player of the 20th century.

"Hutson was just amazing," Kahler said. "You could call him the [Michael] Jordan of our sport back then."

Hutson, who also doubled as a defensive back and a kicker, went on to set NFL records in touchdown receptions and 200-yard receiving games (four). During two different seasons, he averaged more than 23 yards per reception, and he averaged a whopping 16.4 yards per catch for his career.

But Hutson's contribution to the game extended far beyond just numbers. When he first broke into the league, most teams had predominantly running offenses. But Hutson changed that in Green Bay. He helped make the Packers one of league's most dangerous passing outfits, and he changed how offense was played.

"Teams used to line their ends in tight," Kahler said. "But teams always had two or three guys on him. Then [Packers coach] Curly [Lambeau] got smart and started splitting the ends out. He was the first one to do that. And defenses didn't know how to react. It really helped the running game and really helped Hutson."

Which is why some of Hutson's better years came during the twilight of his career. In 1942, Hutson's eighth year in the league, he set career highs in receptions (74), yards (1,211), and touchdowns (17). In fact, Hutson accounted for 46 percent of his receptions, touchdowns, and receiving yards over his final four years in the league—a time several players were also called away to World War II.

Hutson's No. 14 was retired in 1951, making him the first Packer to receive that honor. He was named to the NFL's All–50-Year Team and 75th Anniversary Team. Then in 1994 the Packers built a $4.7 million, state-of-the-art, indoor practice facility. Its name? The Don Hutson Center. Three years later, one of the greatest Packers ever passed at the age of 84.

"He just had great speed and great hands," Hall of Fame receiver Raymond Berry said of Hutson. "Lean and swift, and, boy, he could catch the heck out of it. And they threw an awful lot of deep balls to him. When Don Hutson played, his numbers and career consistency are practically unsurpassed."

5 Bart Starr

Before there was Joe Montana or Tom Brady, there was Bryan Bartlett Starr, known affectionately as Bart.

Accurate. Composed. Precise. Flawless.

Starr was the perfect leader for a Green Bay Packers team that had it all and won five world titles in the 1960s. And at the end of the day, Starr will be remembered as one of the greatest quarterbacks—and winners—in NFL history.

"You couldn't find a quarterback better suited for our offense than Bart," running back Jim Taylor said of Starr. "For my money, he's the best quarterback of all time."

Starr often gets overlooked in those discussions because he didn't put up the gaudy statistics so many other passers have. But Starr played in a run-first era, and his résumé of winning matches anyone who has ever played the position. Starr won five world championships between 1961 and 1967, including two Super Bowls, giving him more titles than any other quarterback. Starr was arguably the greatest postseason quarterback ever, compiling a 9–1 playoff record with wins in his last nine games.

Starr won MVP honors in both Super Bowls I and II. He was named to four Pro Bowls, led the NFL in passing three times, and was the league's MVP in 1966. Most important, though, was the fact Starr helped guide Green Bay to a 74–20–4 regular-season record between 1961 and 1967, a .787 win-loss percentage.

Green Bay's offense always started with the run game. But when the Packers needed a play by air, Starr rarely let them down.

"Bart almost never made a mistake," said Jerry Kramer, the Packers' right guard at the time. "He was a caretaker for the offense, but he could be more than that if we needed him to be. Bart was exactly what we needed at that position."

It still seems remarkable that Starr is in the discussion of greatest quarterbacks of all-time when you consider the path he took to arrive there.

Starr missed much of his junior and senior seasons at the University of Alabama due to back injuries. With NFL brass leery of Starr physically, he wasn't chosen until the 17th round of the 1956 draft.

Starr endured three rather nondescript seasons in which he played under coaches Lisle Blackbourn and Scooter McLean and threw 13 touchdown passes and 25 interceptions. He also could never win the starting job outright in that time. Then Lombardi was hired, and Starr's career skyrocketed.

The son of a career Air Force master sergeant, Starr had the mental fortitude that was perfect for the fantastically demanding Lombardi. By the end of Lombardi's first year, Starr had won over his new coach with sensational performances in victories over the Los Angeles Rams and San Francisco 49ers to help Green Bay close the year 7–5.

"In Bart Starr, we're going to have one of the great quarterbacks in football," Lombardi told Frank Gifford on his radio show following the season.

Lombardi was right. While Starr's arm was far from cannonlike, and he didn't scare anybody physically, few have ever been smarter. Starr understood every intricacy of Lombardi's offense, recognized all the complexities a defense could throw at him, and almost always made the right decision.

Starr led the Packers to the 1960 NFL Championship Game, where they lost 17–13 to Philadelphia. It would be the only postseason game Starr would ever lose. Over the next seven seasons, Green Bay dominated the NFL unlike any team in history. There were NFL championships. The Ice Bowl. And later Super Bowl titles. And at the center of them all was the steady hand of Starr.

"The reason we had success is because that was a great football team," said Starr, who was inducted into the Pro Football Hall of Fame in 1977. "I was just one part of a great team. You look at the quality players and look at the leadership we had, and it's easy to understand why we won. I was just so blessed to be in Green Bay when I was and to be led by a gentleman [Lombardi] who's difficult to describe."

Starr retired following the 1971 season. But four years later, he returned as coach and general manager of a franchise heading south in a hurry. Unfortunately for Starr, the Packers never changed directions during his nine-year tenure. In that time, Green Bay went 52–76–3 and qualified for the playoffs just once. Starr was replaced following the 1983 season.

"Going back to coach in Green Bay was the biggest mistake I ever made in my life," Starr said. "I was approached by the organization, and it turned out to be an enormous mistake. I was extremely disappointed. I disappointed the Packers and their fans. I accept all responsibility. I just didn't get it done. I haven't ever really sat down and analyzed what went wrong. Early on, my inexperience hurt us, but in the later years, we had some good draft choices and we were beginning to make progress. But I don't want it to sound like I'm making excuses. I just didn't get it done."

Those who enjoyed Starr's legendary playing career know he almost always got it done on the field. That's why the most vivid memories of Starr are still from his terrific playing days—not his failed coaching stint.

"I would hope people remember the playing days first, and not the coaching years," Starr said. "Being part of a team that was so unselfish was amazing. What we were able to accomplish was very meaningful, and the fact we were able to get it done as a team."

Thanks largely to one of the greatest triggermen of all-time.

6 The Ice Bowl

Willie Wood walked out to his car on December 31, 1967. His battery had died. Wood was shivering from the frigid temperatures. Never, ever, did Wood think the NFL Championship Game between his Green Bay Packers and the Dallas Cowboys would be played that day.

"Never," Wood said. "I didn't think there was a chance in hell they'd make us play that day."

If that had that been the case, the most famous game in NFL history would have never taken place. One of the most memorable endings in league history wouldn't have transpired. And the Green Bay Packers may have never claimed their fifth world championship in seven years.

Instead, all of the above unfolded on a day that will never be forgotten.

Not only did Green Bay defeat Dallas 21–17 that afternoon, when Bart Starr scored on a one-yard touchdown run with 13 seconds left. The Packers also achieved greatness in some of the most miserable conditions ever.

The temperature at kickoff was 13 degrees below zero and –46 with the wind chill. The game was played on a sheet of ice after the field's $80,000 heating system broke—or was turned off by Packers coach Vince Lombardi, as some believe. The referees' whistles froze. One fan died due to exposure, and several others were treated for frostbite. Making it even worse, Lombardi wouldn't allow anyone except linemen to wear gloves. Immediately afterward, the game was dubbed the "Ice Bowl."

"The Ice Bowl was just incredible," said former linebacker Jim Flanigan, a rookie that season. "Lombardi wouldn't let you wear gloves, and we had cut-off long johns and just regular shirts and T-shirts. But once you're cold, you're cold. We'd come back to the sideline and warm up by the space heaters. But I've never been through anything like it."

No one who competed that day was ever part of something like it again. Yet the league had no intention of ever halting the game, which appeared to be a good thing for Green Bay early on. Packers quarterback Bart Starr engineered an 82-yard touchdown drive— one he capped with an eight-yard TD pass to Boyd Dowler—on Green Bay's first possession. Then early in the second quarter, Starr and Dowler hooked up for a 46-yard scoring pass and a 14–0 lead.

Dallas closed to 14–10 by halftime, though. First, Starr was sacked and fumbled deep in his own territory, and George Andrie returned it seven yards for a Dallas score. Then the normally sure-handed Wood fumbled a punt, setting up a Dallas field goal shortly before intermission.

On the first play of the fourth quarter, the Cowboys took a 17–14 lead when Dan Reeves threw an option pass to Lance Rentzel for a 50-yard TD. It stayed that way until late in the game, when the Packers took over on their own 32-yard line with 4:50 remaining. For this proud but aging Green Bay team, the next few minutes would determine their place in history.

Mount a game-winning drive against Dallas' vaunted Doomsday Defense, and become the first team in NFL history to win three consecutive championships. Fail, and see their dynasty come to an end. Anyone who knew these Packers understood failure wasn't an option.

Green Bay methodically marched down the field to the Cowboys' 1-yard line. But after Donny Anderson was stopped for no gain on second down, the Packers used their final timeout with 16 seconds left. Starr went to the sideline to discuss what play to run with Lombardi, and the two chose a wedge play, in which fullback Chuck Mercein would get the ball. Immediately after calling the play, though, Starr worried that Mercein might slip on the ice rink that was Lambeau Field and decided to keep the ball himself.

Right guard Jerry Kramer found a rare piece of the field that wasn't iced over, came off the ball fast and hard, and immediately cut Dallas tackle Jethro Pugh. Center Ken Bowman finished Pugh off, knocking him back into a linebacker. The fantastic double-team block gave Starr just the room he needed. And when Starr crossed the goal line, the Packers had one of the most dramatic victories in league history.

"People want to always talk about that play. But what personifies the character and make-up of that football team was the drive," Kramer said. "That was a perfect example of what those teams were all about. On that drive, we were absolutely brilliant. Chuck Mercein, Donny Anderson, Boyd Dowler, Bart, the entire offensive line. They were all outstanding."

Starr was in full agreement. "In so many ways, that drive kind of summed up everything that era stood for," Starr said. "[Lombardi] always preached perfection, and on that last drive, we almost had to be perfect. And we were."

As Packers QB Bart Starr calls the signals, steam escapes from his mouth during the bitterly cold Ice Bowl. Starr tossed two TDs and dove for another with time running out to lead the Packers to a 21–17 win over the Dallas Cowboys and their third consecutive NFL title on December 31, 1967.

Afterward, the Packers rushed to the locker room, hoping to warm their frozen bodies. But warming up just wasn't in the cards on this day.

"When the game finally ended, everybody went in looking to take a hot shower, but all we had was cold water," Flanigan said. "All the hot water had gotten used in the bathrooms through the game. It was that kind of day."

An unforgettable day is what it was. And it made for a perfect ending to Green Bay's brilliant run in the 1960s.

The Packers went on to defeat Oakland 33–14 two weeks later in Super Bowl II. That gave Green Bay its second straight Super Bowl title and its fifth NFL championship in seven years. But the win over the Raiders truly was secondary. What had taken place 14 days earlier, a game that will be discussed for generations to come, was the real championship that year.

It's a game that will forever be frozen in time.

"That game was the focal point of everything," Dowler said. "The Super Bowl was almost anticlimactic. And I think that game against Dallas and that season was kind of the climax to the whole period."

7 Super Bowl XXXI

There are times former Packers running back Edgar Bennett allows himself to drift back to 1996. Oh, sure, raising that Lombardi Trophy as champions of Super Bowl XXXI was the ultimate highlight for Bennett and the Green Bay Packers. But the entire ride remains the greatest memory of Bennett's football life.

"I really enjoyed the journey of it, from start to finish," said Bennett. "From training camp through the end of the season, I enjoyed all of that. And I really enjoyed a lot of off-the-field stuff. It kind of gave us an indication of what we were in store for at the end of the year.... I enjoyed the coaches, the people, my teammates. We made the most of the opportunity. We had fun. We had fun at practice. We had fun off the field. It was a brotherhood. We went over to each other's homes, and just the camaraderie was amazing."

So were the results.

Green Bay ranked first in the NFL in total offense and total defense, something no NFL team has done since. The Packers outscored their opponents by a remarkable total of 456–210.

Then, after rolling through the NFC playoffs, the Packers toppled a spunky New England team 35–21 in Super Bowl XXXI. Green Bay, which entered the game a 14-point favorite, captured the organization's first title in 29 years.

"The biggest thing I remember was holding that trophy up and seeing [Vince] Lombardi's name," said former Packers safety LeRoy Butler. "It brought a tear to my eye because we said the trophy was coming back home. It was supposed to represent this city and these fans. They named the trophy after a former Green Bay Packer. I mean, it can't get any bigger than that."

Green Bay's heroes that night in New Orleans were abundant:

- Return man Desmond Howard, in danger of being cut from the team in August, set a Super Bowl record with 244 return yards and became the first special-teams player to earn MVP honors. Howard's 99-yard kickoff return for a TD in the third quarter broke open a six-point game and was the biggest moment in Green Bay's win.

- Quarterback Brett Favre, playing less than an hour away from his hometown of Kiln, Mississippi, threw two touchdown passes and no interceptions. His 54-yard TD strike to Andre Rison came on the Packers' second play of the game, and he later hooked up with Antonio Freeman for an 81-yard TD that, at the time, was the longest reception in Super Bowl history.

- Reggie White, the greatest free-agent acquisition in NFL history and the man who made it chic to play in Green Bay, had three sacks of New England quarterback Drew Bledsoe.

- Green Bay's defense intercepted Bledsoe four times, with cornerbacks Doug Evans and Craig Newsome, safety Mike Prior, and linebacker Brian Williams all notching picks.

"It's hard to express right now," Packers coach Mike Holmgren said that night. "I look at the faces of my players and my coaches, and I see their expressions. And I am humbled by that. I am overwhelmed by it. I'm sure it will set in some time [today]. I'm so happy for those guys. They worked very, very hard for this."

Green Bay's journey to this point was remarkable. The Packers began the season 8–1, but a slew of injuries at the wide receiver position—including that of standout Robert Brooks (ACL)—began to take a toll. Green Bay lost back-to-back games that November—including a Monday night setback in Dallas—and its dream season appeared in danger. But the Packers turned things around with a 24–9 win in St. Louis, a game in which Green Bay rallied from an early 9–0 deficit. That started the Packers on a roll, and the team finished the year with five straight wins and earned the NFC's top seed.

Green Bay steamrolled San Francisco and Carolina by a combined score of 65–27 in the NFC playoffs, then awaited upstart New England.

"We really didn't think there was a team out there that could beat us," Butler said. "That's not to disrespect anybody. We were just playing terrific football, and that's how we felt."

Early on in Super Bowl XXXI, though, Bledsoe was having his way with the Packers' defense. After New England fell behind 10–0, Bledsoe threw for a pair of scores, and at the end of the highest-scoring first quarter in Super Bowl history, the Patriots held a 14–10 lead.

But the Packers took control in the second quarter. Just 56 seconds into the period, Favre and Freeman hooked up on the 81-yard strike that gave Green Bay a 17–14 lead. Freeman got one-on-one coverage against rookie safety Lawyer Milloy, a talented player, but one who couldn't run with Freeman. The Patriots blitzed, but Favre beat it and delivered a strike to Freeman. Green Bay never trailed again.

"I saw [Lawyer Milloy] come up," Freeman said that night. "He was aggressive. There was nobody behind him. I knew all I had to

Brett Favre celebrates his second-quarter touchdown in Super Bowl XXXI with tight ends Jeff Thomason (83) and Keith Jackson (88). Favre's two-yard end-zone run put the Packers ahead 27–14, a lead they never relinquished en route to a 35–21 victory.

do was beat him at the line and Brett [Favre] would deliver a great ball. When I was running, all I could think about was all of those people who doubted me coming out of college. They said I couldn't run across the middle. They said I didn't have 4.3 speed. Now, America, you have to be a believer."

Green Bay's lead grew to 27–14 by halftime. But, late in the third quarter, New England running back Curtis Martin ripped off an 18-yard TD run to make it 27–21. On the ensuing kickoff, however, Howard fielded Adam Vinatieri's kickoff at the 1-yard line. The Packers' wedge sprung Howard loose, and 99 yards later, he was in the end zone. Favre and tight end Mark Chmura hooked up on a two-point play that gave the Packers a 35–21 lead.

"Desmond's the man," defensive tackle Gilbert Brown said. "If you give him just a little block, he's going to take it all the way."

From there, the Packers teed off on Bledsoe, as well as New England's entire offense, and were never challenged again.

It was an amazing ending for arguably the most popular team in Packers history.

A generation of Packers fans had watched miserable football, as Green Bay made the postseason just two times between 1968 and 1991. But things changed when Holmgren and Favre arrived in 1992, and White joined them a year later.

"You can't replicate what it is we did," Packers guard Aaron Taylor said. "That was an unbelievable team, an unbelievable time, an unbelievable experience."

The state of Wisconsin and Packers fans everywhere rejoiced as their long wait for a championship was over. And inside the victorious locker room, Holmgren stood proud and delivered the following message: "This trophy, men, is named after Vince Lombardi. As important as it is to every player in the league, it's more important to us. This is where it belongs. This trophy is for everyone in the Green Bay Packers organization."

And on January 26, 1997, it came home to where it belonged.

8 1962 Packers

Norm Masters kept the letter his whole life. The one where Vince Lombardi expressed tremendous gratitude to his 1962 Green Bay Packers. Where the legendary coach thanked his team for their mental toughness, applauded their character, and reminded them that there is no substitute for winning.

Then, in conclusion, Lombardi wrote that he was sending every player a color television.

"A color TV was big-time back in those days," said Masters, an offensive tackle. "But, really, that letter has meant a lot to me. I've used it many times in my life, and I used so much of what Coach Lombardi taught us."

Those 1962 Packers taught Lombardi a thing or two, as well. And of the 12 NFL championships that have been won in Green Bay, those '62 Packers are widely regarded as the finest team in franchise history.

"That probably was the best year we had during the glory years," quarterback Bart Starr said. "Everything just kind of aligned right that season. We avoided injuries that season. It was our fourth year with Vince, so we all knew just what he wanted. And a lot of our core guys were in their prime. It was an incredible season."

Boy, was it ever.

The Packers went 13–1 during the regular season that year, the second-best winning percentage in team history. They defeated the New York Giants 16–7 to win their second straight NFL championship. And Green Bay outscored its opponents 415–148, a ratio of nearly 3:1. Only a loss to Detroit on Thanksgiving stopped the Packers from achieving perfection.

"That was a great football team, probably the best of any we had there," safety Willie Wood said. "I look back now, and it's incredible how close we were to going unbeaten. That was an incredible football team. There won't be many like that one again."

That's for sure.

Green Bay raced to a 10–0 start, and just two of those games were decided by single digits. After the Packers' loss in Detroit, they won their final three games—including road contests against the San Francisco 49ers and Los Angeles Rams—and won the Western Conference by two games over Detroit.

That set up a repeat of the 1961 NFL Championship Game, where the Packers defeated the New York Giants 37–0. The game was played in brutal conditions at Yankee Stadium, with winds gusting to 40 miles per hour and a game-time temperature of 13 degrees.

But Green Bay beat both the Giants and the elements 16–7. Ray Nitschke, the game's eventual MVP, had a pass deflection that led to an interception and recovered two fumbles. Jim Taylor set a playoff record with 31 carries and a touchdown. And Jerry Kramer banged home three field goals. The Giants' only score came when they blocked a Max McGee punt for a touchdown.

"That team was incredible," said former tight end Ron Kramer, who spent seven years in Green Bay. "Everybody was in their prime, everybody had a great year."

Taylor bulldozed for 1,474 yards and 19 touchdowns that year, two marks that stood for 41 years before Ahman Green broke them in 2003. Starr had his best season yet, completing 62.5 percent of his throws and finishing with a 90.7 passer rating.

The dynamic pass-catching duo of Boyd Dowler and McGee combined for 98 receptions, more than any pair of receivers in the Lombardi era. And the offensive line of left tackle Bob Skoronski, left guard Fuzzy Thurston, center Jim Ringo, right guard Jerry Kramer, and right tackle Forrest Gregg was unparalleled.

Jim Taylor (31) scampers through a gaping hole in the New York Giants defense to score the Packers' only touchdown in the 1962 NFL title game at Yankee Stadium. Green Bay held on to win 16–7 for their second straight championship.

Individual defensive statistics from that time weren't kept, but the Packers' unit included future Hall of Famers in Nitschke, Wood, defensive end Willie Davis, and cornerback Herb Adderley. That group allowed just 10.6 points per game and forced a remarkable 50 turnovers.

It's easy to see why Lombardi took the time to write a letter to everyone who played on that team.

"I'm one of the few guys who saved that letter," said Masters, who played with the Packers from 1957 to 1964, but died in 2011. "Even Vince Lombardi Jr. asked me once where I got it, and I said, 'Your dad sent it out to the team.' It's really special to me."

Just like that 1962 team remains special to Green Bay's fans.

9 Ron Wolf

When Ron Wolf arrived in Green Bay in November 1991, the Green Bay Packers had posted just five winning seasons in 24 years. They had made just two playoff appearances in that time, gone through five coaches who all posted losing records, and suffered through nearly a quarter-century of futility. When Wolf left nearly a decade later, the Packers had become arguably the NFL's most successful franchise.

"What we did up there defies description," said Wolf, who has since been nominated for the Pro Football Hall of Fame. "No one thought the Green Bay Packers could win again."

But win they did, like no other time since Vince Lombardi was in charge.

Among Wolf's most impressive accomplishments:

- NFC championships in 1996 and 1997, with a victory in Super Bowl XXXI
- The NFL's best regular-season record from the advent of free agency in 1993 to 2000 (83–45, a .648 winning percentage)
- Seven consecutive winning seasons (1992–1998) and nine years in a row without a losing mark
- Six consecutive playoff appearances (1993–1998) and three consecutive NFC Central Division titles (1995–1997)
- A 25-game regular-season winning streak at Lambeau Field, the second-longest in NFL history
- 101 total victories in nine seasons

"I was very, very fortunate with Ron Wolf because a lot of people didn't know who he was, and a lot of people questioned that," said Bob Harlan, the Packers president at the time and the man who hired Wolf. "In 1991 we had been bad for so long, and there was nothing to indicate we were going to get better. And when I hired Ron, a lot of people didn't know him and questioned it. But in my mind, he was the strong type of leader we needed. We needed someone to come in here and take this thing by the neck and just change it. And he did it."

Just 10 weeks after the Packers hired Wolf, he traded a first-round draft pick to Atlanta for quarterback Brett Favre. The following season, Favre led the Packers to just their second winning season since 1989, and he'd go on to establish himself as one of the finest quarterbacks in league history.

In April 2000, Wolf also sent disappointing cornerback Fred Vinson to Seattle for running back Ahman Green. Green would later become the Packers' all-time rushing leader.

"Those were two pretty good ones, weren't they?" Wolf chuckled, when asked of those trades. "Favre's a certain first-ballot Hall of Famer. Ahman Green...that's not bad."

Wolf's foray into free agency wasn't too bad, either. Wolf signed defensive end Reggie White in 1993, a move that gave the Packers instant credibility among free agents. Wolf also signed free agents such as defensive end Sean Jones, defensive tackle Santana Dotson, and return-ace Desmond Howard, who all made enormous contributions to the Packers' run to Super Bowl XXXI.

"Ron is a tireless worker," Bill Parcells said during a 1998 interview. "I don't think there is a better personnel guy. He has a tremendous understanding of the game, and he is smart. He always wants to learn, his mind is always working."

As skilled as Wolf was with trades and free agency, his calling card was always the NFL Draft. Wolf began his career as an NFL scout in Oakland, and even while he was in charge of the Packers, scouting came first. During an average week in the regular season, Wolf would be on the road scouting from Tuesday through Saturday.

"I look for guys who make plays," he once said. "If I watch a guy, and he isn't making plays at the college level, how can he make them at this level?"

Wolf's keen eye for talent helped him assemble some of the best draft classes in team history. Wolf's 1995 draft included cornerback Craig Newsome, fullback William Henderson, linebacker Brian Williams, wideout Antonio Freeman, and guard Adam Timmerman—who all started on the 1996 Super Bowl championship team. Wolf's 2000 draft was another gem, as he found future Pro Bowlers in tight end Bubba Franks, tackle Chad Clifton, and defensive end Kabeer Gbaja-Biamila, as well as standout tackle Mark Tauscher.

He also drafted players such as running back Dorsey Levens, safety Darren Sharper, wideouts Donald Driver and Robert Brooks, linebacker Wayne Simmons, tight end Mark Chmura, guard Marco Rivera, cornerbacks Doug Evans and Mike McKenzie, and quarterback Matt Hasselbeck.

"He likes to say he owes me a lot, but I think it works both ways," Favre said of Wolf. "He'll be talked about like Vince Lombardi was for a long time."

Rightfully so.

10 Ted Thompson

Ted Thompson was going to do it his way—no matter what the outside world said and no matter how unpopular the decision was.

On August 6, 2008, Thompson made the most controversial move in Green Bay Packers history and traded future Hall of Fame quarterback Brett Favre to the New York Jets.

Thompson elected to turn his team over to young, unproven Aaron Rodgers. And Thompson was fully aware that if the move blew up, he'd have one of the most soiled legacies in Packers history.

"When the trade papers actually came, and I was going to sign it, which would be my job, I almost wanted someone else to sign it," Thompson said.

Three years later, though, Thompson had gotten the last laugh.

Rodgers proved he was ready for greatness. Favre hit the wall in the latter stages of his glorious career.

And Thompson assembled a deep and gifted roster that vaulted the Packers to a championship in the 45th Super Bowl.

"I don't get into this satisfaction of showing people up," Thompson said. "I think most Packer fans are good people and they want the Packers to do good. And when we do good, they pat us on the back, and when we don't they don't. That's the way the NFL is."

Still, Thompson wasn't getting many pats on the back in the summer of 2008.

Favre was arguably the most popular player in Packers history. And as his messy divorce from Thompson and the Packers played out nationally, most sided with the beloved quarterback.

Thompson and Favre were never tight. Thompson's first-ever draft pick was spent on Rodgers in 2005, and Favre saw that as a sign the organization was pushing him out the door. Favre contemplated retirement well into the off-season for several years, something Thompson certainly didn't appreciate. Finally, Favre announced his retirement on March 6, 2008, then had a change of heart that June. The organization had already committed to Rodgers, though, and wanted Favre to stay retired. When Favre refused, a showdown between he and Thompson ensued.

Favre asked for his release. Thompson said no. Favre wanted his starting job back. Thompson said he could be a backup. Favre asked for a trade to Minnesota or Chicago, both divisional foes of the Packers. Thompson balked. Instead, Thompson and the Packers organization tried persuading Favre to stay retired.

"Them moving on does not bother me. It doesn't," Favre said during an interview that summer on Fox News Network. "I totally understand that. By me retiring March [6], I knew that could possibly happen. You guys have a different path, fine. What does that mean for me?… That means, either you give me my helmet, welcome [me] back, you release me, or attempt to trade me. We all know that that's a possibility, but a way-out-there possibility. And [Thompson] says, 'Playing here is not an option, but we can't envision you playing with another team, either.' And I thought, *So, basically, I'm not playing for anyone.*"

That certainly wasn't true either.

Favre was reinstated to the NFL and returned to the Packers' active roster on August 4, 2008. And for trivia buffs everywhere, the Packers placed cornerback Condrew Allen on injured reserve with a knee injury that day to make room for Favre. But Favre never suited up for Green Bay. On August 6—a Wednesday that Packers fans will never forget—Favre was traded to the Jets for what became a third-round draft choice.

It will undoubtedly go down as the most controversial decision in team history. And Thompson was the one who had the final say.

"This is a high-risk business," Thompson said immediately after trading Favre. "This is the National Football League. We understand that when we sign on. Yeah, that does put us at risk. There's all kinds of risks in the NFL, there's all kinds of risks in life. You make the best decisions you can based on what you believe is in the best interests of the Green Bay Packers, and you do it firmly and you do it the way a leader is supposed to do it. That's what we try to do every day with every decision we make."

Thompson's decision seemed ill fated at first. Green Bay, which went 13–3 during Favre's final season and reached the NFC

Championship Game, plummeted to 6–10 with Rodgers in charge in 2008.

But Thompson's approach of building through the draft and keeping your own players began paying dividends. Green Bay went 11–5 and reached the playoffs in 2009. Then the Packers got red hot at the end of the 2010 season, won their final six games, and toppled Pittsburgh in the Super Bowl, 31–25.

"I take my hat off to him," former Packers receiver Donald Driver said of Thompson. "Not too many people would have done what he's done. Not a lot of guys would have taken that criticism and went out there and jumped over that broomstick."

Packers coach Mike McCarthy agreed.

"I can't say enough about Ted," McCarthy said about the man who hired him. "Ted built this house. He is responsible for everything that goes on. He is our leader and he is our point man."

Thompson's scouting acumen allowed him to largely build Green Bay's 2010 championship team through the draft. That team had 14 starters selected by Thompson, and three others that he plucked as undrafted free agents.

"Ted is a scout by nature and a really good scout at that," said Reggie McKenzie, Green Bay's former director of football operations. "And that's allowed him to find some really good talent in some unorthodox places."

Thompson's legacy was on the line after pulling the trigger on the Favre trade. But just three short years later, Thompson emerged smelling like a rose.

"I don't take any personal satisfaction," Thompson said. "I am proud of our staff, our coaches, the players on this team because they did what they had to do to get this far."

Thompson's role should never be forgotten. He had a plan—albeit a risky one—that paid off handsomely for both Thompson and the Packers.

11 Mike Holmgren

Green Bay, Wisconsin. For a quarter century, it's where NFL coaches went to kill their careers. After Vince Lombardi stepped down following the 1967 season, Phil Bengtson, Dan Devine, Bart Starr, Forrest Gregg, and Lindy Infante all tried to reverse the Packers' fortunes. Each one failed miserably.

"Well, it wasn't exactly the No. 1 destination in the NFL," former Packers president Bob Harlan said.

But Mike Holmgren did something many believed was impossible. He proved you could win in Green Bay. The Packers hired Holmgren in January 1992 to take over a team that had produced just five winning seasons in 24 years. Holmgren proceeded to lead the Packers to seven straight winning seasons before leaving after the 1998 campaign for total control in Seattle.

Holmgren led a renaissance in Green Bay that saw the Packers go 75–37 during his tenure and reach the playoffs six times. Green Bay won three division titles, split its two trips to the Super Bowl, and reached three NFC Championship Games.

Holmgren had a terrific 9–5 postseason record, and his total mark of 84–42 (.667) is tied with Curly Lambeau for the second-best winning percentage in team history behind Vince Lombardi (.766). And by winning at least one game in five consecutive postseasons (1993–1997), Holmgren joined John Madden (1973–1977) as the only two coaches in league history to accomplish the feat.

"There's three critical things that eventually helped get us over the hump and win a Super Bowl," former Packers general manager Ron Wolf said. "I hired Mike Holmgren, traded for Brett Favre, and signed Reggie White [in free agency]. People can argue all day over which one of those was the most important. But they were all huge."

Holmgren brought back the discipline and toughness that were missing from previous administrations. He combined a terrific offensive mind with a menacing presence. He was respected, feared, loathed, and eventually loved.

"He's very tough," Favre said of Holmgren. "I know he was extremely tough on me. I can only speak for the years I played for him, but he's very demanding. To say he's a perfectionist is an understatement. I can remember numerous times in practice I'd make a good throw, tight situation, and I'd turn around, and he says it's not good enough, and I'm thinking, *What do I gotta do?*"

But Holmgren's players grew to appreciate the tough love. They also realized their head coach was more than just a coach.

"Coach Holmgren was different than most coaches," former Packers safety LeRoy Butler said. "Most coaches just coach, but [Holmgren] would call you up and ask, 'How's your family?' He knew all of our wives' names. And he would protect his players like I've never seen before. I don't think I've ever seen a guy go to bat for his guys like coach Holmgren did.

"We had full protection, full, full protection. If you had a bad game, he'd blame it on himself. He wouldn't let you blame yourself because he had another game to worry about next week. He couldn't have us bitching about the one that just ended."

A major key to Holmgren's success in Green Bay was turning Favre from a wild stallion into a three-time NFL MVP. It wasn't easy, of course, and the two had a rocky relationship at times. But Holmgren helped turn Favre into the game's top player, and the Packers' rise to greatness followed.

"He allowed me to flourish and make plays when plays were not there," Favre said. "He trusted me in that sense, and this sounds crazy, but we would repeat plays that worked. He'd run the same play eight times in one game. Where I see a play work

Head coach Mike Holmgren looks on during a game against the Chicago Bears at Lambeau Field on December 1, 1996. The Packers won 28–17, en route to a 13–3 regular season and a victory in Super Bowl XXXI, Green Bay's first since Super Bowl II.

watching any game—college, pro—where a play works and the coach has a tendency to think, *They've probably caught on to that. It's worked, but I'm not going to go back to it.* He would call it until they stopped it. You had to stop it first, and I thought he was an unbelievable play-caller, especially being that he's the head coach and he's involved in everything."

After three straight 9–7 seasons, Holmgren led the Packers to an 11–5 record and the 1995 NFC Central Division title—their first divisional crown in 23 years. The Packers followed that with a stunning win at San Francisco in the divisional playoffs and a trip to the NFC Championship Game, where they fell to Dallas.

The Packers steamrolled through the league in 1996, going 16–3 overall and winning their first Super Bowl since 1967. Green Bay reached the Super Bowl again in 1997 and entered as an 11½-point favorite against Denver. But in Holmgren's most bitter defeat—and a game in which he was thoroughly outcoached by Denver's Mike Shanahan—the Packers fell to the Broncos 31–24.

The following year the Packers went 11–5 in the regular season and fell to the 49ers 30–27 in one of the more memorable NFL wild-card games ever played. Shortly thereafter, Holmgren took the dual role as Seattle's head coach and general manager. Holmgren remained in Seattle for 10 years and later became the Cleveland Browns president. But his time in Green Bay has been—and will continue to be—hard to duplicate.

"Every time I get a chance to come back there…that's a special time," Holmgren said. "Green Bay is a special place for me and my family, and it always will be a special place.… I have friends there, I get to see some of them once a year, maybe twice a year, and it's special."

Just like Holmgren's tenure was.

12 Birth of the GBP

A simple conversation between two extremely dedicated men. Who would have ever guessed this would lead to the start of the Green Bay Packers?

Back in 1919, George Calhoun was the sports editor at the *Green Bay Press-Gazette*. One day, Calhoun bumped into Curly Lambeau, a player he had covered when he was a star athlete at Green Bay East High School, and the men discussed starting up a football team. Calhoun ran a story in the *Press-Gazette* a short time later, targeting local athletes to try out for the team. Then on August 11, 1919, the group met in the *Press Gazette*'s editorial room, and a football team was organized.

Shortly thereafter, Lambeau's employer—the Indian Packing Company—agreed to put up the $500 needed for blue-and-gold uniforms and allowed the team to practice on company ground. Naturally, the nickname "Packers" developed.

That modest beginning started a remarkable relationship between Lambeau and the Packers. The 21-year-old Lambeau became player/coach when Green Bay played its first game against the Menominee North End A.C. in 1919. And it wasn't until 1949 that he resigned.

"The story really is remarkable and so unique," former team president Bob Harlan said. "The history of this team and the entire organization really is unlike any other."

The Packers won almost as soon as Lambeau got them started. In 1919 Green Bay went 10–1 playing non-league games against teams throughout Wisconsin and upper Michigan. That team out-scored its opponents 565–12, as Lambeau led a high-flying offense that loved to throw the ball.

The team played its games at Hagemeister Park, a vacant lot next to Green Bay East High School. The Packers didn't charge for games back then, instead staying afloat by having patrons "pass the hat." By 1921, the Packers had become so successful that Lambeau got the backing of two officials at the packing plant, which had been bought out by the Acme Packing Company. They purchased a franchise in the American Professional Football Association, which later became the NFL.

Calhoun worked as the team manager, publicist, and traveling secretary from 1919 to 1947. And he wrote about the team in the *Press-Gazette*, as well. Andrew B. Turnbull was the general manager of the *Press-Gazette*, as well as the Packers' president from 1923 to 1927. Turnbull helped keep the Packers afloat in 1922 when financial woes hit the team. Then in 1923 Turnbull convinced local businessmen to purchase stock in the team and turn it into a nonprofit corporation, something the Packers still are today.

From those modest roots has come the most successful franchise in football. In the 90-plus years since the Packers were formed, they've won 13 championships, more than any team in football. Through the 2012 season, Green Bay's all-time record in league games is 690–530–36 (.565) and it's 30–18 in the postseason (.625). The Packers have also won 20 division titles.

The Packers, located in a town of 104,868 people, continue to succeed despite being in the smallest market of any professional sport. And the Packers' David vs. Goliath tale makes them a feel-good story every time they're on the national stage. The Packers also remain one of sport's most unique stories in the fact that they operate without an owner. Instead, 364,114 stockholders own 5,014,545 shares of the team—and none receives a dividend on those shares.

"There aren't a whole lot of stories in sports better than that one," former Packers general manager Ron Wolf said. "If there are, I can't think of them."

13 Super Bowl I

In 2013 advertisers paid as much as $4 million for a 30-second commercial during the Super Bowl. Fans who had the rare chance to land a ticket may have needed a small loan to do so. And Super Bowl XLVII itself, between the Baltimore Ravens and San Francisco 49ers, averaged 108.4 million viewers, putting the broadcast at No. 3 on TV's list of all-time-most-watched programs.

Back on January 15, 1967, when the Green Bay Packers routed Kansas City 35–10 in Super Bowl I, no one could have predicted the game would become the spectacle it is today. Tickets that afternoon went for $12. More than one-third of Los Angeles' Memorial Coliseum sat empty. And both CBS and NBC carried television rights to the game.

"We had no idea how big of a game that would become," former Packer Willie Davis said. "None whatsoever. Who could have ever predicted it?"

Perhaps Green Bay coach Vince Lombardi, who felt great pressure not to let the NFL down by losing to the newer American Football League's representative. Lombardi's practices leading into the game were as intense as training camp. Fines for missing curfew went to record amounts. Lombardi was so maniacal about the game that his wife, Marie, had to get away from him and went to Las Vegas for two days.

"Vince made it very clear from our first day out there that we had to win that game," Red Cochran, Lombardi's offensive assistant, said in the best-selling book *When Pride Still Mattered*. "And he didn't want to make a squeaker out of it."

It wasn't. Behind 250 passing yards and two touchdown passes from Most Valuable Player Bart Starr, the Packers outscored the

Chiefs 21–0 in the second half and rolled to the title. Many will remember this contest for bringing the two leagues together. Some will reflect on the magnitude of Green Bay's winning its fourth championship in six years. To others, this will simply be remembered as Max McGee's big day.

McGee, an aging and little-used wide receiver, had just four receptions all season. But when starter Boyd Dowler went down on the Packers' first series, McGee stepped up and caught seven passes for 138 yards and two touchdowns. What made McGee's heroics even more impressive was that he was operating on virtually no sleep. The night before the game, McGee risked the $15,000 fine and sneaked out of his hotel room to meet up with two stewardesses he'd met earlier that day.

The Chiefs had to be wishing McGee would have never come back. His 37-yard touchdown from Starr in the first quarter was a brilliant one-handed grab that gave Green Bay an early 7–0 lead. "I was so surprised that I expected to open my other hand and find a silver dollar," McGee told reporters after the game.

Then, late in the third quarter, McGee hauled in a 13-yard TD strike to give Green Bay a commanding 28–10 lead. McGee did most of his damage on Kansas City cornerback Willie Mitchell, who the Packers planned to attack from the get-go.

"It was our plan to throw a lot to the receiver on the weak side," McGee said after the game. "I just happened to be the one."

McGee and Starr weren't the only heroes.

Green Bay led just 14–10 at halftime, and Lombardi was livid. The Packers had allowed Chiefs quarterback Len Dawson to scramble around and keep his team in the game. But on Kansas City's first possession of the second half, right linebacker Lee Roy Caffey deflected a Dawson pass that Willie Wood intercepted. The Packers safety rumbled to the Chiefs' 5-yard line, and Elijah Pitts scored on the next play. Green Bay rolled from there, outscoring the Chiefs 21–0 after intermission. The Packers finished the game with a 358–239 edge in total yards and completed 73.3 percent of their third downs (11-for-15).

"I was disturbed in the first half," Starr said. "We weren't moving the ball at all. Then we settled down and did just what we were supposed to do—get out there and win the ballgame."

The victory was a relief to Lombardi, who certainly wanted to prove his league was the best. And afterward, he could boast that it was.

"Kansas City has a real top team," Lombardi said. "But I don't think it compares with the top teams in the National Football League."

Kansas City owner Lamar Hunt, a major force in the merger of the two leagues, said, "I'm disappointed. I told somebody they didn't keep the time right. The first half didn't run long enough, and the second half ran too long."

For McGee and the Packers, though, things ran just right. "After I had scored those two touchdowns, [Paul] Hornung came over to me and said, 'You're going to be the MVP,'" McGee said. "Well, I wasn't. But it was a heck of a game."

One that got the ball rolling for the greatest spectacle in sports today.

14 Super Bowl II

The end of a glorious era—arguably the finest in NFL history—came on January 14, 1968. The Green Bay Packers that took the field for Super Bowl II were aging rapidly. The rest of the NFL was quickly gaining ground. And these Packers had a strong hunch that Vince Lombardi was coaching his final game with the

Head coach Vince Lombardi is carried off the field by his team, including All-Pro guard Jerry Kramer (64), after the Packers defeated the Oakland Raiders 33–14 in Super Bowl II in Miami. The win capped an unmatched run of dominance.

team. So the Packers did what all great teams do—they exited in style.

Green Bay dominated Oakland from start to finish and rolled to a 33–14 victory. It was the Packers' second straight Super Bowl win and fifth title in seven years.

"There were a lot of guys getting a little long in the tooth that year," right guard Jerry Kramer said. "You can't play forever, no matter how much you'd like to. There was nothing easy about that year, and [Lombardi] drove us harder than ever. He knew what we could accomplish, and that was to become one of the greatest teams of all-time."

That's exactly what happened. But first Green Bay needed to dispose of Oakland, the champions of the American Football League. The Packers, who had survived the Ice Bowl just two weeks earlier, were a model of efficiency against the Raiders. Green Bay didn't have a single turnover and had just one penalty. Quarterback Bart Starr had a 96.2 passer rating, threw for 202 yards and a touchdown, and was named the game's MVP for the second straight year. Kicker Don Chandler banged home four field goals. And defensive end Willie Davis sacked Raiders quarterback Daryle Lamonica three times.

"We've played several games that were better than that one," Starr said years later. "But we were very good that day. If that game marks the end of our dynasty, that's not a bad game to go out with."

That's for sure.

Green Bay led 6–0 early in the second quarter, when Starr and Boyd Dowler hooked up on a 62-yard TD. Dowler beat the initial jam of cornerback Kent McCloughan, caught Starr's pass 20 yards downfield, then outran safety Rodger Bird to the end zone to make it 13–0. Oakland answered with a TD a little more than four minutes later that made it 13–7. But Green Bay proceeded to score the next 20 points and make this one a laugher.

Running back Donny Anderson had a two-yard TD run in the third quarter to give Green Bay a 23–7 lead. Then early in the fourth quarter, All-Pro cornerback Herb Adderley picked off a Lamonica pass and brought it back 60 yards to make it 33–7.

"You can't get better than that," Adderley said years later of his Super Bowl interception. "That was such a great time and a great group of men. But that game was kind of the end of our run."

Seventeen days later, Lombardi announced he was stepping down as head coach, but would remain general manager. He handed the coaching reins to Phil Bengtson, but by 1968 the Packers were clearly a team in decline and finished 6–7–1.

That 1967 group, though, certainly provided a storybook ending to the Lombardi years. By winning Super Bowl II, the Packers allowed Lombardi to exit with six Western Conference championships, five NFL titles, and two Super Bowls. Since that time, no NFL coach has matched that success.

"Not everything came as easy that year as maybe it did in some past years," Dowler said. "I think we had to work a lot harder that season than we did in the past. But when you look back now, it sure was worth it. That was a great ride for all of us."

15 Lambeau Field

There was talk of a new stadium. Discussion that it might be time to start over rather than revamp what already existed. Bob Harlan would have none of it.

"I just never believed that building a new stadium was the way to go," the former Packers president said. "There's just too much history and tradition at Lambeau Field to tear that down."

So as Lambeau Field became outdated in the 1990s, Harlan helped put together a renovation plan for the historic stadium that asked for $169 million from taxpayers. The main goal was to increase the stadium's capacity by roughly 11,000.

Then for eight months during the 2000 season, Harlan spent the majority of his waking hours making appearances, shaking hands, and persuading voters. The measure eventually passed by a 53–47 margin, with the Packers contributing $125.9 million to the $295 million project. Now Lambeau Field remains one of the meccas in the sport and should keep the Packers thriving financially for years to come.

"Every time a team moved into a new stadium, we were falling further and further behind financially," Harlan said. "We had to do something."

What Harlan and the Packers did was make one of the most historic venues in sports even better, while ensuring an aging, out-of-date stadium wouldn't bury the organization financially. Lambeau Field, which completed its 56th season in 2012, is now the longest continuously occupied stadium in the league.

Built in 1957 for a cost of $960,000, Lambeau Field has long been placed atop the food chain of stadiums. In both 2007 and 2008, SI.com ranked Lambeau as the No. 1 stadium experience in the NFL. Lambeau's sightlines are completely unobstructed, meaning there truly isn't a bad seat in the house. And even with the recent rise in seating capacity, the stadium maintains an intimate feel.

The facility was originally called City Stadium when it opened on September 29, 1957. But after Curly Lambeau, the Packers' founder and first coach, died in 1965, it was renamed Lambeau Field. The stadium had a capacity of 32,150 when it first opened, a number that grew to 60,890 before the renovation. But the redevelopment increased capacity to 72,928, leading to new revenue for a publicly owned team that has to generate income from its home.

That wasn't all the renovation project did, though. The team also built the Lambeau Field Atrium, a 366,000-square-foot, five-story structure on the building's east side. Inside the Atrium are several dining, entertainment, and retail options aimed at making Lambeau Field a year-long destination. During the 2008–2009 fiscal year, nearly 500 events were held at the Atrium, including several wedding receptions.

The Packers haven't stopped either. Lambeau Field recently concluded a $286.5 million expansion project that added 7,000 new seats and increased capacity to roughly 80,000, the fourth highest total in the league.

The second phase of the construction project will revamp the Lambeau Field atrium.

With all of the upgrades in recent years, the Packers have moved from the bottom third of the league in revenue to the top third.

"When we went after the stadium, we said that we've got to do this because it's going to help us in revenue," Harlan said. "It's going to keep us competitive. It's going to keep us a viable part of the National Football League. It's going to bring visitors to Green Bay from literally around the world. And it has done all of those things. Everything we said to the voters in 2000 has come true."

That, of course, has thrilled Packer Nation, which always believed renovating their beloved stadium was the way to go.

"Almost every place in the National Football League where history has occurred has been torn down and replaced with a new stadium," Harlan said. "This is still Lambeau Field."

Amen.

16 Super Bowl XLV

Bold. Brash. Bombastic.

That's how the 2010 Packers operated from day one and throughout the entire season.

When the Packers concluded their off-season program that spring, they lightened the mood by holding a home run-hitting contest. Rookie offensive tackle Bryan Bulaga won the event, and for his efforts, was presented a broken-down car.

While many chuckled at Bulaga's new vehicle, the message on the car was no laughing matter. On the driver's side, it read: "To the Super Bowl—Dallas."

"I definitely think we're positioned to do that," veteran wideout Donald Driver said. "Super Bowl's the goal and I don't think we're going to be shy about saying it."

Later that summer, quarterback Aaron Rodgers and several of his teammates showed up at the annual "Welcome Back Packers Luncheon." They did so wearing cowboy hats and bolo ties— which are popular apparel in Texas.

By all accounts, the stunt was Rodgers' idea. The message was also crystal clear: Green Bay's goal was to finish its season in Arlington, Texas, home of the 45th Super Bowl.

"I have every intention and belief that we have the capability of winning the Super Bowl," Packers coach Mike McCarthy said.

Many teams talk the talk. Few back it up.

But those 2010 Packers did exactly that.

Green Bay struggled to an 8–6 start that year, but got red hot down the stretch and won its final six games.

The Packers capped their miraculous late-season charge by defeating the Steelers, 31–25, in Super Bowl XLV.

Rodgers was the game's MVP after throwing for 304 yards and three touchdowns. And the Packers won their 13th NFL Championship, tops among all franchises.

"The character in that locker room is like nothing I've ever been a part of," Rodgers said. "It's just a special group of guys who believe in each other and love each other. When someone goes down, somebody steps up and picks each other up."

That was Green Bay's mantra all season long.

The Packers had 15 players land on the injured reserve list that season, including standouts like running back Ryan Grant, tight end Jermichael Finley, right tackle Mark Tauscher, linebacker Nick Barnett, and safety Morgan Burnett.

But Green Bay stayed the course, then rallied down the stretch with huge home wins over the New York Giants and Chicago to reach the playoffs as the NFC's No. 6 seed.

"It feels incredible," said Packers outside linebacker Erik Walden, who had a career night with two sacks and 11 tackles in the season finale against Chicago. "It didn't always look great for us, but we got it done."

The Packers kept getting it done during a memorable postseason.

Green Bay held on for dear life and posted a 21–16 win over host Philadelphia in the wild-card round. Cornerback Tramon Williams intercepted a Michael Vick pass in the endzone in the final minute to preserve the win.

The Packers routed Atlanta 48–21 in the divisional playoffs. Rodgers was a remarkable 31-of-36 for 366 yards and three TDs and Williams had two more interceptions, including one he returned 70 yards for a touchdown on the final play of the first half.

Green Bay defeated Chicago—its oldest rival—in the NFC Championship Game, 21–14, and clinched a berth to its first Super Bowl in 13 years.

"I'm numb," said McCarthy, who grew up in Pittsburgh and was an assistant coach at the University of Pittsburgh from 1989–'92. "It's a great feeling. I'm just so proud of our football team."

With good reason.

When the Packers were 8–6, things looked remarkably bleak. Rodgers had just missed a game with a concussion, and Green Bay was on the outside looking in when it came to the postseason.

But McCarthy took a borderline cocky approach with his team down the stretch, proclaiming they were "nobody's underdog." The Packers proved that, too, on their way to the Super Bowl.

Then, the night before the biggest game of their lives, McCarthy continued his daring approach to the 2010 season and had his team fitted for Super Bowl rings. Traditionally, teams get fitted after winning a title. But the McCarthy Way was operating much differently than many of his peers.

"I felt the measurement of the rings—the timing of it would be special," McCarthy said. "It would have a significant effect on our players doing it the night before the game.

"I just told them, 'We're going to get measured for rings tonight.' Scheduling is so important during the course of the week. You want to do certain things at certain times. I thought that was a perfect time. I thought it would be special and give us a boost of confidence to do it the night before the game."

The Packers certainly weren't lacking confidence. And they took the fight to Pittsburgh immediately.

On Green Bay's second possession, they hit paydirt. The Packers drove to the Steelers' 29-yard line, where on third-and-1, they lined up with two tight ends and wideout Jordy Nelson the lone receiver split to the right. Pittsburgh anticipated a run, and that left Nelson one-on-one with William Gay, Pittsburgh's No. 3 cornerback.

Gay played press coverage at the line of scrimmage, but Nelson beat him after faking inside, then releasing down the right sideline. The Packers' offensive line did its job and Rodgers lofted a perfect fade to the right corner of the end zone.

Gay's coverage wasn't terrible, but Nelson had a step on him and won a hand-fight between the two. Nelson then hauled in Rodgers' gorgeous toss to give the Packers a 7–0 lead with 3:44 left in the first quarter.

"It was just press [coverage]," Nelson said. "Aaron gave me a little signal if it was press to go deep. It was actually a screen play, but he checked to a go route. That's what we hit."

The hitting had just begun.

Pittsburgh began its next drive on its own 7-yard line following an illegal block penalty. And on the Steelers' first play, quarterback Ben Roethlisberger made the game's biggest blunder.

Green Bay rushed four, but Roethlisberger was trying to hit a home run to Wallace, so he needed substantial time for the play to develop. That allowed beefy defensive end Howard Green, who was signed off the street in October when the Packers were ravaged by injury, to get home in 3.4 seconds.

Green whipped left guard Chris Kemoeatu, then drilled Roethlisberger as he let loose a bomb for Wallace. But Green's pressure caused Roethlisberger's pass to be severely underthrown and Packers safety Nick Collins intercepted.

The following season, Collins' Green Bay career ended when he suffered a neck injury in the second game of the year. On this play, though, Collins was magical.

Collins, who was named to three straight Pro Bowls, took off down the right sideline and made a nifty cut back inside. When Collins reached the 3-yard line, he jumped and reached the endzone. In a matter of 24 seconds, Green Bay had surged to a 14–0 lead.

"Oh man, that was the highlight of my day right there," Collins said. "I was able to read Big Ben [Roethlisberger] and got a nice jump on the ball. I made a couple cuts to get into the endzone."

The Packers led 21–3 shortly before halftime, when the Steelers were given new life.

At the two-minute mark, Packers nickel cornerback Sam Shields left with a shoulder injury. Shields would return, but not until the fourth quarter.

One play later, cornerback Charles Woodson—Green Bay's best free agent since Reggie White—suffered a broken collarbone and wouldn't return. Earlier in that second quarter, wideout Donald Driver left with an ankle injury and he didn't come back, either.

With the Packers shorthanded and scrambling defensively, Pittsburgh took full advantage. Roethlisberger threw for all 77 yards of the drive—highlighted by an eight-yard TD to Hines Ward—and the Steelers pulled within 21–10 just 39 seconds before halftime.

With Woodson and Shields still sidelined, Green Bay was searching for defensive answers. But the Packers didn't have any early in the third quarter.

After the Packers went three-and-out to start the half—a series that included a drop from wideout James Jones that might have gone for a touchdown—the Steelers took over at midfield. Pittsburgh called five straight running plays and ripped off 50 yards, capped by an eight-yard Mendenhall TD run.

Green Bay's lead, once as many as 18 points, had been whittled to 21–17.

"It was tough," Packers defensive coordinator Dom Capers said. "We were scrambling there for a while, because a big part of our game plan went out the window. We planned on playing a lot of man coverage, and when those guys went out we had to become more of a zone team."

The Packers got a huge lift at the start of the fourth quarter when linebacker Clay Matthews forced a fumble from Steelers running back Rashard Mendenhall deep in Green Bay territory. Rodgers then drove the Packers to Pittsburgh's 8-yard line, where they faced second-and-goal.

Green Bay employed an empty backfield, and after the ball was snapped, Rodgers quickly looked left. Rodgers had no intention of ever going left, mind you. He was simply trying to get Troy Polamalu—the NFL's Defensive Player of the Year—to drift that way.

It was a continuation of a 60-minute battle that Rodgers waged—and won—with Polamalu.

"He's a guy that you have to be aware of him, where he's at all times," Rodgers said of Polamalu. "He's a great player, had a great season, but guys have to respect where my eyes are looking so it was important to me to use good eye control on the field and not stare anybody down because he can cover a lot of ground quickly."

Rodgers was sublime on this play. Polamalu watched Rodgers' eyes and cheated back to the left, which allowed wideout Greg Jennings to come free in the right corner. Rodgers lofted another perfect ball and Jennings' TD grab gave Green Bay a 28–17 lead.

"It was a corner route," Jennings said. "I had a corner route the entire time and they dropped me and let me run free the play before. They dropped me on another corner route and we came back to it and scored on that play."

Pittsburgh answered right back, though, as Roethlisberger engineered a 66-yard TD drive that took just seven plays and slightly more than four minutes. The Steelers then converted the two-point play and pulled within 28–25.

Green Bay added a field goal with 2:07 remaining and went ahead, 31–25. But that left Pittsburgh plenty of time to notch a dramatic win.

In the 43rd Super Bowl two years earlier, Roethlisberger led the Steelers 78 yards in the closing moments and hit Santonio Holmes with a six-yard TD pass to win the game.

Then in 2009, Roethlisberger and Mike Wallace hooked up on a 19-yard TD on the final play of the game to defeat Green Bay, 37–36.

Not this time, though.

The Steelers quickly faced a fourth-and-5 and Roethlisberger threw to his left for Wallace. But Williams—who had a memorable postseason—broke on the ball perfectly and knocked it to the ground. The Steelers wanted a pass interference call, but Williams' technique was perfect and no flags were warranted.

Green Bay had held. This group that had talked about Super Bowl championships starting in June was about to hoist the Lombardi trophy.

"I did some things that were different, but frankly, just trust your instincts," McCarthy said of his late-season strategy. "I think the No. 1 responsibility as the head coach is to have your finger on the pulse of your football team and react and respond accordingly. That's what I felt myself and our coaching staff did. We stayed true to our operation. We didn't change the way we prepare for games, we didn't change the way we practice.

"There is a belief in how we operate and I think that was the biggest key for us down the stretch. I just felt we were a consistent football team all year. I never felt we were as bad as our record may have been some time or as good when we had the blowout win. I felt we were just a very consistent football team and I think that is why we ended up being the Super Bowl champions."

17 Ray Nitschke

Twenty-five years after he put on a uniform for the final time, Ray Nitschke's presence could still be felt in the Green Bay Packers locker room. The 1996 Packers were on their way to the organization's first Super Bowl in 30 years. But even that great Packers team could feel Nitschke breathing down their collective necks.

"I think Ray Nitschke thinks we stink," former Packers defensive end Sean Jones said that year.

Not quite. But Nitschke had that effect on people—he made you sweat. Nitschke was one of the most ferocious middle linebackers in NFL history. He played in Green Bay from 1958 to 1972 and was the anchor of the Packers' great defenses that helped produce five NFL championships in the 1960s.

With a toothless, prison-yard look to him, Nitschke was dubbed "the Animal." And it's doubtful many creatures of the wild would have wanted to battle him. Nitschke didn't just tackle people. He punished them. And to this day, the debate rages over

Hall of Fame Packers linebacker Ray Nitschke (66) closes in on Oakland Raiders running back Hewitt Dixon (35), with a little help from Lee Roy Caffey (60) during Super Bowl II, a 33–14 Packers victory at the Orange Bowl in Miami on January 14, 1968.

whether Nitschke or Chicago's Dick Butkus was the game's best middle linebacker ever.

"He could put the fear of God into people," said Bart Starr, the Packers quarterback during their glory years. "Getting hit by Ray was not a fun thing. But off the field, Ray was one of the nicest guys you'll ever find."

Nitschke grew up in Elmwood Park, Illinois, as a die-hard Chicago Bears fan. After a rough childhood in which he lost both his parents, Nitschke played fullback and linebacker at the University of Illinois.

The Packers saw him as a linebacker, though, and moved Nitschke there after drafting him in the third round in 1958. It didn't take long for Nitschke to get acclimated, as he started as a rookie and eventually played in 190 games—the third most in team history.

"He was the man," Packers safety Willie Wood said of Nitschke. "He was a guy who played with a lot of great tenacity. Every time you saw him, you knew he was ready to play."

The NFL didn't keep tackle totals back in Nitschke's day. If they did, someone might still be adding them up, as Nitschke was a tackling machine. Nitschke was also Green Bay's emotional leader on defense, a player whose intensity and fire seemed to rub off on those around him.

"He was our spark," former defensive end Willie Davis said of Nitschke. "Ray was the guy who could fire you up with his words. Or you'd watch him lay somebody out, and that would certainly fire you up, too."

Nitschke's career highlights are numerous:

- He had an interception that led to a touchdown in Green Bay's 37–0 destruction of the New York Giants in the 1961 NFL Championship Game.
- He was named the MVP of the 1962 NFL Championship Game, a 16–7 Packers' win over the Giants. In that game, Nitschke recovered two fumbles and deflected a pass that was intercepted.
- Nitschke had a sack and six tackles in Super Bowl I.
- And in Super Bowl II, Nitschke led the Packers with nine tackles.

"Ray was terribly frustrating to block because he used his linemen so well," former Bears center Mike Pyle said. "You couldn't get to him. He also had the ability to give the center coming out to block him a forearm that could knock you upside down."

By the time Nitschke's unparalleled career in Green Bay ended, he was named All-Pro by the Associated Press five times. He also had 25 interceptions, and his 20 fumble recoveries still ranks second in team history. Nitschke was later named to the NFL's All–50-Year Team and its 75th Anniversary Team. He was inducted into the Pro Football Hall of Fame in 1978, had his No. 66 retired by the Packers in 1983, and had the east practice field named in his honor.

Nitschke died of a heart attack at just 61 years old in 1998.

"There will be a lot of people who will play middle linebacker for Green Bay and in the National Football League," Davis said in 1998 after Nitschke's funeral. "In my opinion, there will never be another Ray Nitschke."

18 Reggie White

It was halftime of the biggest game of his life, and nothing was going the way Reggie White had hoped. The most dominant defensive end of his era had been stymied by the upstart New England Patriots for 30 minutes of Super Bowl XXXI. So, during halftime, White turned to the Bible and teammate Eugene Robinson for encouragement.

"Eugene kept coming to me and saying, 'Isaiah 40:31 says we must mount up with wings of an eagle, run and not get weary, walk and not get tired,'" White told reporters afterward.

White didn't get weary—only stronger.

And in one of the most dominant halves in Super Bowl history, White notched three sacks and helped the Packers capture a 35–21 win. It was Green Bay's first Super Bowl title in 29 years.

"God sent me here [to Green Bay]," White said. "Some of you guys thought I was crazy four years ago, but now I'm getting a ring. How crazy do you think I am now?"

Back in the spring of 1993, much of the football world thought White was crazy. White, known as "the Minister of Defense," was arguably the most attractive player to ever hit the free-agent market. And when White signed with Green Bay—a team that hadn't reached the postseason since 1982—eyebrows were raised throughout the league.

"The Bible says God is not of confusion, but of peace and a sound mind," said White, an ordained minister from the time he was 17. "That's what I was looking for, and I've gotten peace about being here and a sound mind about being here."

White also got one of the biggest contracts in league history, one that paid him $17 million over four years and made him football's third-highest-paid player. By the time the deal expired, most would agree that White was a bargain. The first thing White did was bring instant credibility to the NFL's smallest city. Green Bay was no longer the NFL's version of Siberia or a place other teams threatened to trade their disgruntled players.

Second, White gave teeth to a defense in dire need of some. The year before White arrived, the Packers ranked 23rd in total defense. Green Bay jumped to second in White's first year and was in the top eight five of six seasons.

"Getting Reggie was the key," former Packers safety LeRoy Butler said. "Without him, we would have been just a vanilla defense because we had no pass rush."

Third, White played a huge role in the recruitment of other free agents to Green Bay, which helped the Packers assemble the necessary talent for their Super Bowl run. "That's what changed the football fortunes of this franchise. It was huge," Packers president Bob Harlan said of signing White. "Everyone thought the last place he would sign was Green Bay, and it was monumental because not

Reggie White celebrates as he walks off the field after a 17–3 victory over the Chicago Bears at Lambeau Field on October 31, 1993. The Hall of Fame defensive end was one of the biggest free-agent signings in NFL history and helped return the Lombardi Trophy to Green Bay. White, a longtime minister off the field, died at the age of 43 in 2004.

only did he sign, but he recruited for Green Bay and got guys [such as] Sean Jones to come here. He sent a message to the rest of the NFL that Green Bay was a great place to play."

And White played great with the Packers. In six seasons, he posted 68.5 sacks, which ranks second in team history, and made six consecutive Pro Bowls. White also was a huge factor in Green Bay reaching two Super Bowls and three NFC Championship Games during that time.

To this day, Packers fans could spend hours arguing over whether general manager Ron Wolf, coach Mike Holmgren, quarterback Brett Favre, or White played the greatest role in Green Bay's rise to greatness. "You can argue all day about what the biggest move was," Packers general manager Ron Wolf said. "But in some order, it's Mike, Brett, and Reggie."

White died tragically on December 26, 2004, at 43 years old from causes related to sleep apnea. White, who began his career in Philadelphia and finished up in Carolina, had 198 sacks when he retired, which was an NFL record at the time. White also holds the record with 12 seasons of 10-plus sacks, was named to 13 Pro Bowls, and was the NFL's Defensive Player of the Year in 1987 and 1998.

White's No. 92 was never worn after his final season in Green Bay (1998). The Packers then retired his number in 2005.

"I had the utmost respect for Reggie White as a player," Favre said. "He may have been best player I've ever seen and certainly was the best I've ever played with or against."

19 Paul Hornung

Paul Hornung was beginning to wonder if the call would ever come.

"I was really getting kind of peeved and worried," the former Green Bay Packers standout running back said.

With good reason. It was 1986, and Hornung's name had been on the Hall of Fame ballot 14 times. In each instance, he fell short of the necessary votes for induction. Finally, on his 15th try, Hornung got the needed support. Today, Hornung is one of 22 Packers in the Hall—10 of whom played under Vince Lombardi.

"Let's put it this way, I didn't give up hope," Hornung said. "But it was a long time in coming.... I thought I might have been used somewhat like a political football because the story was, 'Why wasn't Paul Horning getting into the Hall of Fame rather than most of the people who were getting in?' But, naturally, I'm happy to be in it now."

Hornung, who won the NFL MVP award in 1961, always had Hall of Fame credentials. But voters couldn't get past the fact that Hornung was suspended the entire 1963 season for gambling. When it came to football, Hornung was one of the dominant players of his era. It wasn't always that way, though.

Hornung, dubbed "the Golden Boy," was an All-American and Heisman Trophy winner at Notre Dame. Green Bay was football's worst team in 1956 and used the No. 1 pick in the 1957 draft on Hornung.

Then–Packers coach Lisle Blackbourn mistook Hornung's versatility for shortcomings. Blackbourn couldn't decide on a position for Hornung, and after two short seasons, Hornung had seen enough and wanted a trade.

The move that may have saved Hornung's career was the hiring of Vince Lombardi as head coach before the 1959 campaign. Lombardi viewed Hornung as a halfback with great power and a player who could throw on the run—two traits that would open up the playbook.

"I suggest that you report to training camp at a maximum of 207 pounds," Lombardi told Hornung in a letter dated May 14, 1959. "You will be heavy enough at that weight, and the left half-back in my system must have speed in order to capitalize on the running pass option play."

The Packers' Golden Boy, Paul Hornung, first earned fame as a Heisman Trophy–winning back at Notre Dame. He floundered in his first years with the Packers but then flourished under Vince Lombardi in a backfield that included fellow future Hall of Famer Jim Taylor.

Under Lombardi, Hornung developed into a standout running back, but also posed danger as a passer, kicker, receiver, and lead blocker. He won three straight NFL scoring titles between 1959 and 1961 and set a league record with 176 points in 1960. That mark stood for 46 years before San Diego's LaDainian Tomlinson broke it in 2006. During that 1960 campaign, Hornung scored 15 touchdowns, kicked 15 field goals, and converted 41 extra points. He also threw for two touchdowns that year, meaning he had a hand in 188 points—or 15.67 per game.

Hornung scored a league-best 146 points in 1961 and was named the NFL's MVP that season. But he nearly missed out on the Packers' NFL Championship Game that year when he was called to duty by the Army. Lombardi called President John F. Kennedy and asked that Hornung be granted leave for the title game, and Kennedy obliged.

"Paul Hornung isn't going to win the war on Sunday," Kennedy said. "But the football fans of this country deserve the two best teams on the field that day."

Hornung played a large role in assuring the Packers were the best. He scored 19 points that day—a title-game record—and led the Packers to a 37–0 rout of the Giants. Lombardi later called Hornung "the most versatile player in football" and "the best clutch player I have ever seen."

Perhaps, but Hornung's off-the-field exploits got him into trouble and kept him out of the Hall all those years.

Hornung had a reputation as one of the country's most successful ladies' men. Hornung and teammate Max McGee were also both hard drinkers who liked to party together. Lombardi could live with that. The gambling was another story. NFL commissioner Pete Rozelle suspended Hornung and Detroit's Alex Karras in April 1963. With Hornung out of the lineup that season, the Packers' run of two straight NFL championships ended, as well.

"Oh, we missed him," Packers quarterback Bart Starr said. "There's no doubt about that."

You bet they did, especially Hornung's incredible versatility.

After missing the 1963 season, Hornung scored 107 total points in 1964. But he also made just 12 of 38 field-goal attempts that year. Don Chandler replaced him as the team's kicker in

1965, and Hornung's last two seasons were injury-plagued and rather nondescript. By the time his terrific nine-year career ended, Hornung had scored 760 points, including 62 touchdowns, 190 extra points, and 66 field goals.

"You have to know what Hornung means to this team," Lombardi said in George Sullivan's *The Great Running Backs*. "I have heard and read that he is not a great runner or a great passer or a great field-goal kicker, but he led the league in scoring for three seasons. In the middle of the field he may be only slightly better than an average ballplayer, but inside the 20-yard line, he is one of the greatest I have ever seen. He smells that goal line."

20 Forrest Gregg

Vince Lombardi didn't throw praise around often. So when the Green Bay Packers' legendary coach once called Forrest Gregg "my best player," people took notice. Gregg certainly put together credentials for such lofty acclaim. The best right tackle in team history, Gregg played in nine Pro Bowls and was named All-Pro eight times during a brilliant 14-year career in Green Bay. He was voted to the NFL's 75th Anniversary Team and inducted into the Hall of Fame in 1977. Gregg held the Packers' record for consecutive games played (187) until Brett Favre later broke it. And Gregg was a major reason the Packers won five NFL championships between 1961 and 1967.

For years, Gregg's name was gold around Green Bay. Then he returned to Titletown, and that all changed. Gregg coached the Packers from 1984 to 1987, compiling a 25–37–1 record and failing to produce a single winning season.

But it wasn't just the losing that drove the players and fan base crazy. Gregg's people skills were deplorable, and he created a divided locker room. The Packers players were running roughshod off the field, and the community became embarrassed by many of the individuals representing the NFL's smallest city.

"I don't think Forrest was right to come back to Green Bay," former Packers defensive end Alphonso Carreker said. "He thought he could be the type of coach who would put you through punishing practices all year long and threaten you with words and that would make you a champion. Forrest wanted to be the Bobby Knight of football, and it's hard to motivate people that way. So I never paid Forrest any attention."

Gregg was Cleveland's head coach for three years and coached Cincinnati for four seasons, leading the Bengals to a Super Bowl appearance. When Green Bay fired Bart Starr after nine seasons in 1983, it thought it hit the jackpot with Gregg. Not exactly.

"Forrest, he was just loony at times," said defensive back Estus Hood. "Forrest would just fly off the handle and get all crazy."

"Forrest? Man, that was scary," added former safety Johnnie Gray. "I remember his opening-day speech. He said, 'I've got a five-year contract here, and I will be here for a while. Most of you won't.' Man, with that personality and that attitude, I was done."

While Starr couldn't get the Packers over the hump in his nine-year run, the players respected the fact he treated them with dignity and respect. With Gregg, it wasn't like that at all.

"Forrest came in and he yelled at you and he insulted you in front of the team," former quarterback Lynn Dickey said. "Some things went on with him that would never work at any level. I remember our first meeting with Forrest, he was berating guys he didn't even know. He said, 'Some of you guys have been living on easy street. Like you, [Larry] McCarren.' Well, Larry McCarren was probably the hardest-working guy on the team, making about $220,000 a year. Forrest knew his Xs and Os, but he had no idea about people skills. And he brought in his own guys, and they walked all over him."

Even worse, the Packers were becoming an embarrassment off the field, as well. Mossy Cade was convicted of rape and sentenced to prison, with Gregg defending him every step of the way. James Lofton stood trial on sexual assault charges, but was found not guilty. The Packers suffered another black eye when defensive lineman Charles Martin delivered one of the league's all-time cheap shots, ending the season of Chicago quarterback Jim McMahon in 1986.

Gregg had one year left on his contract after the 1987 season and realized his days in Green Bay were numbered. So when SMU asked Gregg to resuscitate a program that had just received the death penalty, he took it. In typical Gregg fashion, he didn't tell his assistants that he was leaving. Many of those coaches never talked to Gregg again, and much of Packer Nation still tries to only remember his time as a player.

"The truth is he was not a good football coach," former tackle Greg Koch said.

He was a remarkable player, though, something Packer Nation will never forget.

21 Clarke Hinkle

Clarke Hinkle loved contact. It didn't matter which side of the ball he was coming from, Hinkle loved delivering blows. He was one of the most versatile and talented players in the history of the Green Bay Packers. In fact, the Packers' west practice field was dedicated as Clarke Hinkle Field in 1997.

Hinkle was one of the best rushers in team history, but also a standout defensive player and the Packers' kicker for much of his 10-year career (1932–1941). He helped the Packers win NFL championships in 1936 and 1939, and was later inducted into the Pro Football Hall of Fame in 1964.

"I vividly remember Russ Winnie—a very dramatic play-by-play announcer in his day—describe Hinkle as a 'hunk of steel,'" former Packers historian Remmel recalled.

"I think he liked to hit people any chance he could," Herm Schneidman, who played in the Packers backfield with Hinkle from 1935 to 1939, said before his death in 2008. "Clarke was a great football player who could do a lot of things well."

That's an understatement.

Hinkle led the Packers in rushing seven different seasons, which is tied with Jim Taylor for the most in team history. Hinkle's 3,860 career yards still ranks sixth all-time, and his 35 career touchdowns are fifth. He was Green Bay's leading rusher from 1932 to 1934, although he shared the lead with Bob Monnett in 1933. Then in 1936 Hinkle tied his career-high with five rushing touchdowns as the Packers went 10–1–1 and won the NFL championship. Hinkle also averaged a career-best 4.8 yards per carry that season, and his 476 rushing yards were his second-most ever. He ran for a career-best 552 yards in 1937, which ranked second in the league, and also scored touchdowns in six consecutive games that season. Then in 1938 Hinkle led the NFL in scoring with 58 points (seven TDs, three field goals, seven extra points).

Hinkle played a huge role on Green Bay's 1939 NFL title team, finishing second to Cecil Isbell in rushing yards (381), scoring five touchdowns, and averaging 40.7 yards per punt. Hinkle was still running strong during his final season of 1941, when he finished with six total touchdowns.

Hinkle's offensive exploits often get more attention than those on defense, largely because the NFL didn't keep defensive statistics during his era. But Hinkle was an extremely fierce linebacker who certainly drew the attention of Chicago Bears standout fullback Bronko Nagurski. Hinkle was recognized as one of the few players tough enough to tackle Nagurski by himself. And when Hinkle went into the Hall of Fame, Nagurski delivered the induction speech.

Hinkle handled the punting duties for Green Bay for three seasons and averaged 40.8 yards on his 87 punts. And over his final four seasons—when the Packers began keeping statistics—he made 14 of 16 extra points (87.5 percent) and 19 of 47 field goals (40.4 percent). Hinkle was a two-time All-Pro and was named to the Pro Bowl from 1938 to 1940. He was also named to the NFL's All-Time Two-Way Team in 1994. Versatile, powerful, dynamic. That's how history will remember Hinkle.

"Hinkle was one of the most versatile players in the Green Bay Packers and NFL history," Remmel said. "He was the first of the great all-around players and one of the first six Packers inducted into the Pro Football Hall of Fame, which is a substantial honor."

One that was well deserved.

22 Willie Wood

Willie Wood didn't think his odds were particularly good. But in the spring of 1960, he sat down with a pen, some paper, and a dream. Wood, a college quarterback at USC, had just gone undrafted in large part because there were no black quarterbacks in the NFL at that time. Wood knew his only hope of playing in the NFL would be at safety, so he studied the teams that needed help, then sent letters to the San Francisco 49ers, Los Angeles Rams,

New York Giants, and Green Bay Packers. In the days before advanced scouting existed, Wood did all he could to detail his collegiate career and explain why he could be an asset.

"Looking back, the odds of somebody signing you certainly aren't very good," Wood said. "There were only 34 men on a team back then. The draft was already over. Your chances really aren't great."

They got even worse when three of the four teams didn't even respond to Wood. But the one that did—Green Bay—hit the mother lode. Wood was the last man to make the 1960 Packers roster. A year later, he was in the starting lineup and on his way to one of the best careers an NFL safety has ever had.

Wood, who patrolled center field from his free safety position as well as any player of his era, is second in Packers history with 48 career interceptions. He led the NFL with nine interceptions in 1962 and led Green Bay in picks five different seasons. Wood was a Pro Bowl player eight times and received all-NFL honors six straight years beginning in 1963. Wood also led the league in punt returns in 1961, averaging 16.1 yards, and still holds the Packers record for career punt-return yardage (1,391).

Wood's interception in Super Bowl I is still regarded by many as the turning point in Green Bay's 35–10 win. Early in the third quarter, the Packers were clinging to a 14–10 lead when Wood intercepted Kansas City's Len Dawson and returned the ball 50 yards to set up a Green Bay touchdown.

In Wood's 12 seasons, the Packers won the first two Super Bowls, as well as NFL championships in 1961, 1962, and 1965. Not bad for a former college quarterback.

"I have no regrets about my career whatsoever," Wood said. "I got more out of it than anyone would have ever imagined." He sure did. In 1989, after several close calls, Wood was elected to the Pro Football Hall of Fame and is one of 22 former Packers in the Hall.

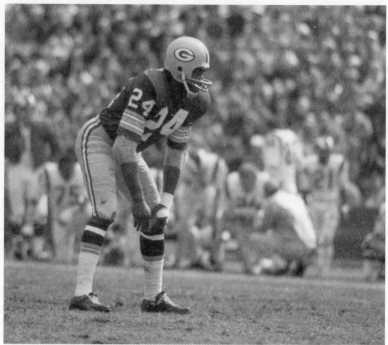

Hall of Fame safety Willie Wood lines up during a 1971 game versus the Los Angeles Rams at Memorial Coliseum. Wood anchored the Packers' defensive backfield during the glory years, collecting 48 interceptions along the way.

"I was ecstatic," Wood said of his selection. "I went numb for about four or five hours. We have quite a few of my teammates in the Hall already. I thought perhaps the people who make the selections might say, 'We have too many of those guys.'"

When Wood finished playing, he earned the distinction of becoming the first black head coach in professional football. Wood took over the Philadelphia Bell of the short-lived World Football League in 1975 and was head coach of the Toronto Argonauts of the Canadian Football League from 1980 to 1981. For a time, many believed Wood had the makings to become the NFL's first black coach. But he left the game in 1982 and never returned.

"When I came to Green Bay in 1960, my goal was not to be in the Hall of Fame," said the 5'10" Wood, who could dunk a basketball. "I just wanted to make the team and prove to myself that I could do it and work hard at it. I was just fortunate that I came to the right place at the right time. That's really what it is. It's probably 75 percent luck."

And a lot of persistence, which started with a letter.

23 Take the Tours

It was a gorgeous July day in the summer of 2009. Green Bay Packers quarterback Aaron Rodgers was walking with a guest from the team's media room out to Lambeau Field. The shortest path was through the team tunnel, which even in the middle of summer, excited Rodgers.

"Isn't this cool?" Rodgers said. "I love going through this tunnel."

Green Bay Packers fans can have that exact same experience—and many more—by taking some of the tours the team offers. There's a trip to the Packers Hall of Fame, which has countless artifacts to celebrate the team's unique history. Then there's the Lambeau Field Stadium Tour, which is highlighted by a trip through the very tunnel the Packers run through each Sunday.

The Hall of Fame remains one of the most popular activities for Packers fans. They can see what Vince Lombardi's office once looked like and sit behind the legendary coach's desk. They can look at the Packers' four Super Bowl trophies. And they can see the lockers of the 22 Packers in the Pro Football Hall of Fame.

"Despite the fact that the Magic Kingdom is generally regarded as 'The Happiest Place on Earth,' I have always told my children that Lambeau Field deserves that title," said 46-year-old Jason Heinze, a lifelong Packers fan from Marshall, Wisconsin. "A big reason for that is the Green Bay Packers Hall of Fame. The last time I was there, my buddy and I spent about four hours, but you could easily double that. The place is a treasure trove of memorabilia."

The 25,000-square-foot Hall of Fame sits one level below the main Lambeau Field Atrium floor. And inside, there's truly something for everyone. The tour starts with a 12-minute movie about the Packers and their unique history, produced by NFL Films. Fans can see the plaques of all 151 members of Green Bay's Hall of Fame. Along the way are countless historical items obtained by chief archivist Tom Murphy. Roughly 99 percent of the objects have been donated, and up to 75 percent are consistently on display. There's also an interactive display, as well as a kids zone, where youngsters can do a Lambeau Leap or throw a football.

When fans finish with the Hall of Fame, they can take the Lambeau Field tour. Tour guides take customers to several behind-the-scenes areas. The tour runs through the Lambeau Field Atrium and up to the exclusive Club Level for a look at the Legends Club. Fans are then taken down to the field, which has been home to countless memories and highlights.

As expected, the tours are most popular in the summer, especially during training camp. Fans can visit: *www.lambeaufield.com/stadium_info/stadium_tours* or *www.lambeaufield.com/hall_of_fame/visit_the_hall_of_fame* to find out specific days and hours the tours run.

"Once you've been there, much like the Magic Kingdom, you look forward to going back," Heinze concluded.

24 Herb Adderley

"Take the best player available." That's the axiom spouted by general managers everywhere when it comes to the NFL Draft. Back in 1961 that's exactly what Green Bay general manager Vince Lombardi did, and it turned out to be a stroke of genius.

The Packers were set at running back heading to the draft that season, with the dynamic duo of Paul Hornung and Jim Taylor in the backfield. Still, Lombardi couldn't pass on Herb Adderley, who had been a terrific running back at Michigan State.

Adderley, the 12th pick in the draft that season, was buried on the offensive depth chart midway through his rookie year. But when cornerback Hank Gremminger was injured, Lombardi switched Adderley to defense. Little did Lombardi know at the time, but he'd just discovered a Hall of Fame cornerback.

"I was too stubborn to switch him to defense until I had to," Lombardi once said. "Now when I think of what Adderley means to our defense, it scares me to think of how I almost mishandled him."

Perhaps, but Lombardi also deserves credit for bringing Adderley to Green Bay in the first place. Both Hornung and Taylor would go on to have Hall of Fame careers, so the last thing the Packers needed was another running back. But the remarkably gifted Adderley was just too good to pass up.

"The things Herb could do out there were just incredible," said safety Tom Brown. "He had gifts and talents that most cornerbacks simply didn't have."

At 6'1", 205 pounds, Adderley was bigger than most of the corners of his era, which allowed him to get physical with receivers at a time when there was a far greater tolerance for contact. Adderley was also a terrific athlete and could run with much smaller wide-outs. In essence, Adderley had the whole package—size, speed, strength and smarts.

During his nine years in Green Bay, Adderley had 39 interceptions, which is more than any cornerback in team history and third on the franchise's all-time list. And Adderley, who was inducted into the Pro Football Hall of Fame in 1980, is widely regarded as the Packers' top corner ever.

"God didn't make a whole lot of Herb Adderleys," Packers Hall of Fame safety Willie Wood said. "Guys like Herb weren't growing on trees."

Adderley's first year as a starter was 1962, when he had a career-best seven interceptions. He was also a huge reason the Packers allowed just 10.6 points a game that season, a mark the team hasn't matched since.

Adderley led the NFL in interception-return yardage in 1965 (175) and 1969 (169). His seven career defensive touchdowns were a Packers record until Charles Woodson broke it with eight in 2009. Adderley was also a dynamic return man and still ranks third in Packers history for career kickoff-return yards (3,080). Adderley's career average of 25.67 ranks fifth in team history, and his 103-yard kickoff return against Baltimore in 1962 is the fourth-longest by a Packer.

As terrific as Adderley was in the regular season, he may have been even better in the postseason. Adderley was a huge part of Lombardi's five NFL championship teams and played in both Super Bowls I and II, as well. In fact, Adderley's 60-yard interception return for a TD against the Raiders in Super Bowl II was the only "pick-six" in the first decade of the Super Bowl.

Adderley later played in Super Bowls V and VI with Dallas, losing the first and winning the second. But in a revised edition of *Instant Replay*, a memoir by former Packer Jerry Kramer, Adderley said, "I'm the only man with a Dallas Cowboys Super Bowl ring who doesn't wear it. I'm a Green Bay Packer."

When his brilliant career finally ended, Adderley had played in five Pro Bowls and was named All-Pro by the Associated Press seven times. Not bad for a former running back.

25 Tony Canadeo

It was 1949 and Tony Canadeo had already given seven years to the Green Bay Packers. That edition of the Packers would eventually finish 2–10 and become the franchise's worst team in its first 31 years. But you wouldn't have known it watching Canadeo run that season.

The little running back known as the "Gray Ghost of Gonzaga" took a beating that year. But he plowed on and gave no quarter. When the season ended, Canadeo had rushed for 1,052 yards and averaged 5.1 yards per carry. Canadeo became the first-ever Packer and only the third back in NFL history to crack the 1,000-yard barrier. Making that accomplishment even more impressive was Canadeo did it on a team that couldn't throw the ball. He also did it when the league played 12 games, not 16 like today.

It was seasons like this that made Canadeo one of the greatest Packers ever and an inductee into the Pro Football Hall of Fame in 1974. The Packers also retired Canadeo's No. 3 jersey after he hung up his spikes in 1952.

"He was probably one of the best all-around players in Packer history," Packers historian Lee Remmel said of Canadeo. "He could do just about anything. He was a good runner, a good blocker, a good returner, and a good receiver. He was one of the toughest players the Packers have ever had, an extremely hard-nosed player."

Nicknamed the "Gray Ghost" for his prematurely graying hair, Canadeo arrived in Green Bay with little fanfare. That's because the Packers had used a ninth-round draft choice on him in 1941, and expectations were certainly minimal. But the 5'11", 190-pound Canadeo quickly showed the versatility and gifts that helped make him one of the better all-around players in team history. Not only did Canadeo excel as a running back, he was also used as a passer, punter, return man, and played defense—finishing his career with nine interceptions.

"He was a good guy, until he got on the football field," Tom Miller, a teammate of Canadeo's in 1946 and one of his best friends, once told the *Milwaukee Journal Sentinel*. "Then he was pretty mean. When he put that uniform on, he changed. He was tough and ready to go all the time. He was one heck of a football player."

It took a while for Canadeo to make his mark, but by 1943, he led the Packers in both rushing (489 yards) and passing (875 yards, nine TDs). Canadeo missed most of the 1944 season and all of the 1945 campaign while serving in World War II. When Canadeo returned, Curly Lambeau made him his primary ball carrier, then watched him excel.

Canadeo led the Packers in rushing each of the next four seasons. But it was that 1949 campaign that best defines his legacy. The Packers were outscored 329–114 that season. Green Bay's quarterbacks threw five touchdowns, 29 interceptions, and had a passer rating of 11.4. The only weapon the Packers had was Canadeo, and opponents knew it. Still, Canadeo had a career year and was Green Bay's lone bright spot.

Canadeo retired after the 1952 season, yet still ranks fourth in Packers history in career rushing yards (4,197) and fourth in consecutive seasons leading the team in rushing (four). Canadeo later served on the Packers' board of directors from 1955 to 1993 and on its executive committee from 1958 to 1993 before his death in 2003. In fact, his 59 years of service were longer than any person in team history. Canadeo also became one of Vince Lombardi's most trusted friends after Lombardi was named Green Bay's head coach in 1959.

"I admired him for what he did as a player, of course," former Packers president Bob Harlan said. "But I also admired him for his loyalty to the organization and his willingness to fight for the Green Bay Packers."

Most who watched or knew Canadeo felt the same.

26 1929–1931

Johnny "Blood" McNally. Verne Lewellen. Lavvie Dilweg. These are players that many Green Bay Packers fans may have never heard of. More than 80 years ago, though, they were among the Packers that were the toast of the town.

Between 1929 and 1931, the Packers won three straight NFL championships. Those Packers were the first teams to ever "three-peat," and the only squads to do it since were Green Bay's 1965 to 1967 teams. Under the direction of head coach Earl "Curly" Lambeau, the Packers went a remarkable 34–5–2 in that time. And on three occasions, they won at least eight games in a row, including 10 straight in the 1929 season.

Lambeau was fantastically ambitious and a terrific player himself until 1929. Lambeau was also ahead of his time when it came to the passing game and threw the ball far more often than several of his foes. He was a terrific recruiter and signed several standout players that helped turn the Packers into a powerhouse.

The 1929 team was a magnificent 12–0–1 and outscored its opponents by a whopping 198–22. The Packers had eight shutouts that season, and nobody scored more than six points against them. Tailbacks Lewellen and McNally scored seven and five touchdowns, respectively, and Dilweg, a standout receiver, had three. In all, the Packers ranked first in the league in defense and second in offense.

Green Bay was 10–3–1 the following year for a .769 win-loss percentage. The New York Giants were 13–4 that season (.765), giving the Packers the title by percentage points. Green Bay struggled down the stretch, earning its only tie and all three losses in its final six games. But an eight-game winning streak to open the season had given the Packers enough cushion to win the title.

Green Bay made it a three-peat in 1931, when it went 12–2 and edged the Portsmouth Spartans (11–3) for the title. The Packers held a 291–87 scoring edge that year and allowed just three foes to score in double figures. The Packers were first in offense, second in defense, and first in point differential that season. McNally had his best year with 11 receiving TDs and 14 total scores.

Green Bay almost won a fourth-straight title in 1932, but there was an NFL rule that stated ties didn't count in the standings. The Packers finished that year 10–3–1 (.769), while the Chicago Bears were 7–1–6 (.875). Under modern rules, ties are treated as a half-win and half-loss. So in today's world, the Packers would have had a .750 winning percentage and outdistanced Chicago (.714). Under that system, though, the Packers would have lost to New York in 1930, negating their three-peat.

As it is, those Packers did amazing things between 1929 and 1931, and set the bar fantastically high for all Green Bay teams to come.

27 Fourth and 26

The 2003 NFL season had been over for weeks. Packers cornerback Al Harris was trying to enjoy a vacation in the Bahamas but wasn't having much luck. That's because everywhere Harris went on that trip—and really that entire off-season—people wanted to discuss a topic that quickly became taboo in Packerland: fourth and 26.

"Man, it was brutal," Harris said. "It was fourth and 26 this, fourth and 26 that. I couldn't take it after a while."

To this day, many Packers fans still can't take the thought of that fateful play—one that helped knock the Packers out of the playoffs and cost defensive coordinator Ed Donatell his job.

It was January 11, 2004, and the Packers were in Philadelphia for an NFC divisional playoff game. Green Bay was one of the hottest teams in football and had rolled off five straight wins. With just 1:12 left, the Packers led 17–14, and Philadelphia faced a fourth and 26 at its own 26-yard line. A math professor at the University of Wisconsin–Green Bay later calculated the odds against the Eagles picking up a first down as 339 to 1. But to the shock and dismay of Packer Nation, this was the Eagles' lucky day. Philadelphia quarterback Donovan McNabb fired a laser to wideout Freddie Mitchell that was good for 28 yards, and the Eagles subsequently drove for the tying field goal to send the game into sudden-death overtime. Following a costly Brett Favre interception in the extra period, the Eagles kicked a game-winning field goal to win it 20–17.

"Let's not sugarcoat it," Donatell said when talking about the play more than a year later. "It's part of Packer history. They'll talk about it for a long, long time."

How it happened will always be a sore spot with Packers fans. Green Bay put the Eagles in this unfavorable situation thanks to a 16-yard sack by defensive back Bhawoh Jue and a pair of McNabb incompletions. Green Bay seemed disorganized before fourth down, though, which led to much second-guessing later.

"Quite frankly, we should have called a timeout," cornerback Michael Hawthorne said. "We should have called timeout to regroup and play the defense that we know will make them catch everything in front of us."

Instead, Green Bay sat in a cover-2 defense and rushed four. And when the pressure was nonexistent, the middle of the field was wide open. Nick Barnett, Green Bay's middle linebacker, had failed to get a deep enough drop with Mitchell. Safeties Marques Anderson and Darren Sharper had inexplicably fallen 30 yards deep into coverage. McNabb threw a bullet to Mitchell, and when Jue made a poor play on the ball and both safeties arrived late, Mitchell picked up 28 yards and the most impossible of first downs.

To this day, Donatell insists he wouldn't have done anything differently. He would just have coached it differently. "I'd coach Nick Barnett to stay back deeper, I'd tell Bhawoh Jue to have awareness, and I'd tell Darren Sharper to buy that route at 20 yards," Donatell said. "But I'm not blaming any player. I'm not blaming any assistant. The buck stops with me. Somewhere along the line, the buck's got to stop, and it's stopping right on me. I'm blaming myself for the way that was coached."

Packers coach Mike Sherman certainly seemed to blame Donatell and fired him after the season.

Green Bay's players, meanwhile, will be haunted by that play for years. The Packers felt they had a Super Bowl team that season but were done in by a play with astronomical odds.

"I still think we could have won the Super Bowl that year," Sharper later said. "Everything was set up for us. We were playing great and had a ton of confidence. Our next game [at Carolina] was against a team we all felt we matched up really well against. But as we all know, fourth and 26…"

Who could ever forget?

28 Jim Taylor

Jim Taylor wasn't blessed with Bo Jackson–like size. He didn't have the speed of a Chris Johnson. But good luck finding a running back any tougher than Taylor was.

Taylor came to the Green Bay Packers as the 15th pick in the 1958 draft out of LSU. He left as the most prolific rusher in Packers history and the proud owner of a career that earned him induction into the Pro Football Hall of Fame in 1976.

During his nine seasons in Green Bay, Taylor rushed for a team-record 8,207 yards. That mark held up until 2009, when Ahman Green passed him. Taylor eclipsed 1,000 yards rushing a team-record five straight years (1960–1964) and led the NFL in rushing in 1962 with 1,474 yards. He led the Packers in rushing seven seasons (1960–1966), a mark equaled only by Clarke Hinkle, who did so between 1932 and 1941. Taylor also averaged 4.53 yards per carry, which ranks second to Gerry Ellis' 4.58. Taylor's 91 career touchdowns also ranks second to Don Hutson (105), who played 11 years in Green Bay.

But perhaps the statistic Taylor remains most proud of is his fumbles—or lack thereof. In 2,166 career touches, both rushing and receiving, Taylor had just 34 fumbles. That equates to one fumble every 63.7 touches, a mark that stood until Barry Sanders shattered it with one fumble in every 83.3 touches.

Hall of Fame Packers running back Jim Taylor (31) slants through a hole in the San Francisco 49ers' defense on December 4, 1966, at a home game in Milwaukee. Taylor rushed for 8,207 yards in his nine seasons in Green Bay.

"I was very conscious to maintain my hold on the ball," Taylor said. "I was always very conscientious of maintaining the football, and that's a record I always cherished. I feel I was above average in maintaining the football."

Taylor was above average in every aspect of the game. He was a bruising runner who sought out defenders as much as they searched for him. He wasn't elusive, but bringing him down often took multiple defenders. Throw in the fact he operated behind one of the greatest offensive lines ever assembled and the passion Vince Lombardi had for the running game, and you can see why Taylor excelled.

"I was clearly running behind the best offensive line in football," said Taylor, who was also inducted into the Packers Hall of Fame in 1975. "And Coach Lombardi stressed that part of the game more than anything. We were going to run the ball 65 percent of the time, or so, and Bart [Starr] was only going to have to throw it about 15 times a game. But as I look back, I can say I feel good about the contribution I made to the Packers' era and the Lombardi era. I feel good about it."

Taylor had more games to feel good about than most players would dream of. But one that stands above the others was the 1962 NFL Championship Game against the New York Giants at Yankee Stadium. The game-time temperature was 13 degrees and falling, and with winds gusting up to 40 mph, many players said the conditions were worse than the legendary Ice Bowl. The field was also hard and frozen, and when players fell, there were pieces of dirt that cut like glass.

In the first quarter, Taylor was drilled by Giants linebacker Sam Huff, tore up his elbow, bit his tongue, and was swallowing blood the rest of the half.

"That had never happened to me before," Taylor said. "It was rough."

But so was Taylor. After getting stitched up at halftime, Taylor played on and played exceptionally well. Despite his multiple injuries, the fact that his hands were nearly frozen, and that the Giants were now gunning for him, Taylor was the impetus in Green Bay's 16–7 win. He finished with 31 carries for 85 yards and a touchdown, as the Packers won their second straight title.

"Did everything I could to that f—," Huff later recalled. And Taylor just stared at him and said, "That your best shot?"

"That was just a brutal, brutal football game," Taylor said. "We didn't wear gloves back then, so that made it even worse. But we accepted it and just went out and did our job."

After years of doing his job as well as anyone in the NFL, Taylor and Lombardi reached an impasse. Prior to the 1966 season, the Packers had given youngsters Jim Grabowski and Donny Anderson big contracts to be their backfield of the future. Taylor, always one of the toughest negotiators among Packers players, became determined to play out his contract and go searching for big money himself. So after the 1966 campaign, he returned home and played one frustrating year with the New Orleans Saints.

Although Taylor and the expansion Saints struggled on the field in 1967, the move proved beneficial. After his career ended, Taylor spent 18 years working as a color commentator and later a scout for the Saints. He and Lombardi also patched up their differences, and when Taylor went into the Hall of Fame, he asked Marie Lombardi to give the introductory speech.

"After Vince went to the Redskins [in 1969], we had dinner one night," Taylor recalled. "And after that, everything was great again."

Almost as great as Taylor's days with the Packers.

"When I got drafted by Green Bay, I didn't know anything about it or where Green Bay even was," Taylor said. "But, for me, it turned out to be a stroke of luck because they needed running backs, and Coach Lombardi came along the next year. At the time, I just said I'll go there and do my job. And I think things worked out fine."

Anyone who got to see Taylor play would certainly agree.

29 New Year's Celebrations

A lamp shade on the head of one guest. Party favors galore. And plenty of adult beverages. Oh, New Year's usually leads to some of the biggest and best parties of the year. And in the mid-1960s, no one had greater reason to celebrate the New Year than the Green Bay Packers and their faithful. In the 1965 and 1966 seasons the Packers played in memorable NFL Championship Games right after the New Year.

Happy New Year? You betcha.

Here's a look at those memorable contests that helped the Packers kick off the New Year in style.

January 2, 1966—Green Bay 23, Cleveland 12

Jim Brown was the NFL's leading rusher and is still widely regarded as the greatest running back in the history of the game. But on this day, the Packers' defense stymied him, and Green Bay's terrific tandem of Jim Taylor and Paul Hornung outperformed Brown. Hornung carried 18 times for 105 yards and scored a critical third-quarter touchdown to give Green Bay a 20–12 lead. Taylor had 96 yards on 27 carries. Meanwhile, Green Bay limited the dynamic Brown—who had 1,544 yards during the regular season—to just 50 yards on 12 carries.

"It was just Green Bay's defense," Brown said afterward. "Then there's Ray Nitschke at middle linebacker. He seems to know where I'm going before I do."

For Taylor and Hornung, it was a bit of redemption. Earlier that season, Green Bay coach Vince Lombardi had spent a reported $850,000 in signing bonuses on Donny Anderson and Jim Grabowski to be his running back tandem of the future. But on this day, Taylor and Hornung—a pair of 30-year-olds—proved they had plenty left.

"Just a couple of old-timers trying to hang on," joked Taylor, who was named the game's Most Valuable Player.

Green Bay grabbed an early 7–0 lead when quarterback Bart Starr hit Carroll Dale for a 47-yard touchdown. But the Browns fought back, grabbed a 9–7 lead, and trailed just 13–12 at halftime.

In the third quarter, the Packers marched 90 yards in 11 plays and capped the drive with a 13-yard touchdown run by Hornung. The Packers added some insurance in the fourth when Don Chandler drilled a 29-yard field goal, his third of the game. And, afterward, it was Taylor and Hornung receiving much of the credit for Green Bay's third title in five years.

"You have to control the ball against the Browns if you are going to beat them," Lombardi said. "We planned to stick to the basics. Yes, I think there is a little spark left in Jimmy and Paul."

January 1, 1967—Green Bay 34, Dallas 27

The NFL-AFL World Championship Game—which later became known as the Super Bowl—was looming for the winner. But that was a first-time event against what was considered a far inferior league. So to those inside the National Football League, what was on deck was almost irrelevant.

This game would prove the real champion of football. And thanks to four Bart Starr touchdown passes and a heroic late-game interception by Tom Brown, the Packers won the NFL championship and advanced to Super Bowl I.

"That was really the championship back then," Starr said. "The Super Bowl was a new game, and we didn't know much about it. But we knew the Dallas Cowboys." Did they ever, as the familiar foes forged another epic game. Green Bay stormed to a 14–0 lead on a 17-yard TD pass from Starr to Elijah Pitts and an 18-yard fumble return for a score by Jim Grabowski.

The Cowboys evened the game before the first quarter expired, but then Green Bay began to take control. Carroll Dale, Boyd Dowler, and Max McGee all scored on touchdown passes from Starr, and the Packers built a 34–20 lead with five minutes remaining.

Dallas wouldn't die, though, as Don Meredith hit Frank Clarke for a 68-yard score, then got the ball back and drove to the Packers'

2-yard line with 2:30 left. The Packers stymied Dallas on the first three downs, then on fourth down with 28 seconds left, Meredith rolled out to pass. Green Bay's Dave Robinson broke through and got a hand on Meredith, who still managed to get rid of the ball. But Brown, a former major league baseball player, leaped high for the game-clinching interception.

"That's probably the play I'll always be best known for … and that's great," Brown said. "We had so many big plays and so many great players. But that was probably my shining moment."

As it turned out, New Year's was all about shining moments for the Packers and their fans.

30 Cal Hubbard

There remains debate over exactly how tall Cal Hubbard was. The Pro Football Hall of Fame lists the former Green Bay Packers star as 6'2", 253 pounds. Green Bay publicity material from the time Hubbard played lists him as 6'5". Either way, he was a giant during his era.

Hubbard spent six of his nine NFL seasons in Green Bay and was arguably the game's most dominant offensive tackle. The Packers won their first three NFL championships during Hubbard's first three seasons with the team (1929–1931), and they compiled a 57–19–4 record during Hubbard's time in Green Bay. Hubbard played at a time when 6' linemen were considered large. Hubbard combined terrific size and skill to earn All-Pro honors in Green Bay from 1931 to 1933.

Herm Schneidman, who played with Hubbard in Green Bay in 1935, was a former Packers halfback and blocking back. He remembered Hubbard as a dominating player but also someone who loved to challenge head coach Curly Lambeau.

"Cal was real smart and a jovial kind of guy," Schneidman said shortly before his death in 2008. "We'd take the train to New York, and Curly would have a quiz on the plays on the train. Cal would miss 'em on purpose, just to get Curly riled up. And Cal was one of the players—with [Arnie] Herber, [Mike] Michalske, and [Milt] Gantenbein—who would help Curly put in the defense and make up the plays for the next game. They were on the [players'] board, so to speak."

Rightfully so.

Hubbard so dominated his position that he was selected to the NFL's All–50-Year Team in 1970. Hubbard, who also was a defensive star his first two years in the league with the New York Giants, was selected to the NFL's All-Time Two-Way Team in 1994.

Hubbard had umpired baseball games for several summers during his NFL days. So, following his retirement after the 1936 season, Hubbard became an American League umpire. A hunting accident ended his umpiring career in 1951. He then served as the umpire director for the American League for two decades and was later enshrined in the Baseball Hall of Fame. Today Hubbard is the only person in the Baseball and Football Halls of Fame.

During his time in Green Bay, Hubbard never made it a secret that he didn't care much for Lambeau. He respected him professionally, but his personal feelings were a different story.

"They won't be able to find six men to bury the so-and-so," Hubbard once was quoted. But Hubbard also added, "He was a hard driver, but he got the job done."

The outspoken Hubbard even questioned Lambeau's football knowledge. In David Zimmerman's book on Lambeau titled *The Man Behind the Mystique*, Hubbard said, "To be frank, Curly really didn't know that much about football. After all, he just spent one year at Notre Dame, how much did he learn? Most of us knew more because we spent more time learning during four years of college and then, for most of us, some professional experience, too. Hell, sometimes Curly would design a new play, draw it up on the blackboard, and we just knew it wouldn't work the way he drew it. He'd have impossible blocking assignments, or the play would just take too long to develop. The defense would mess it up before it got going. We'd have to tell him that, and one of the veterans would go right up to the blackboard and change it around."

No matter how they did it, Hubbard, Lambeau, and those Packers eventually got things right. And Hubbard was a huge reason for Green Bay's first three NFL titles.

31 Packers-Colts 1965

The question wasn't even completed, and Don Chandler already had the answer.

"It was good," the former Green Bay Packers kicker said. "I'm sure of it."

Nearly 40 years after one of the most controversial kicks in NFL history, Chandler is still being asked about its validity. To this day, Chandler, the Packers, and referee Jim Tunney insist the kick was good. The Baltimore Colts still feel differently.

On December 26, 1965, the Packers and the visiting Colts were playing for the Western Conference championship. The winner would face Cleveland the following week for the NFL championship. The Packers trailed 10–7, when Chandler trotted out for a 22-yard field goal with just 1:58 left in regulation.

While kickers' accuracy averaged roughly 50 percent in that era, Chandler still called the kick "a chip shot." The kick flew high above the right upright, and Chandler's initial body language indicated he missed the attempt. But Tunney, who was standing directly under the goal post, said the kick was good.

"The kick went down the middle, but the wind was blowing," Tunney said years later. "I was the only official standing under the goal post, and it went over the crossbar, and then after it crossed, from the kicker's standpoint, the wind blew it past the right post. In those days, the posts were only 10 feet above the crossbar, so I drew an imaginary line up that side."

After that season, the NFL raised goalposts from 10 feet to 20 feet so officials could make clearer judgments on similar kicks. On this day, though, all that mattered was Tunney called it good. That sent the game into overtime, where Chandler drilled a 25-yard field goal to lift the Packers to a 13–10 win. Afterward, Shula and the Colts insisted the kick was wide right—something they stood by years later.

"I saw [Coach] Shula years later, and we laughed about it," Chandler said during an interview shortly before his death in 2011. "He still didn't think it was good, but I know it was good. Plus Bart [Starr] said it was good, and Bart never lied. But that's all water under the bridge now. A lot has gone on since then."

One week later, Green Bay defeated Cleveland 23–12 to win its first of three straight championships. And it seemed like Chandler was the ultimate lucky charm.

Chandler spent his first nine seasons with the New York Giants and played in six NFL Championship Games, winning just one. The two sides parted ways after the 1964 season, and the Packers signed Chandler to upgrade the kicking position. Chandler did exactly that, making 65.4 percent of his kicks in 1965, a substantial upgrade from Paul Hornung's 31.6 percent in 1964. Chandler made a combined 54.4 percent of his kicks over the next two seasons and helped the Packers win two more NFL championships and Super Bowls I and II before his retirement.

"I was very fortunate," Chandler said. "Not many people had the luck I did. I was kind of disenchanted with the Giants, and they were disenchanted with me. The Packers needed a kicker, and it was the perfect place to wind up."

Chandler, who also handled punting duties, was named the punter on the NFL 1960s All-Decade Team. Chandler also still holds the record for most field goals in a Super Bowl with four in the 1968 title game against the Oakland Raiders, which helped clinch the championship for the Packers.

Still, when talk of his brilliant career comes up, the topic of choice is almost always the 1965 Western Conference Championship Game.

"That seems to be what I'll always be remembered for," Chandler said. "And I guess that's not too bad."

32 Henry Jordan

Henry Jordan had heard the threats. Play lousy, screw up, or do something your team didn't approve of, and the punishment was simple: you'll get traded to Green Bay.

So after two uneventful years as a reserve defensive tackle in Cleveland, Jordan got the news in 1959: he'd just been traded to Green Bay, which was coming off a 1–10–1 season. The thing is, Jordan wasn't depressed. He was thrilled.

"He came back to the room [after his first practice] and said, 'Momma, we've found a home,'" said Olive Frey, Jordan's widow. "He was ecstatic. Everything was falling into place. They really wanted him."

Jordan never could make a dent in Cleveland, where he was a fifth-round draft choice. But Lombardi thought enough of Jordan to send a fourth-rounder to the Browns for his rights. At the time of the trade, Jordan didn't even know where Wisconsin was. Lombardi told him he had 24 hours to report, so after grabbing a map, Jordan drove all night. It didn't take Jordan and the Packers long to realize this would be a productive marriage. The ever-rebuilding Packers needed help up front. Jordan was looking for a place to play, and the fit was natural.

"I know Henry was like me and just wanted to play," said former teammate Willie Davis, who was traded to Green Bay the following year. "I'd say it worked out pretty well for both of us."

Jordan was a former collegiate standout wrestler, who was runner-up in the heavyweight division at the 1957 NCAA Championships. Jordan was undersized in his day (6'2", 248), but he used his strength, leverage, and technique to become a terror in the trenches. Six different times Jordan was named All-Pro by the Associated Press (1960–1964 and 1966). He was named to four Pro Bowls and was the Most Outstanding Lineman in the 1962 game.

More important, of course, was the fact that Jordan played on five championship teams and two Super Bowl winners between 1961 and 1967. The defenses Jordan helped lead were a huge reason for Green Bay's success. Jordan played 11 years and 139 games with the Packers, and they allowed an average of just 15.5 points per contest in that time. The 1962 team that Jordan starred on allowed just 10.6 points per game, and the 1966 squad gave up only 11.6 points per contest.

Although the NFL didn't keep statistics for sacks and tackles when Jordan played, he is credited with making 3.5 sacks of Los Angeles Rams quarterback Roman Gabriel in the 1967 Western Conference Championship Game. He also was second on the Packers with six tackles in Super Bowl I.

While things were always intense under Lombardi, the fun-loving Jordan helped keep them light. Of Lombardi, Jordan once said, "He was very fair. He treated us all the same—like dogs." Or this one: "When [Lombardi] says, 'Sit down,' I don't look for a chair."

Jordan retired in 1969, but he never left Wisconsin. He became director of Milwaukee's Summerfest before dying of a heart attack in 1977 at age 42. Jordan became the fifth member of those great Green Bay defenses to be inducted into the Pro Football Hall of Fame in 1995. That day, his son, Henry Jordan Jr., wrapped up an emotional acceptance by saying, "I love you, Dad. You're my hero. Congratulations. You've earned it."

33 Willie Davis

Willie Davis was ticked. It was 1960, and Davis—a defensive lineman for the Cleveland Browns—was driving in his car. Davis flipped on the radio and heard he had been traded to the Green Bay Packers.

The Green Bay Packers? Seriously?

"The way I heard about the trade, first of all, was on the radio, so I wasn't really happy about that to begin with," said Davis, who was a second-year defensive end out of Grambling State at the time. "Then my only knowledge of Green Bay came from [coach] Paul Brown telling players he would ship them there if he wasn't happy with them. Green Bay was like a Siberia back then."

Davis gave some initial thought to playing in Canada. But within 24 hours, Davis knew he was fooling himself with any thoughts of crossing the border.

"I got on the phone with Coach Lombardi, and he said, 'I hope you're ready to come and be part of our team,'" Davis recalled. "And by the time I hung up that phone, I knew I was going to be a Green Bay Packer. He was that convincing."

Which was fortunate for the Packers. Davis had played both defensive tackle and end for the Browns, but when Lombardi was coaching with the New York Giants, he was enamored with Davis' skills at end. So Lombardi moved him there permanently, and over the next 10 seasons, Davis became as feared as any pass rusher in football. The NFL didn't keep official sack totals when Davis played, but if they had, Davis would have certainly cemented himself among the all-time leaders.

"I remember," Davis recalled, "Lombardi once said to me, 'I know why you play the way that I coach. It's because you want to prove to the world, and I want to prove to the world, and we both want to prove what we're capable of doing.' And he was right."

One of the keys to Davis' success was he kept himself in tip-top shape year-round. And, at the end of football games, when many players were exhausted, his tank still had something left.

"To me, I always accepted my personal situation that it was going to be up to me to make plays at the end of the game," said Davis.

And more often than not, he did just that.

"I could always hear Lombardi above the crowd yelling, 'Get in there, Willie!'" Davis recalled.

Davis, whose greatest payday came during his final season when he made $46,000, was named to five Pro Bowls, won All-Pro honors five times, and also holds the Packers' all-time record for fumble recoveries with 21. He was named to the Pro Football Hall of Fame in 1981 and was inducted into the Packers Hall of Fame in 1975. Along the way, he helped guide Green Bay to five NFL titles, including three consecutive championships, from 1965 to 1967.

Hall of Fame defensive end Willie Davis (87) gets ready to pummel Lions running back Nick Eddy (40) during a 28–17 Packers victory on October 12, 1969, in Detroit. Davis was one of the NFL's most feared pass-rushers during Green Bay's glory years.

Lombardi was once asked what made a great player and said, "You look for speed, agility, and size. You may get two of these qualities in one man, and when you have three, you have a great player. In Willie Davis, we have a great one. For a big man, 6'3" and 240 pounds, he has excellent agility, and he has great sincerity and determination."

Today, when Packers fans look at the 22 names that make up the team's "Ring of Honor" inside Lambeau Field, Davis' name rests between Ray Nitschke's and Lombardi's.

"For me, playing in Green Bay was a love affair," Davis said. "Now I couldn't imagine playing anyplace else."

Davis has kept close ties to the state after his retirement in 1969. He owns five radio stations, including three in Milwaukee and two in

California. He serves as a trustee at Marquette University and also sits on the board of directors of several major companies in Wisconsin.

"I fell in love with Green Bay and the state of Wisconsin," Davis said. "Who would have guessed it?"

Certainly not Davis back in 1960.

34 Bob Harlan

You've experienced it countless times. You have a problem and call the company with your complaint. After a lengthy wait on hold, you're bounced from lackey to lackey, and they offer little help. You never get the answer you want, eventually give up, and simply hang up more frustrated than you were at the start.

That was never the case during Bob Harlan's presidency.

Harlan was the Green Bay Packers' president from 1989 to 2006, then again for half of the 2007 season. If ever there was a man of the people, it was Harlan, who believed customer service came first and even answered his own phone throughout a memorable tenure.

"I like to avoid all the confusion of going through secretaries if people are trying to reach me," Harlan said during an interview late in his presidency. "I feel like I owe the fans that. I think since these people own this team, if they want to reach me, they should be able to do so. I don't want them saying, 'Well, you can't find Harlan.' Well, yes, you can."

The thing is, most of those folks should have been thanking Harlan when they called. That's because Harlan was largely responsible for turning the Packers from the NFL's version of Siberia into one of the league's most competitive franchises.

"The perception of Green Bay wasn't always the best," Harlan said. "We had to do a lot of work to change that."

And Harlan was never one to shy away from work. Because he was so successful, the case can certainly be made that Harlan was the most influential—and successful—president in team history. Harlan joined the organization in 1971 as an assistant general manager and rose through the ranks, eventually becoming the ninth president in team history in 1989. He then became the driving force behind some of the largest moves in franchise history.

Harlan's greatest success was hiring Ron Wolf as the team's general manager in 1991. Wolf proceeded to hire Mike Holmgren as coach and surround him with a talent-laden roster led by Brett Favre and Reggie White. Those moves helped the Packers win Super Bowl XXXI and NFC championships in 1996 and 1997.

"He was great to work for," said Wolf, the Packers' general manager from 1991 to 2000. "He did exactly what he promised. He put me in charge of the football operations and never once did he interfere. I think he did a lot for the Packers' operations, and the Packers are back on the map because of it."

Off the field, Harlan's greatest success was lobbying for a county-wide referendum for the redevelopment of Lambeau Field. For eight months during the 2000 season, Harlan spent the majority of his waking hours making appearances, shaking hands, and persuading voters. The measure eventually passed by a 53–47 margin, drawing $169.1 million in public funds to complement the $125.9 million the Packers ponied up. The $295 million project increased the stadium's capacity from 60,890 to 72,515 and helped the Packers move from the bottom third of the league in revenue to the top third.

"Every time a team moved into a new stadium, we were falling further and further behind financially," Harlan said. "We had to do something. And thank God we did it when we did it, because right after we got our vote, the economy went downhill, and the next year we had 9/11. Our timing was probably perfect. And I've always said, 'Hey, God tapped us on the shoulder and told us it was time to go with this.'"

While those were the crowning jewels of Harlan's career, he had several other landmark moves, as well. Harlan helped launch the fourth stock sale in team history in 1997, a move that produced more than $20 million of "new money" and more than 100,000 new shareholders. He authorized the construction of the Don Hutson Center, giving Green Bay one of the league's top indoor practice facilities. And he presided over the Packers' controversial decision to stop playing home games in Milwaukee in 1994.

Through the good and bad, Harlan always picked up his phone—regardless of how happy or irate the caller might be.

"I just don't want people feeling we're sitting up on this high hill, sold out, and don't have time for anybody," Harlan said. "It's still a people business first."

Harlan understood that better than most, which was a huge reason he had such tremendous success.

35 Instant Replay

"After further review, we have a reversal…touchdown!"

Those words, spoken by referee Tom Dooley, still make Green Bay Packers fans smile. The Chicago Bears and then-coach Mike Ditka still almost refuse to admit it ever happened.

It was November 5, 1989. Green Bay trailed Chicago 13–7 with just 41 seconds left and faced a fourth-and-goal from the Bears' 14-yard line. Packers quarterback Don Majkowski dropped to pass, was forced out of the pocket, and scrambled to his right. Majkowski got perilously close to the line of scrimmage, then fired back across his body and hit Sterling Sharpe with an apparent 14-yard TD pass. But line judge Jim Quirk ruled Majkowski had crossed the line of scrimmage, took away the touchdown and a potential Green Bay victory.

"Mike Singletary walked up to me and whispered, 'Sorry, kid. Too bad it won't count,'" Majkowski said of the Bears' standout linebacker. "He was a great player. He stared at me with those intense eyes during games for six years, and I stared right back."

But then the call went to the instant-replay booth. After a delay of nearly five minutes, the ruling on the field was reversed, and the touchdown was reinstated.

"When the call was made," recalled Majkowski, "I didn't trash talk or anything like that. I just winked at him [Singletary]."

Replay official Bill Parkinson said the deciding factor in his decision was where the ball was released from, not where Majkowski's feet were. "On stop and start on the instant replay, the initial line feed showed that the ball did not cross the line of scrimmage, the 14-yard line," Parkinson said. "This was a very important play. The ballgame hinges on this play. We took our time and looked at both feeds."

The Bears have never agreed with either feed. Chicago bemoaned the ruling afterward, and to this day, the Bears' media guide has an asterisk next to that game. "It was a bad call—period," Ditka said recently. "Remember one thing: instant replay was put in to get the call right. I don't care how long it takes, but get the call right. Of course, it was controversial, and we were very disappointed at the time. It was agonizing for both teams to wait while they reviewed it. But human beings make mistakes, and the call went Green Bay's way. It is what it is. You win some, you lose some. It was just one game in a long series between the Bears and the Packers—a series based on competition, which got out of hand for a couple of years. I was proud to be a part of those competitions and that rivalry."

Back in the 1980s, it was unique for the Packers to defeat the Bears. Chicago had won eight straight games against Green Bay— its longest streak in a series that dates back to 1921. Packers fans were desperate for a win over the hated Bears. But late in the game, Green Bay's chances for victory appeared slim after Majkowski fumbled and threw an interception inside Chicago's 20-yard line. Today, of course, nobody remembers those blunders. All they remember is Majkowski's heroics, Sharpe's catch, and the eventual words of Dooley that sent the state of Wisconsin into euphoria.

"That's probably my defining moment as a Green Bay Packer, my most famous play," Majkowski said. "And I'm proud to be remembered from that game. That game had such significant meaning to the Packers fans because the Bears of the mid-'80s and late '80s were so dominant. And to finally end the streak at home on the last play of the game in such dramatic fashion is pretty memorable. And to this day, that game goes down as one of the five most memorable games in Lambeau Field."

36 Jim Ringo

Jim Ringo wanted a raise. He didn't want a trade. And he most certainly didn't have a player agent. The greatest center in the history of the Green Bay Packers wants his loyal followers to understand all of the above.

"That's the thing I really want people to know," said Ringo, a Packer from 1953 to 1963, who was traded before the 1964 season. "I didn't have an agent. They were only for the elite players back then. I really don't know how that story got going. Sometimes people create their own stories, and such fallacies are not good things."

The details of Ringo's trade have been debated for years. Here's the story Packers coach and general manager Vince Lombardi wanted the world to believe: Before the 1964 season, Ringo was unhappy with his annual salary of $17,500 and went to Lombardi to ask for a $7,500 raise. Just one catch. Ringo brought a player agent with him. While agents are status quo today, they were new to the sporting world at that time. And Lombardi was downright insulted by the mere presence of such creatures. So after Ringo—who had played in seven Pro Bowls and started 126 consecutive games for Green Bay—issued his demands, Lombardi excused himself. A few minutes later he returned and told Ringo and his agent to talk to the Philadelphia Eagles, the place Lombardi had just traded Ringo.

While Ringo was indeed traded, Lombardi's move wasn't made in haste. Lombardi had determined that Ringo was nearing the end of his career and had been working on a deal with the Eagles for months. When Lombardi decided Ringo's demands were too high, he completed a trade that brought linebacker Lee Roy Caffey and a first-round draft choice (which eventually became fullback Donny Anderson) to Green Bay for Ringo and fullback Earl Gros.

As the tale grew through the years, it only added to the Lombardi mystique. Bring in an agent, deal with the consequences. Just ask Jim Ringo. The last person who was going to quash such a tale was Lombardi himself, who relished the tough-guy role. However, as Ringo pointed out, "There's a lot of stories how the trade existed, but I never had an agent that day."

Despite winning NFL championships in 1961 and 1962, Ringo wasn't crushed to exit Titletown. His four children and wife at the time were all in eastern Pennsylvania, and Ringo said his wife wouldn't come to Green Bay. So if Ringo was going to be traded anywhere, Philadelphia was the ideal spot.

"My life was back on the East Coast," said Ringo, who played four more seasons for the Eagles and would stretch his string of consecutive starts to 182, then an NFL record. "So it was nice to get back there. I commuted back and forth every day and never had to move out of the house. It was ideal for me. Who knows? Maybe Vince did it for my blessing."

That's doubtful, but make no mistake about it, Ringo was a blessing for the Packers. Green Bay selected him in the seventh round of the 1953 draft out of Syracuse, and Ringo went on to start every game from 1954 to 1966. Despite never weighing more than 235 pounds, Ringo's quickness and agility helped make him one of the game's elite centers. Ringo's blocking was essential to Green Bay's signature play, the Power Sweep, or Packer Sweep.

"What tenacity he had as a center in the NFL," former teammate Willie Davis told the Associated Press of Ringo. "Probably, no one was better."

Lombardi agreed.

"A bigger man might not be able to make the cut-off blocks on our sweeps the way Jim does," Lombardi once said. "The reason Ringo's the best in the league is because he's quick and he's smart. He runs the offensive line, calls the blocks and he knows what every lineman does on every play."

During Ringo's first six years in Green Bay, the Packers never cracked the .500 barrier. But in 1959 Lombardi arrived, and things changed in a hurry.

"Everything was completely different," Ringo said. "This man came in a complete unknown and turned everything around. The man was just one of the greatest coaches you'll ever find, a great philosopher and a great man. Any phase, he was there."

And the results were fantastic. By Lombardi's third year, Green Bay won its first of back-to-back NFL championships and had gone from doormat to dominator.

"That experience was just incredible," said Ringo, a captain on those title teams. "To be a champion in a community that small was something else. No matter where you went, somebody knew you. You'd walk down the street, and people would say hi and want to talk about the Packers."

Ringo went on to play in 10 Pro Bowls and was named first-team All-Pro six times. Ringo was named to the 1960s All-Decade team, then received the ultimate honor when he was named to the Pro Football Hall of Fame in 1981. Ringo died in November 2007, after battling Alzheimer's. His trade to Philadelphia, though, will always remain one of the more intriguing stories of Lombardi and those great Packers teams.

37 James Lofton

The entire Hall of Fame process was getting downright agonizing for James Lofton. Each year between 1999 and 2002, Lofton's hopes would rise when he learned he was among the 15 finalists for pro football's greatest honor. And each time, those hopes were crushed when the former Green Bay Packers great learned he fell just short.

"Each year you don't make it, it's kind of painful," Lofton said.

Finally, in 2003 Lofton's pain came to an end. On his fifth crack at it, Lofton was one of five players elected to the Pro Football Hall of Fame. Lofton is one of 22 players or coaches in Packers history to be enshrined in Canton, and he became the first from the post–Vince Lombardi era.

"I wouldn't say I was confident," Lofton said, when assessing his chances of reaching the Hall of Fame. "I would say I'm very humbled that it could happen. But in the same breath, I'm over-whelmed by it and very humbled by it."

Lofton's play on the field often humbled defensive backs. With world-class speed and the grace of a gazelle, the 6'3", 197-pound Lofton was a nightmarish matchup for secondaries. Lofton, who Green Bay selected with the sixth overall pick in the 1978 draft, became a dominant player rather quickly. He made the Pro Bowl in seven of his nine years in Green Bay and led the team in receptions in eight of nine seasons. Lofton's 9,656 career receiving yards is second in team history, and his 530 catches as a Packer ranks third all-time.

"Just a treat to play with," said Lynn Dickey, Lofton's quarterback. "He could run down balls that almost no one else in the league could. Just a dynamite talent."

Lofton was traded to the Los Angeles Raiders for third- and fourth-round draft choices following the 1986 season. The move came after Lofton was acquitted of second-degree sexual assault charges in May 1987, stemming from an incident at a downtown Green Bay nightclub. After spending two years with the Raiders, Lofton was released and found paradise when Marv Levy and the Buffalo Bills took a chance on him. Lofton made it pay off, starting for four years and helping the Bills reach three Super Bowls.

His career totals include 764 catches for 14,004 yards (18.3 yards per catch) and 75 touchdowns. At the conclusion of his playing career, Lofton's 764 receptions ranked 10th in league history, while his 14,004 yards were the most in NFL history. Lofton was inducted into the Packers Hall of Fame in 1999, and his name is on the façade inside Lambeau Field's bowl.

"That is an amazing statistic [average yards per catch] for somebody with that many catches [764]," Levy said of Lofton. "He made some electrifying, game-breaking plays for us. I'm old enough to say he reminds me of Don Hutson."

Hall of Fame wide receiver James Lofton gets a breather in a game against the Los Angeles Rams on December 17, 1978, at Memorial Coliseum. As a rookie, Lofton grabbed 46 receptions for 818 yards and six TDs, earning his first of eight trips to the Pro Bowl.

Amazingly, Lofton didn't seem destined for such honors as a child. Lofton wasn't typically the first kid picked on the playground. And Lofton was considered too skinny in high school to ever play collegiate football. In fact, it took Lofton until his senior year before he became a starter at Stanford. But he always had blazing speed, and combined with an exceptional drive, he became a Hall of Fame talent.

"The one thing I was never able to get over was I was always the skinny player from high school who wasn't good enough," Lofton recalled. "And I don't know if that's what fuels you while you're learning to compete at the NFL level, but I never thought of myself as a can't-miss guy." That's exactly what Lofton turned out to be, though, which made him a treat for Packers fans everywhere.

38 Aaron Rodgers

Aaron Rodgers spent nearly a decade playing the waiting game.

He waited for NCAA Division I colleges to notice his rare gifts. He waited for what seemed like an eternity to hear his name called during the 2005 NFL Draft.

He waited three long seasons for Brett Favre to move on. And he waited three more years before finally winning over all of Packer Nation.

Today, Rodgers has a Super Bowl championship, an NFL MVP, and a Super Bowl MVP on his résumé. He's one of the league's brightest stars and seems well on his way to a Hall of Fame career.

Truthfully, no one except perhaps Rodgers himself could have seen this coming.

"He's always been talented," Packers coach Mike McCarthy said of Rodgers. "I had a chance to evaluate the guy every game in college when he came out. I've never questioned that man's talent. He's put it all together. He's the most accomplished player I've ever coached."

Considering McCarthy coached both Joe Montana and later Favre, that's saying a mouthful. But Rodgers—and his rags to riches ascension—have been something to behold.

Rodgers has faced doubters every step of his remarkable journey. And it could be argued that of the 30 quarterbacks to win

Super Bowl titles, Rodgers overcame the most obstacles and longest odds to reach football's pinnacle.

Undersized in high school, Rodgers didn't receive a single NCAA Division I scholarship offer. He went the junior college route, before University of California coach Jeff Tedford discovered him.

Rodgers waited, waited and waited some more during the 2005 NFL Draft before the Packers finally took him with the 24th overall pick. Then Rodgers played the waiting game for three years while he sat behind Packers-icon Brett Favre.

"He has had a hard road for no reason," Packers wideout Jordy Nelson said. "He was behind Brett. Give him credit for learning and not just sitting there and waiting for Brett to be done. He went about and perfected his game."

That he did, although there was plenty of turbulence along the way.

During Rodgers' first year as a starter, Green Bay went just 6–10 after going 13–3 in Favre's final season. Although the season was a bust, Rodgers ranked fourth in the NFL in passing yards (4,038) and touchdown passes (28), was sixth in passer rating (93.8), and kept his interceptions to a manageable number (13).

"For all the pressure that was on him, he had a great year," former Packers wideout Donald Driver said of Rodgers. "And he's only going to get better. He's gotten better every year he was here, and we all expect him to keep getting better."

He did.

Rodgers guided the Packers to an 11–5 mark in 2009 and their first playoff appearance in the post-Favre era. Green Bay fell, 51–45, to Arizona in the wild-card round when Rodgers fumbled and Karlos Dansby returned the loose ball 17 yards for a game-winning score.

Overall, though, Rodgers' second season as a starter was a smashing success. Rodgers finished fourth in passer rating (103.2),

Aaron Rodgers, Green Bay's franchise quarterback, scrambles during the NFC wild-card playoff game against the Arizona Cardinals on January 10, 2010, in Glendale, Arizona. The Cardinals won the game in overtime 51–45, despite a stellar performance by Rodgers in a comeback effort.

passing yards (4,434), and TD passes (30), and earned his first trip to the Pro Bowl.

"Aaron Rodgers is a Pro Bowl quarterback, and that's the fact," McCarthy said. "Trust me, I fully understand the greatness of Brett Favre, and I had the opportunity to be part of his career, and he deserves everything that comes his way. But this is the beginning of potentially another great career at quarterback here in Green Bay."

McCarthy was right—and Rodgers proved exactly that in the 2010 postseason.

Green Bay rallied late in the year to make the playoffs. Then Rodgers had a postseason for the ages.

Rodgers led the Packers to three road wins and helped Green Bay become the NFC's first No. 6 seed to ever reach a Super Bowl. Then, McCarthy put the entire offense on Rodgers' shoulders in the title game, and he was the No. 1 reason Green Bay defeated the vaunted Pittsburgh Steelers.

Rodgers carved up a Pittsburgh defense that was allowing an NFL-best 14.5 points per game by throwing three touchdown passes and completing 24-of-39 passes for 304 yards in Green Bay's 31–25 win. Rodgers then joined Bart Starr as the only quarterbacks in Packers history to be named MVP of a Super Bowl.

"He is the reason they won," Steelers defensive lineman Brett Keisel said of Rodgers.

That capped a memorable postseason in which Rodgers threw for 1,094 yards and nine touchdown passes. The only quarterback prior to Rodgers to throw for more than 1,000 yards and nine TDs in one postseason was Kurt Warner.

"I think he's a very mature young man," Packers GM Ted Thompson said of Rodgers. "In some ways sitting for three years and then playing is helpful. That's the way it was back in the day. You always brought quarterbacks in and you developed them for about two or three years before you actually played them—that's hard to do anymore. I think that was helpful. He was able to sit back, watch, listen, and learn. Like I said, he's a very good quarterback and I think the best is yet to come."

Thompson was right.

Rodgers threw for 45 touchdowns, six interceptions and more than 4,600 yards in 2011 when he won NFL MVP honors. Rodgers also posted a passer rating of 122.5 that season, which was a new NFL record.

Rodgers led Green Bay to a franchise-record 15–1 regular season in 2011, although the Packers were upset in the NFC Divisional playoffs by the New York Giants.

Rodgers followed that with a terrific 2012, when he threw 39 touchdowns, eight interceptions, had nearly 4,300 passing yards and led the NFL in passer rating (108.0) for a second straight season.

Before the 2013 season began, Rodgers signed a five-year, $110 million contract extension making him the highest paid player in NFL history.

"The guy has overcome a ton," teammate Jordy Nelson said. "A ton."

The next challenge will be for Rodgers to keep improving and help the Packers win multiple Super Bowls in the years ahead. After proving people wrong for years, it would seem foolish to bet against Rodgers now.

"I'm always looking for challenges," Rodgers said.

And more often than not, he's conquered them.

39 Jerry Kramer

Jerry Kramer still doesn't get it. During Kramer's 11 years as a standout right guard in Green Bay, he played on five NFL championship teams. Kramer received some type of All-Pro honors on six occasions and he played in three Pro Bowls. Kramer was named to the NFL's 50th Anniversary All-Time Team. And Kramer's block on Dallas' Jethro Pugh sprung Bart Starr for a game-winning touchdown in the Ice Bowl, one of the most famous football games ever played.

To this day, though, Kramer's omission from the Hall of Fame is one of the great mysteries of the sport.

"Out of every guy who was on the [NFL's 50th Anniversary] team, I'm the only one not in there," Kramer said. "Does it bother me? A little bit, but not a lot. The way I look at it is football has been so good to me. It's given me so many presents. After so many years, it would seem a little childish to be pissed off over an honor you didn't get."

Kramer looks back and laughs when he thinks how close he came to not getting anything that football eventually provided him. Green Bay's fourth-round draft choice in 1958, Kramer played his first season under the loosey-goosey Scooter McLean. And when Vince Lombardi came in the following season, his in-your-face approach didn't sit well with Kramer initially.

In the early 1960s, the *Chicago Tribune* had just published a story calling Kramer and Fuzzy Thurston the best pair of guards in football. Later that same week in practice, a Packer Sweep went nowhere, and Lombardi went ballistic.

"He came running up, screaming, 'The best pair of guards in football, my ass!'" said Kramer, who scored 156 points as the Packers' place-kicker in 1962 and 1963. "And I was already playing hurt. I had broken two ribs the week before in San Francisco, and I just snapped. I was dead-set on punching him in the mouth. I got off the pile and I thought, *Okay, I'll be suspended. I'll get docked my salary. And I'm sure I'll get traded.* And I just said, '[Screw] it! I'm going to hit him.' I was so angry and so out of control. So I walked over by him, and he wouldn't look at me. He just stayed turned away. Finally, I got over my anger and decided to walk the sidelines. Well, after five or six minutes, just the right amount of time for me to cool off, Lombardi came down and pats me on the shoulder and rubs my hair. It was good for both of us that I didn't hit him."

That it was. Kramer became a prototype NFL guard, pulling on sweeps and helping see to it that Starr was almost never touched.

But when history remembers Kramer, it will always be linked to the Ice Bowl. Trailing Dallas 17–14 in the 1967 NFL Championship Game, the Packers were out of time-outs, facing a third-and-goal from the Cowboys' 1-yard line with 16 seconds left. Lombardi bypassed a potential tying field goal and elected to go for the victory instead. The play was supposed to be a handoff to Chuck Mercein, but Starr was leery of Mercein slipping and decided to run a quarterback sneak instead. Kramer found a rare piece of field that wasn't iced over, came off the ball fast and hard, and immediately cut Pugh. Center Ken Bowman finished Pugh off, giving Starr the wedge opening he needed. Starr snuck in, the Packers had one of the most dramatic victories in league history, and Kramer was part of the NFL's most legendary block.

"People want to always talk about that play. But what personifies the character and make-up of that football team was the drive," Kramer said, referring to the 12-play, 68-yard march to win the game. "That was a perfect example of what those teams were all about. On that drive, we were absolutely brilliant. Chuck Mercein, Donny Anderson, Boyd Dowler, Bart, the entire offensive line. They were all outstanding."

The legendary play also provided the ideal ending for a book Kramer and sportswriter Dick Schaap were working on. Throughout the 1967 season, Kramer kept a diary of the Packers' season, one which ended with a victory in Super Bowl II. And the publicity generated by the Ice Bowl—a game that was later voted the greatest game in NFL history—helped *Instant Replay* become one of the best-selling sports books of all time.

"It was an interesting experience, and it was fun to see that world," Kramer said. "Pro football is a very closed world. You're either part of the team or you're not. But the whole experience was pretty great. Those were incredible times and some incredible men. You won't get groups of guys like that very often."

40 Mike McCarthy

Mike McCarthy was bold, daring, and courageous.

McCarthy had just been named the 14th head coach in Green Bay Packers history. And McCarthy, who rarely made headlines with his words, did so on this day.

"I'd like to acknowledge the fans of Green Bay and just to let you know that there will be an unconditional commitment... to bring a World Championship back to Green Bay," McCarthy said during his introductory press conference. "I think that's very important to state that right up front."

At the time, many undoubtedly chuckled. The Packers were coming off a dysfunctional 4–12 season, had an aging roster, and lacked young stars.

But to the surprise of many, just more than five years later, McCarthy was holding up the Lombardi Trophy after his Packers defeated Pittsburgh 31–25 in Super Bowl XLV.

"I've been talking about the Super Bowl since...the first day I stood up here," McCarthy said. "The first overlay I ever put up in front of our team was to win the Super Bowl. This is always the goal. It will always be the goal as long as I'm the coach here. It's part of coaching the Green Bay Packers. The standard has been set, the history is in place, and it's our responsibility to make sure we get that done."

While many were amazed McCarthy led the Packers to a Super Bowl title, several were just as surprised he landed the job in the first place.

McCarthy was a dark-horse candidate, at best, to replace Mike Sherman. McCarthy had never been a head coach at any level. And the offense he coordinated in San Francisco in 2005 ranked 32nd in the NFL.

But Packers general manager Ted Thompson saw something different in McCarthy, and gave him the job at the age of 42.

"I kind of liked that Pittsburgh macho stuff, you know?" Thompson said after hiring McCarthy, who was born and raised in Pittsburgh. "I like the fact that he's a tough guy. I think he's a players' coach, but also understands the bounds of that. I think he's a good fit for us."

McCarthy has certainly been that.

In McCarthy's first seven seasons, he's compiled a 74–38 overall record. That .661 winning percentage ranks fourth in team history behind only Vince Lombardi (.754), Mike Holmgren (.670) and Earl "Curly" Lambeau (.668).

McCarthy led the Packers to the Super Bowl title in 2010, joining Lambeau, Lombardi and Holmgren as the only coaches in franchise history to win a championship. And McCarthy's six postseason wins are third in team history behind only Lombardi and Holmgren (nine each).

According to those closest to McCarthy, consistency and communication have been enormous reasons for his success.

"I think Mike's very consistent," Packers defensive coordinator Dom Capers said. "I think he's had a plan since he's been here and a vision of what he wants this team to look like. This is a business that's a roller-coaster business and we're all evaluated on what we do right now. What we did yesterday really has no relevance.

"So I think being able to be consistent with that message and be demanding and consistent in terms of the effort and the focus, in the meeting room and practice field and weight room and everything you do, you create a culture that's just standing operating procedure in the way we do business. And that benefits you in the long haul."

McCarthy doesn't get too high or low. Whether the Packers are in the midst of a 13–0 start—like they were in 2011—or struggling through a 6–10 season like they were in 2008, McCarthy is the exact same guy. No craziness. No unpredictability. No tirades.

Instead, McCarthy is innovative, bold, confident, and imaginative on game days. During the week, McCarthy is organized, consistent, straightforward, and honest.

"He's consistent every week," former Packers center Scott Wells said of McCarthy. "He's clear, he's concise, and there's no ifs ands or buts about it. You know exactly what's expected of you."

Thompson, the man who made the surprise move of hiring McCarthy, agreed.

"He does a very good job of being organized," Thompson said. "He does a very good job of handling the chaos coming from the job and he keeps a fairly even keel. I like all those things. I think those are good qualities."

The Packers' philosophy under McCarthy and Thompson has always been to draft and develop players. That's means Green Bay almost always has more youth than most teams.

Therefore, McCarthy's steadiness is vital.

From the start, McCarthy established a plan, stayed true to it and his players bought into it.

One of the first things McCarthy did was try and improve communication throughout the entire building. Things had become fantastically corporate under former coach and general manager Mike Sherman, a man who many players said lacked a personal side.

By the end of Sherman's regime, some players were terrified to make a mistake. There was tension everywhere. Morale was low. And coming to work each day had become a job, not a passion.

McCarthy did all he could, though, to change that. Today, players rave about his communication abilities, and while they understand he's their boss first, they seem to have a bond that's greater than simply player-coach.

"Coach [Sherman] was all business," quarterback Aaron Rodgers said. "I would have never just gone up to his office. I think [McCarthy's] a good communicator and there's an open-door policy. He listens to people and he's able to allow the other coaches on the staff to coach and to speak up, which I think is really important."

On the field, there's been a lot of respect earned, too.

McCarthy often uses the term "stack successes," and his teams have done a terrific job of that.

Green Bay reached the postseason in 2009, then followed that with a Super Bowl championship in 2010. Then in 2011, the Packers went an NFL-best 15–1, before being upset in the playoffs.

A big reason for that has been McCarthy's work with quarterbacks.

When McCarthy first arrived, Brett Favre was coming off the worst year of his career. But McCarthy helped Favre get back on track and lead the Packers to the NFC Championship Game in 2007.

Rodgers' mechanics were a mess when McCarthy showed up in 2006. But McCarthy and then-quarterbacks coach Tom Clements coached Rodgers to lower his carriage. When he did, Rodgers became a more natural and effortless thrower, eventually winning a Super Bowl title in 2010 and the league's MVP award in 2011.

"In Aaron Rodgers' particular situation, he had a very high ball carriage, which I felt there was a stiffness to the way he carried the ball," McCarthy said. "It wasn't as natural, because he is a very good athlete, and it's something you didn't see in my opinion in his earlier days, how good of an athlete he was. I think it's something that we've adjusted and he's very natural with it. Every quarterback that I've ever coached, you're always looking to improve their mechanics."

In McCarthy's first seven seasons, he led Green Bay to the playoffs five times. The Packers had just one losing season in that stretch, as well.

McCarthy's run of success is probably more than even the most optimistic of Packers fan could have hoped for back in 2006. But no one is complaining.

"I just don't believe in the crash-and-burn theory," McCarthy said. "I believe in winning and learning. I don't believe in that other word [losing]. I don't even like to say it.

"I believe you keep building and keep working at it, keep winning. And as long as they keep giving you opportunities, make the best of it.

"I'm not satisfied with coming close. I'm going to do everything I can to win the championship and that will never change. And when that does change, I probably need to step out and let someone else take a swing at it."

That's not likely to happen for quite some time, which seems like terrific news for Packer Nation.

41 Johnny "Blood" McNally

Johnny "Blood" McNally led the Green Bay Packers to four NFL championships between 1929 and 1936. He had blazing speed, was a terrific running back and receiver, and even played defense. But McNally was also one of the most colorful players in Green Bay Packers history. And his off-the-field exploits are even more legendary that his on-field accomplishments.

"Johnny gave [coach] Curly [Lambeau] fits over the years with his nocturnal escapades, of which there were many," former Packers historian Lee Remmel said. "On one occasion, Lambeau locked him in his hotel room the night before a game against the Bears in Chicago so he wouldn't break curfew and go out on the town. Being resourceful, Johnny had other ideas and reportedly tied bed sheets together and climbed down through the hotel window. Though I can't confirm it, another story told of Johnny missing the team train and then stopping it with his car."

If you like those, how about this one?

"Before the 1929 season, Johnny Blood played for the Pottsville Maroons," Remmel said. "Curly offered him $100 per game to play in Green Bay via a letter, with a P.S. that, if he stopped drinking by Wednesday night of each game week, he'd pay him $110 per game. Johnny wrote back: 'I'll take the $100.' That was typical Johnny Blood."

On the field, McNally was just as memorable.

McNally created his alias—Blood—in 1922 while playing collegiately at St. John's. Like many college players, McNally wanted to make some money by playing professionally on the side. McNally chose the name "Blood" after seeing a billboard for the movie *Blood and Sand* starring Rudolph Valentino. He was then able to sneak through and played for the Duluth Eskimos as Johnny Blood.

McNally had already played four years of professional football when he arrived in Green Bay in 1929 at the age of 26. During his first year with the Packers, McNally led Green Bay in rushing yards (406) and helped it win its first-ever NFL title. In 1931 McNally's 14 total touchdowns (11 receiving, two rushing, one return) led the NFL. His exploits were also integral to the Packers winning their third-straight NFL title. McNally also had a career-high 25 receptions in 1935 and helped the Packers to another NFL championship in 1936.

"I remember him well," said Dan Rooney, the Pittsburgh Steelers' chairman of the board. "I always thought, of the guys from the past who could play in the NFL today, Johnny Blood was one of them. In my opinion, he'd have been a first-round draft choice. He was fast and versatile and an excellent receiver. And he was versatile off the field, as well."

McNally was inducted into the Pro Football Hall of Fame in 1963. The Packers later named a banquet room after him in the Lambeau Field Atrium.

"Foremost, Johnny Blood was truly a great football player," Remmel said. "He played a significant role on the Packers' early championship teams and was a charter inductee in the Pro Football Hall of Fame in 1963, along with three other Packer greats [Lambeau, Don Hutson, and Cal Hubbard]. That honor speaks for itself. I never did see him play, but...he was probably the most colorful character to ever wear a Packer uniform and one of the most interesting and intelligent people I've ever met. I don't think there will ever be another one quite like him. I believe the best summation of Johnny Blood was authored by his wife [Marguerite], who said, 'Even when Johnny does the expected, he does it in an unexpected way.'"

42 Jack Vainisi

The typical Green Bay Packers fan has never heard the name Jack Vainisi. And that's a shame. Because, in many ways, Vainisi was as vital to the Packers' success in the 1960s as Vince Lombardi, Bart Starr, or Ray Nitschke.

Vainisi was a Packers scout, scouting director, and personnel director from 1950 to 1960. In that time, Vainisi was credited with discovering seven Packers Hall of Famers and several other standouts who helped the Packers win five championships in seven years, beginning in 1961. Unfortunately, Vainisi suffered a massive heart attack and died at just 33 years old in 1960.

"Jack Vainisi was highly regarded as a talent scout," said Lee Remmel, the Packers former team historian and public relations director. "He helped build a dynasty, and his 1958 draft is considered the best in team history."

The Pittsburgh Steelers' draft of 1974 is often pointed to as the greatest in NFL history. That year the Steelers became the only team to ever select four future Hall of Famers in the same year, when they drafted wideouts Lynn Swann and John Stallworth, linebacker Jack Lambert, and center Mike Webster.

But Vainisi's 1958 draft certainly rivals that of the 1974 Steelers.

Vainisi's first-round selection was used on linebacker Dan Currie, a seven-year starter in Green Bay. In the second round, Vainisi drafted fullback Jim Taylor, who was Green Bay's all-time leading rusher until 2009 and was inducted into the Hall of Fame in 1976. In the third round, Vainisi took Nitschke, who played 15 years in Green Bay and went into the Hall of Fame in 1978. And he used a fourth-round pick on Jerry Kramer, the Packers' All-Pro primary starter at right guard from 1958 to 1968.

Vainisi's magic extended far beyond that draft, though. He drafted future Hall of Famers, such as Jim Ringo in 1953, Forrest Gregg and Starr in 1956, and Paul Hornung in 1957. Vainisi also signed Willie Wood, an undrafted free agent, in 1960, and Wood had a Hall of Fame career himself.

"I loved Jack Vainisi—all the players did," Hornung said. "He even got along with Lombardi. He was a football man—that's what he was. Pure and simple. He brought so much talent to Green Bay."

Vainisi was hired as a scout by Packers coach Gene Ronzani in 1950 and developed a network of college and high school coaches. He used those contacts to rank more than 4,000 players, which helped revolutionize the position of scout. While Vainisi was ahead of his time as a scout, his legacy may be getting Lombardi to come to Green Bay.

The Packers had just completed a 1–10–1 season in 1958 when Vainisi reached out to Lombardi to gauge his interest. Lombardi, who was the New York Giants' offensive coordinator at the time, told Vainisi he was interested. Vainisi then went to the Packers' executive board and recommended the team hire Lombardi as its coach and give him total autonomy as their general manager. Just three years later, the Packers were NFL champions for the first time since 1944. Many of the players Vainisi had selected were integral in Green Bay's resurgence. Lombardi, the coach and GM Vainisi lobbied for, was equally responsible.

Unfortunately for Vainisi, he never saw the fruits of his labor fully materialize. The Packers never forgot Vainisi, though, and he was inducted into the team's Hall of Fame in 1982.

"He was the unsung hero of that whole era," said Starr, who was drafted in the 17th round. "Jack gets forgotten sometimes, but his eye for talent made it all possible."

43 1996 NFC Championship Game

The wait was brutal. Nearly 30 years of futility. Three decades of being a punch line, a punching bag, and a city few wanted to play in. All the painful memories came to an end on January 12, 1997.

The Green Bay Packers defeated the Carolina Panthers 30–13 that day to advance to Super Bowl XXXI. And while the Packers captured their third Super Bowl title two weeks later, there's still something about the NFC Championship Game that remains even more special to many.

"Out of all our wins, that was the best," free safety Eugene Robinson said.

"That was the game that showed we had arrived," former general manager Ron Wolf said. "I'll never forget it. Playing in our stadium in front of our fans and going up to the podium to accept that [NFC Championship] trophy. That was some kind of experience."

Green Bay locals, who eat, drink, and breathe football, had been waiting for a champion since Super Bowl II. They had watched miserable outfits led by Dan Devine, Bart Starr, Forrest Gregg, and Lindy Infante trip over themselves. But here they were, back within one game of the Super Bowl when the second-year Panthers came calling.

"We were confident," Carolina coach Dom Capers said during a 2009 interview. "Watching the tape, you knew it would take an awful lot to beat a team like Green Bay in their building. But we were confident."

And the Panthers played that way, racing out to leads of 7–0 and 10–7. Carolina was taking the fight to the Packers, despite the fact the kickoff temperature was just 3 degrees above zero (minus-17 with the wind chill).

But, before the first half was over, Antonio Freeman caught a six-yard touchdown pass from Brett Favre, and Chris Jacke drilled a 31-yard field goal to give the Packers a 17–10 lead. Jacke and Carolina's John Kasay traded third-quarter field goals as Green Bay retained a 20–13 lead. But the game changed late in third quarter behind the Packers' two-headed monster at running back. Dorsey Levens, who had a 29-yard reception for Green Bay's first touch-down, went 66 yards on a screen pass. On the next play, Edgar Bennett went untouched from four yards out for a TD that gave the Packers a 27–13 lead and total control of the contest.

"All year, everyone said the weakest part of the team was the running game," Levens said. "We wanted to prove a point. Nobody gave us any respect all year. We wish quarterbacks had no arms so we could run every time."

The Packers finished with a team playoff-record 479 yards in an effort that was an offensive coordinator's dream. Favre threw for 292 yards, completed 19 of 29 passes, and threw two touchdowns.

Defensive end Reggie White (92) embraces quarterback Brett Favre during the NFC championship trophy presentation at Lambeau Field on January 12, 1997, after the Packers defeated the Carolina Panthers 30–13 to advance to Super Bowl XXXI in New Orleans.

Bennett rushed for 99 yards on 25 carries, and Levens carried for 88 yards on just 10 attempts. The Packers finished with 201 rushing yards, and Levens added another 117 receiving yards on just five catches (a 23.4-yard average).

"In the second half, once the Packers got things going, they got rolling," Capers said. "The Packers were the best team, and they did something that year that I'm not sure has been done since, and that's led the league in offense and defense. Usually a team is very good on offense or very good on defense, but it's hard to get both sides of the ball. And I remember the second half, as the Packers started picking up momentum and the crowd got into the game and we got out of the game, it got really cold out there."

Not to the Packers or their faithful, who celebrated well into the memorable night.

"I don't think anybody can stop us now," Favre said.

Nobody did, as Green Bay won Super Bowl XXXI two weeks later. But the game that got the Packers to Super Sunday was just as memorable for many.

44 Freeman's Miracle

To this day, Antonio Freeman has no clue how the ball found his hands. He's uncertain how Cris Dishman didn't come up with a sure interception, how the ball didn't fall harmlessly to the ground, or how he eventually scored the winning touchdown in the Green Bay Packers' 26–20 overtime win in a *Monday Night Football* game on November 6, 2000.

"It's the craziest catch I ever made," Freeman said. "Brett [Favre] could throw that pass my way 100 times, 1,000 times, and the way that ball ended up bouncing won't happen more than once. A 'Monday Night Miracle,' I guess."

Miracle is the perfect word for Freeman's heroics, as well as the Packers' stunning win. When the Vikings arrived in Green

Antonio Freeman (86) leaps into the stands at Lambeau after making one of the most improbable, incredible TD catches in NFL history, as Donald Driver (80) looks on. The game-winning reception came on a Brett Favre pass in overtime to beat the Vikings 26–20 on Monday Night Football, *November 6, 2000.*

Bay that night, the Packers were just 3–5 under first-year coach Mike Sherman. The Vikings, who would go on to win the NFC Central that year, were 7–1 and entered as 3½-point favorites. But the Packers played one of their more spirited games of the year and forced overtime, thanks largely to a 5–0 advantage in the turnover department.

Green Bay won the coin toss in overtime and drove to the Minnesota 43, where it faced a third-and-four. Minnesota blitzed six, forcing Favre to throw off his back foot and get rid of the ball in just 1.59 seconds. Favre took a shot deep down the right sideline for Freeman, who was working one-on-one against Dishman, a better-than-average cornerback.

Freeman slipped and fell to the ground on a field that had been getting pelted with rain, giving Dishman a clear shot at an interception. Dishman had inside position on Freeman, and the ball hit his right hand first. It then caromed off his left hand and appeared to fall incomplete. In fact, the *Monday Night Football* audience heard this call from play-by-play man Al Michaels: "Favre puts it up for Freeman, and it's incomplete." Hardly.

When Dishman hit the ball the second time, it ricocheted toward Freeman, who was lying face down on the ground. The ball hit Freeman's left shoulder, and as he spun back around, the ball bounced up, and he somehow managed to get his right hand underneath it. Dishman was certain the pass was incomplete and jumped around, five yards behind Freeman, stewing over his missed interception. Freeman knew the ball was still alive, though, and leapt to his feet after he had secured it.

"It was a lucky, lucky play," Freeman said. "But I knew that ball never hit the ground."

After Freeman rose up, he eluded safety Robert Griffith at the 14-yard line, then raced to the end zone for one of the most improbable touchdowns you'll ever see. The play was reviewed and upheld, marking the only time all night Green Bay had the lead. Afterward, Freeman received the hero's treatment, getting carried off the field by his teammates.

"As I rolled back, I got an early Christmas gift, I guess," Freeman said. "Hey, who said football was all skill? Tonight, we got our lucky bounce."

While the bounce was certainly lucky, the hook-up itself was premeditated. Freeman was supposed to run a slant route, but when he noticed Dishman didn't have any safety help, he got Favre's attention.

"I was just standing there waiting, and I heard, 'Brett,'" Favre said afterward. "I knew it was Free. When I looked out, he kind of gave me the signal, and I kind of nodded my head. Your star player wants the ball, give it to him. He made the play. I don't even know if you can call it a play. That was remarkable, unbelievable."

Freeman, who spent eight of his nine NFL seasons in Green Bay, had several memorable moments as a Packer. He caught an 81-yard touchdown pass in Super Bowl XXXI. He led the NFL in receiving yards in 1998, and he ranks sixth in Packers history in catches (431) and yards (6,651). But Freeman's version of the "Immaculate Reception" is something that Packers fans will remember for years to come.

"If that's what you're going to be remembered for, that's not a bad thing," said Freeman, who was inducted into the Packers Hall of Fame in 2009. "I know I'll never forget that play."

Who could?

45 Phil Bengtson

Phil Bengtson never really stood a chance. The roster was aging. The legend he was replacing was still in the building. Expectations were completely out of whack. So it shouldn't have shocked anyone when Bengtson—who replaced Vince Lombardi as Green Bay's head coach in 1968—lasted just three seasons. Bengtson compiled a 20–21–1 record, then stepped down after the 1970 season.

"Guys who were at their peak kind of started on their downside when Bengtson took over," said former linebacker Jim Flanigan. "And it was kind of a no-win for Phil. Had he won, people would have said he was winning with Lombardi's guys. When he didn't win, he was cast as the villain. Lombardi definitely got out at the right time."

As Green Bay's defensive coordinator from 1959 to 1967, Bengtson played a huge role in the Packers' success. During that nine-year stretch, the Packers finished in the top three in total defense seven times and were first twice. So when Lombardi stepped down as Green Bay's head coach following the Packers' win in Super Bowl II, Bengtson was a natural choice to replace him. The low-key approach Bengtson had was much different from the often-volatile Lombardi. At the end of the day, though, Bengtson simply didn't win enough football games. Whether or not that was his fault will always be debated around Green Bay.

"Even with Vince, I don't think we would have made the play-offs," former running back Jim Grabowski said. "There were a lot of guys who had been around quite a while. We had a lot of injuries occur. And in Phil's defense, he was considered by almost everybody to be one of the brightest defensive minds around. We just had a lot of guys who had been around a while who weren't at the same level."

Grabowski's point is well taken. The Packers had become one of the older teams in football, filled with players past their prime.

Lombardi, who remained as general manager, wasn't bringing in the talent he had earlier in his regime. And even Lombardi saw the writing on the wall and left after the 1968 season for a head coaching job with the Washington Redskins. Bengtson did what he could to try getting an aging roster to recapture its glory years. But that never happened, and the Packers missed the postseason in each of Bengtson's three seasons.

"[Lombardi] didn't do Phil any favors," said Gary Knafelc, who played on Green Bay's early championship teams. "To win the Ice Bowl and the last Super Bowl was amazing. But the Packers were old and dead. [Lombardi] didn't want to go down a loser."

Instead, Bengtson was left to fall on the sword.

After he was fired in Green Bay, Bengtson was the New England Patriots' interim head coach in 1972. He later was New England's director of pro scouting. While Bengtson's tenure as head coach didn't go as planned, he was still highly respected and fondly thought of around Green Bay.

"Phil was a magnificent gentleman and a great human being," Hall of Fame linebacker Ray Nitschke once said. "I truly loved the man. Phil was one of the classiest people I ever met in my life."

46 Training Camp

National Football League players have always hated training camp. The practices are long. The days are monotonous. The summer heat is unyielding. For Green Bay Packers fans, though, taking in a training camp practice is a memorable experience. It's also one of the more popular destinations for the green-and-gold faithful.

For years, the Packers held most of their practices at Clarke Hinkle Field on South Oneida Street. There were roughly 20 units of bleachers outside a fence that could seat up to 1,000 fans. The rest of the folks were left to fend for themselves, and considering there were days when practices could draw up to 5,000 people, overcrowding and safety were often an issue. But in 2009 the Packers moved their practices to the brand new Ray Nitschke Field. The state-of-the-art facility seats roughly 1,500 fans on the east side and includes a 170-yard natural grass field.

Fans are allowed carry-ins, while concessions are also sold. Today, what was already a good experience has been elevated to great.

"I love the field," former Packers wideout Donald Driver said. "I just love the atmosphere of it. Love it, love it, love it. You've basically got the fans right there in the stands enjoying everything with us, they're not sitting outside the gates. They're experiencing what we get to experience. The fans cheer you on. We love that."

Packers linebacker A.J. Hawk rides the bike of a fan to practice. This has been a long-standing tradition in Green Bay and a way for fans to get closer to their heroes.

The Packers held 22 training-camp practices in 2013—roughly half the number of a decade ago. But one unique change in the past decade has been the addition of night practices. Mike McCarthy introduced the concept when he was hired as Green Bay's coach in 2006 to break up the boredom and help keep his team fresh. McCarthy has fewer night practices today than he once did. Overall, though, the experiment has been a hit.

"There's a lot of benefits to it, obviously, from the players' wear-and-tear standpoint," McCarthy said. "Today's game is different…. You don't have as many people in camp, and the salary cap obviously is a focus. So that's definitely the benefit of it. Also, it's fan-friendly and it's coaching-friendly."

One unique tradition of training camp in Green Bay is that Packers players often ride the bicycles of young fans to practice. The ritual dates back to the days of Vince Lombardi. Young fans are encouraged to line up in front of the Oneida Nation Gate, which is where the players enter and exit Lambeau Field. And while some players elect to walk or use their vehicles, many still snag a youngster's bike.

"It's fantastic. It really is," said former Packer Aaron Kampman, who played collegiately at Iowa. "I come from a place where people love football, and I just think they take it to another level here. The whole training-camp experience is great for people. They have a lot of chances to get up close to the game and to the players, and I know that means something to a lot of people."

47 Brett Favre in Purple

They say divorce is far harder on the children than the adults. Packer Nation can certainly relate.

On November 1, 2009, Brett Favre prepared to play his 140th game (including playoffs) at Lambeau Field. Only this time, the legendary quarterback was wearing the purple of the hated Minnesota Vikings, not the Packers' green and gold he'd donned the previous 139 times. For Favre, it was like going to visit his first wife with his new mistress. For fans, it was one of the most surreal sporting events they'll ever attend.

"It didn't seem weird until I got into around DePere," Favre said. "Everything was real familiar to me, obviously. Then I came up Ridge [Road], and all the Packer fans were there. There was some purple. I saw just a mixture of everything. Cheers. A couple [middle] fingers."

He probably saw a lot more when he left.

On that bizarre November day, Favre was surgeon-like, carving up Green Bay's secondary with remarkable precision and accuracy in leading the Vikings to a critical 38–26 win. Favre threw four touchdown passes for the 21st time in his career, which tied him with Dan Marino for the most in NFL history, and posted a lights-out passer rating of 128.6.

Afterward, Favre raised both arms to the sky before being hugged by several former teammates, as well as Packers head coach Mike McCarthy and Jerry Parins, the Packers' longtime director of security. Fans watched in amazement, not sure how to react. Favre had previously said he'd like to "stick it" to Packers general manager Ted Thompson, the man who traded him. And on this day Favre did exactly that.

"It had nothing to do with trying to prove myself to anyone," said Favre, who also led the Vikings to an earlier 30–23 win over the Packers in the Metrodome. "I still have a passion for it. But I'm glad it's over, I'm glad we won both, but I'm not going to sit here and throw any daggers."

Favre's breakup with the Packers was arguably the most hotly debated sports topic in state history. It caused chaos throughout the Packers locker room, left Favre bitter toward the organization he helped carry for years, and divided one of the most loyal fan bases in sports.

"It was not an easy thing to get through," Packers president Mark Murphy said.

There was still a lot of love for Favre during the 2008 season, after Thompson shipped him to the New York Jets. To many, Thompson was the villain, especially after the Packers slumped to a 6–10 season. Favre was seen as a sympathetic figure by some, a master manipulator by others, and everything in between. The majority of fans still cheered for their longtime hero, bought Favre's new jersey, and made the Jets their favorite team in the American Football Conference.

But that all changed in 2009, when Favre maneuvered his way to Minnesota. Favre had retired again, asked the Jets for his release, then un-retired to play for the Vikings. To the majority of Packers fans, Favre immediately became a Judas—choosing to play for Green Bay's No. 1 rival. So throughout the game at Lambeau Field that November day, a regular-season record crowd of 71,213 booed Favre at a frenzied pace.

"It was about what I expected. It was probably worse every time I took the field," Favre said of the booing. "Although I wasn't expecting a standing ovation, I know what I've done, what I stand for. What I've done here speaks for itself. What I was a part of was awesome. That will never change."

Time, of course, heals all wounds. In all likelihood, Favre will return to Green Bay to have his jersey retired and perhaps reestablish a relationship with the organization. For now, the messy split has left most people siding with the Packers—at least since Favre chose to don purple.

"Packer fans cheer for the Packers first," said Favre, who retired from the Vikings after the 2010 season and hasn't played since. "I know that. But I hope that everyone in the stadium watching tonight said, 'I sure hate those jokers on the other side, but he does play the way he's always played.'"

Perhaps, but that didn't make it any easier on the kids.

48 Bobby Dillon

The 1950s were a forgettable time in Green Bay. The Packers' only winning season came in the final year of the decade after Vince Lombardi arrived. Green Bay's first three coaches in the '50s— Gene Ronzani (1950–1953), Lisle Blackbourn (1954–1957), and Scooter McLean (1958)—still have the three worst winning percentages in team history.

Clearly, there wasn't much positive happening. But the Packers did have this going for them: Bobby Dillon.

Dillon, a magnificent free safety, played in Green Bay from 1952 to 1959 and still holds the team record with 52 career interceptions. He also averaged nearly 20 yards per return. History often overlooks Dillon, though, because the teams he played on were brutal. But to this day, Dillon remains one of the most dynamic defensive players in team history.

"It's a shame he played when the Packers were not very successful," former Packers historian Lee Remmel said. "Bobby was a very special player and a very special human being, one of the finest gentlemen I've ever known. With where he stands statistically, I think he's the No. 1 defensive back in team history and one of the best ever in the NFL. I don't think his career merits were appropriately rewarded. In my humble opinion, Bobby Dillon deserves to be in the Pro Football Hall of Fame."

Remarkably, Dillon's accomplishments came with just one working eye. Dillon lost an eye during a childhood accident and played with a glass one.

"The only adjustment I made was I learned to have my head on a swivel," Dillon said during a 2004 interview with the *Milwaukee Journal Sentinel*. "Those guys would look for you from the blind side. Everybody knew I had only one eye. In fact, [quarterback] Bobby Layne was playing at Detroit, and he'd come by and say, 'You one-eyed son of a bitch, I'll get you today.' He'd laugh."

Opponents weren't usually laughing when Dillon was done with them. Dillon led the Packers in interceptions every year between 1952 and 1958. That string of seven straight seasons remains a team record. Dillon had nine interceptions in 1953, 1955, and 1957, which remains tied for the second-most picks in a single season. (Irv Comp's 10 interceptions in 1943 ranks first.) Dillon also had four interceptions in a 1953 Thanksgiving game at Detroit that the Packers lost 34–15. Dillon and cornerback Willie Buchanon (1978) still share the team record for most interceptions in a single game.

Football is hard enough for great athletes with full sight. Amazingly, Dillon was accomplishing this all with severe visual limitations, as well as an unusual concern.

"I only had the eye knocked out one time during a game," he said. "We had to call timeout and look around on the ground for it until we finally found it. They just popped it back in."

Dillon retired following the 1958 season, but Lombardi talked him out of it. Lombardi called Dillon "by far the best defensive halfback in the league" and knew he needed the standout to succeed. Dillon had a career-low one interception during his final season of 1959. But he went out as a winner for the first time, as the Packers posted a 7–5 record under Lombardi.

Dillon was named to four Pro Bowls in his career and was named first-team All-Pro by the Associated Press four times, as well. His brilliant career was capped off when he was named to the Packers' Hall of Fame in 1974. The NFL Hall of Fame never came calling, though.

"It just wasn't in the cards," Dillon said.

49 Max McGee

On the field, he produced one highlight after another. Off the field, he assembled even more. Whether he was playing for the Green Bay Packers or broadcasting their games, Max McGee was arguably as colorful as anyone who ever passed through the organization.

A standout wide receiver during the team's glory years, McGee built a reputation for having as much fun away from the field as he did on it.

"Yeah, I think that's safe to say," McGee said during an interview shortly before his death in 2007. "I was fortunate to spend my whole time in Green Bay, because we had a hell of a time."

Boy, did he ever.

McGee came to Green Bay in the fifth round from Tulane in 1954. He was called up to serve as a pilot in the Air Force from 1955 to 1956, then returned to Green Bay in 1957. McGee led the team in receptions in 1958 and from 1960 to 1962. He was a starting wide receiver through 1964, as the Packers dominated the rest of the NFL.

By the time Super Bowl I rolled around, though, McGee was a little-used reserve who had caught just four passes all season. But when Boyd Dowler was injured on Green Bay's first series, it was McGee to the rescue. Over the remainder of the afternoon, McGee produced one of the greatest games in Super Bowl history, catching seven passes for 138 yards and two touchdowns, as Green Bay routed Kansas City 35–10.

"After I had scored those two touchdowns, [Paul] Hornung came over to me and said, 'You're going to be the MVP,'" McGee said. "Well, I wasn't, but it was a heck of a game."

And a heck of an evening before the game. Because McGee believed he had virtually no shot at playing in the game, he says he risked the $15,000 fine and sneaked out the night before to meet up with two stewardesses he had met earlier that day. McGee claims he had been out all night and went into Super Bowl I on virtually no sleep.

Dave "Hawg" Hanner, who was in charge of bed checks, claimed that McGee was full of hot air and his story of dodging curfew was sheer fiction. McGee, though, says otherwise.

"Hawg's one of my favorite buddies, but he's trying to cover his ass on this one," McGee said. "I was rooming with Hornung, and Hornung didn't want to risk going out because the fine was the same as our game check was going to be. But when Hawg stuck his head in, I said, 'Are you going to be checking late?' He screamed, 'You damned right I am!' Then he stuck his head back in and shook it no. Well, I almost ran him over trying to get out."

McGee was notorious for such antics. He and Hornung both loved the nightlife, and often seemed to divvy up as much in fines as they brought home. While McGee would often drive coach Vince Lombardi nuts, there was a mutual respect between the two.

"Not to pat myself on the back," McGee said, "but he was very confident when I was playing that I could give him some big plays."

One play that proved how much McGee could push the envelope came in the 1960 NFL Championship Game in Philadelphia. McGee, who also punted, loved to fake a punt and take off running under former coaches Lisle Blackbourn and Scooter McLean. But when Lombardi arrived, he told McGee that wouldn't be tolerated unless the instruction came from him. With Green Bay needing a spark in the fourth quarter, McGee took off running on a fake punt from his own goal line and picked up 35 yards. McGee later capped the drive with a seven-yard TD reception from Bart Starr for a 13–10 Green Bay lead. Although the Eagles rallied back for a 17–13 victory, McGee's run remains legendary.

"If I hadn't made it, I would have never played another down in Green Bay," McGee said. "I know that much."

Packers wide receiver and unlikely hero Max McGee makes a juggling TD catch during Super Bowl I, a 35–10 victory over the Kansas City Chiefs. McGee, past his prime by the 1966 season, filled in for an injured Boyd Dowler in the Super Bowl with seven catches for 138 yards and two scores.

Little did McGee know then that he'd still be with the Packers nearly 40 years later. When McGee's playing days ended following the 1967 season, he did some television and radio broadcasting and was broadcasting Penn State football with Ray Scott in 1980. Jim Irwin and Lionel Aldridge were calling Packers games for WTMJ radio at the time, but when Aldridge became ill, McGee got the call.

"They told me the game was in L.A.," McGee said. "And I said, 'I'll be there. Maybe I can find those stewardesses again.' Had it been in St. Louis or something, I would have probably said no."

Many Packers fans feel fortunate he didn't. Over the next 19 years, McGee and Irwin developed a cult following through the state that many were sad to see end when the two retired following the 1998 season.

"I never claimed to be an announcer," McGee said. "What it did was give me a platform to tell people the truth and what was really going on. We saw a lot of bad football early on, and I'd tell people when a guy made a dumbass play. And I'd tell jokes and be funny, and Jim was kind of a homer who people liked. I think it worked perfectly."

Just like his Packers career.

50 LeRoy Butler

LeRoy Butler was just eight years old. And when his mother, Eunice, asked what he wanted to be, Butler was quick with his response.

"I told her I wanted to play professional football," Butler said. "I knew what I wanted to be. I was very focused. I don't think you've ever seen a more focused kid. I made an agreement with God that I'd get my Mom out of the projects by playing professional football."

That certainly seemed like a pipe dream. Butler had just gotten out of a wheelchair and was still wearing braces on his legs. And those closest to Butler would have been thrilled to see him live a life of normalcy.

But Butler always aimed for the sky. He was the ultimate over-achiever, someone who defeated every challenge ever placed in front of him. And his fire, passion, and zeal helped him become one of the greatest Packers of all-time and arguably the NFL's top safety in the 1990s.

"The kids who have dreams and aspirations to want to go out and be a lawyer or a doctor or a professional football player and have an element that presents a different challenge—whatever it is, you can still get to those dreams," Butler said. "But in order for those dreams to come true, you have to work hard accordingly."

No one would know better than Butler. When he was born, the bones in his feet were extremely weak, creating a misalignment, which, as he grew older, allowed him to walk only short distances and prevented him from running. For much of Butler's childhood, his feet were in braces or casts, and there were periods he was confined to a wheelchair.

In addition, Butler had to escape the Jacksonville projects. Butler succeeded on both counts and went on to become Green Bay's top safety since Willie Wood in the 1960s.

"He's one of the best football players I've ever been around," former Packers general manager Ron Wolf said of Butler. "He really helped make us go."

Butler, a second-round draft choice out of Florida State in 1990, spent his first two seasons at cornerback. But when Mike Holmgren's staff arrived in 1992, they moved Butler to strong safety, and his career took off.

"[Defensive coordinator] Ray Rhodes was the one who convinced me," Butler said. "He called me up and he said, 'We're going to take [Terrell] Buckley with the fifth pick and we're going to move you to safety.' And I said, 'Ray, I'm only 191 pounds. I can't play safety. I'm going to get killed.'

"He said, 'No, no, no. I've got this thing about moving guys. You're one of my best cover guys. I want to move you on the inside on third downs, so I need to move you to safety so I can put [Terrell] Buckley at corner.' And it worked. It worked. And I loved corner, but I absolutely loved safety."

There wasn't anything Butler couldn't do on a football field. He was a terrific tackler. He could take tight ends out of a game.

He could cover wideouts in the slot. He could blitz quarterbacks. He was a ballhawk. And he was the verbal and emotional leader of Green Bay's defense.

Butler's finest year may have come in 1996, when the Packers won Super Bowl XXXI. That season, he finished second on the team in sacks (6.5), had five interceptions, and spearheaded the NFL's No. 1–ranked defense.

"That's one of the best years I've seen a safety have," Wolf said.

Butler played in more games (181) than any defensive back in Green Bay history. Butler originated the "Lambeau Leap" and was always a fan favorite for his honesty and candor. Butler's career ended in 2001 when he suffered a broken shoulder blade against Atlanta. Still, his 12-year career is the seventh-longest tenure by a player in team history. In that time Butler was named to four Pro Bowls, played in two Super Bowls, and was named to the NFL's 1990s NFL All-Decade Team.

"My game was always positive and about being a leader," Butler said. "And people always associated me with trying to win, thanking the fans for spending their hard-earned money to come and see us play, the Lambeau Leap—stuff like that. All that's real positive nice stuff, and people like that."

People always loved Butler for his performance both on and off the field. While Butler shined on Sundays, he was also a terrific sound bite, and fans always appreciated his honesty and candor.

"I just always thought the fans deserved to know what was going on," Butler said. "They were the ones buying the tickets. They were the ones buying our jerseys. If there was stuff they wanted to know, I thought it was part of our job to tell them."

When Butler's career ended, he hoped to land a coaching job with the Packers. But when that didn't work out, Butler took it hard.

"I was very disappointed, especially because they didn't even give me a reason," Butler said. "When you've been in one situation

Packers safety LeRoy Butler, originator of the "Lambeau Leap," jumps into the crowd after intercepting a Cincinnati Bengals pass in the end zone in the fourth quarter of a game on December 3, 1995, in Green Bay. The Packers held on to win 24–10.

for so long and then it just comes to an abrupt stop, you'd think that if it was a family atmosphere, they'd take care of you. So, when it didn't happen, I just had to move on."

These days, Butler is involved in several projects, including the LeRoy Butler Foundation. And he remains one of the most popular Packers of the last generation.

"My time in Green Bay was terrific," he said. "I played with some great players, made some great friends, and we won a lot of games. That's tough to top."

Especially considering where Butler came from.

51 Fuzzy Thurston

Frederick Charles "Fuzzy" Thurston never expected to be a football star. Thurston played basketball his first two years at Valparaiso before switching to the gridiron. He rode the bench for a year in Baltimore before the Packers traded linebacker Marv Matuzak for him. And the undersized Thurston (5'10", 230 pounds)—who was born in Altoona, Wisconsin—was uncertain what kind of impact he could make in Green Bay when he arrived in 1959.

But Thurston was the exact type of pulling left guard that coach Vince Lombardi wanted. And Thurston was a huge reason the Packers became the dominant team of the 1960s, winning five NFL championships and two Super Bowls between 1961 and 1967.

"Right place, right time," Thurston said.

Green Bay's Power Sweep (also known as the Packer Sweep) was the signature play in Lombardi's offense for nearly a decade. And the performance of Thurston and right guard Jerry Kramer was integral in making it go. On the play, the guards pulled and tried to form a convoy around an end. The lead guard would then take out the cornerback, with the offside guard picking up the middle or outside linebacker.

While everybody had a critical job in making the play go, Thurston and Kramer had arguably the toughest roles. The player with the most difficult task was the off guard, who had to pull farthest away from the play, yet still get to the outside in time to lead the convoy. "I know it's a difficult maneuver," Lombardi once said. "But [the off guard] has to get there. I don't give a damn whether he enjoys getting there or not."

Thurston and Kramer certainly didn't mind.

An offensive guard might be the least glamorous position in sports. But the Packer Sweep gave this terrific pair a chance for their own bit of glory.

"Generally speaking, there's nothing more anonymous than playing guard," Kramer wrote in his book *Farewell to Football.* "After they announce the lineups, you never hear your name over the loudspeaker. But in Lombardi's offensive system, with the guards pulling and leading the attack, Fuzzy Thurston and I emerged from obscurity. Every time there'd be a photograph in the papers of Hornung scoring a touchdown—which was pretty often—there'd be me or Fuzzy or both of us in the picture, leading the way."

Thurston started 112 games in Green Bay between 1959 and 1967. And in those nine seasons, the Packers ranked first in rushing offense three times and second three times. Thurston may have been undersized in most offenses, but his speed and strength made him a natural to run Lombardi's favorite play.

"There is nothing spectacular about it," Lombardi once said of his sweep. "It's just a yard-gainer. But on that sideline, when the sweep starts to develop, you can hear those linebackers and defensive backs yelling, 'Sweep!' 'Sweep!' and almost see their eyes pop as those guards turn upfield after them. It's my No. 1 play because it requires all 11 men to play as one to make it succeed, and that's what *team* means."

Thurston was named to the 1961 and 1962 All-Pro teams, retired following the 1967 campaign, and was inducted into the Packers Hall of Fame in 1975. Thurston was diagnosed with throat cancer in 1982 and given one year to live. But more than three decades later, Thurston is still going strong—although he barely speaks above a raspy whisper these days. He still remains wildly popular in Wisconsin, largely because he's the last player from the Lombardi era still living in Green Bay. In fact, he owns a bar called "Fuzzy's" that is something every Packers fan should experience.

52 Ahman Green

Ron Wolf had soured on Fred Vinson. Mike Holmgren had done the same with Ahman Green. So when the two former colleagues decided to exchange unwanted parts in the spring of 2000, it wasn't exactly big news. Years later, it ranks as one of the best trades in Green Bay Packers history and one of the more lopsided deals the NFL ever saw.

Wolf, the Packers' general manager, had fallen in love with Green prior to the 1998 NFL Draft and was eager to trade for him. Still, not even Wolf could have predicted Green would someday become the Packers' all-time leading rusher.

Holmgren, the head coach and general manager in Seattle at the time, was tired of Green's fumbling woes and happy to move him. What he got in return was the oft-injured Vinson, who lasted just one year with the Seahawks and never played in the NFL again.

Ahman Green breaks a tackle during a 35–13 thrashing of the Seattle Seahawks on October 5, 2003, at Lambeau Field. Green, the Packers' all-time leading rusher, had a dream season in 2003, running for 1,883 yards and 15 TDs.

"People talk about my trade for Brett [Favre] as my best ever," Wolf said. "And they're right. That was a great trade. But our trade for Ahman isn't far behind."

Green, who played with the Packers from 2000 to 2006 and then returned for part of the 2009 campaign, plastered his name throughout the team's record book. He has the most rushing yards in a career by a Packers back (8,322) and the most attempts (1,851). He led Green Bay in rushing six different years, including five straight between 2000 and 2004. Green has the two highest-rushing games in team history, including a 218-yard performance against Denver in 2003. His 98-yard run in that game is a team record. And Green eclipsed the 100-yard mark a franchise-best 33 times, including 10 times in 2003.

Of all Green's highlights, though, his most impressive was his 2003 body of work. That season, Green ran for 1,883 yards, which remains a Packers record and is tied for eighth in NFL history.

"A year like that is something else," Packers offensive coordinator Tom Rossley said at the time. "You just won't see many like it. He's a special back, and he proved it."

Green's 1,883 rushing yards in 2003 have only been surpassed by Eric Dickerson of the Los Angeles Rams (2,105 yards in 1984), Minnesota's Adrian Peterson (2,097 in 2012), Baltimore's Jamal Lewis (2,066 in 2003), Detroit's Barry Sanders (2,053 in 1997), Denver's Terrell Davis (2,008 in 1998), Tennessee's Chris Johnson (2,006 in 2009), Buffalo's O.J. Simpson (2,003 in 1973), and Houston's Earl Campbell (1,934 in 1980).

In Green's magical 2003 season, he also did something few believed was possible. Even with Favre in tow, the Packers became a run-first operation. That season, Green Bay ran the ball on 51.7 percent of its plays, its largest percentage of running plays since the 1979 outfit ran on 52.1 percent of its carries. And in the Favre era, the most a Green Bay team had ever run was 46.7 percent in 1997.

"Everything just kind of went right that year," Green said. "The line was great that year, and I was healthy, and we were just in sync. That year was a lot of fun."

The Packers set a new team record with 2,558 rushing yards that season. And they finished with the top rushing offense in the NFC and the third-best in all of football.

"I think Ahman is probably the best back I've played with," said former Packers tight end Wesley Walls, who also played with Roger Craig and Ricky Watters in San Francisco. "Those other guys I played with were really good. I mean really good. But I think Ahman has got a little more burst, and he's definitely in that caliber."

Green was just a third-round draft pick coming out of Nebraska in 1998, and five running backs went before him that season. But Green (6', 218 pounds) combined his tremendous speed with terrific strength to become the top rusher in Packers history.

"I'm fortunate enough to be a part of that elite group of guys who has a chance to be in the record books for the Green Bay Packers," Green said after setting the mark in 2009. "One day somebody's going to come down after me when I'm done and break my record. But for now, hats off to all the guys who helped me get there from 2000 to now."

And hats off to Green, as well.

53 Dan Devine

Maybe this is all you need to know about the Dan Devine era in Green Bay: Bart Starr, who rarely says a negative word about anyone or anything, was asked about Devine. "I don't even want to go there," said Starr.

Few Packers fans care to, either.

Devine, who was Green Bay's coach and general manager from 1971 to 1974, died in 2002 at the age of 77. He will forever be remembered as one of the more overmatched coaches the Packers have ever had. Devine went just 25–28–4, including a playoff loss to Washington in 1972. Devine also made the most damaging trade in team history, when he acquired quarterback John Hadl midway through the 1974 season. Desperate to save his job, Devine sent two first-round draft picks, two seconds, and a third to the Los Angeles Rams for the 34-year-old Hadl, the reigning MVP of the National Football Conference.

"I was still fine," Hadl said. "I was just coming off an MVP season in '73. I was throwing the ball good enough."

Hardly. Hadl was clearly on the downside of his career and, over the next two seasons, threw 29 interceptions, nine touchdowns, and had a passer rating of 53.2. After the Packers failed to reverse course in the 1974 season and missed the playoffs, Devine bolted for the head coaching job at Notre Dame before the Green Bay brass could fire him.

While Devine landed on his feet with the Fighting Irish, his short-sighted trade set the Packers back several years and left the cupboard bare for Starr, his eventual successor. For that, many Green Bay fans never forgave him.

"He knew what was coming," Perry Moss, an assistant under Devine, said of what would have been his firing. "We were eating breakfast before the last game of the year [vs. Atlanta]. The staff was sitting around the table, and Devine asked, 'What's the greatest coaching job in America?' Some guys said Oklahoma, and some said Texas or whatever. And Devine said, 'Notre Dame.' Well, sure enough, a few days later he's in South Bend, being introduced as Notre Dame's coach."

Lee Remmel, Green Bay's longtime director of public relations, recalled Devine's final weekend with the team. The Packers lost

10–3 to the Falcons in Atlanta on a rainy Sunday that featured 48,000 no-shows. The next afternoon, Devine announced he was resigning and leaving for Notre Dame.

"He had all his ducks in a row because that Monday morning he had his attorney negotiate a settlement with the Packers of his contract," Remmel said. "On the Friday before the Atlanta game, he had an aide mail two letters: one to Seattle, apparently declining the University of Washington job, and the other to South Bend, apparently accepting the Notre Dame job. That's speculation, but that's the way it appears."

Devine's stint in the college ranks proved far more successful than his days in Green Bay. Devine, who also coached at Arizona State and Missouri, won the 1977 national championship with Notre Dame and compiled a 172–57–9 record as a college coach. In Green Bay, though, Devine never could get it done. He had a hard time dealing with the ghosts of Vince Lombardi, purged the roster of those players, and never found suitable replacements. Moss also said Devine's failure to be up front with people rubbed many the wrong way and left Green Bay with a locker room that was completely divided.

"He called me in and offered me a bribe," former guard and team captain Gale Gillingham recalled. "I said, 'I'm not changing anything I am. I'm not changing the way I treat you or the players. I'm the captain, and I represent the players.' I don't think anybody he didn't pay off had a good relationship with him. I think pretty much everybody had a crummy relationship with him."

The Packers' greatest success under Devine came in 1972, when they won the NFC Central Division with a 10–4 record before losing to the Redskins in the first round of the playoffs. The rest of the Devine years were a mess, with the Packers going 15–23–4 in the other three seasons.

"It wasn't all successful, obviously, but the man won a division and had a knack for landing on his feet," said former Packers president Bob Harlan, who was hired by Devine in 1971. "He went from Missouri to Green Bay, and when he was in trouble in Green Bay, he landed at Notre Dame. So he found a way to move someplace and be successful."

That place wasn't Green Bay, though. And because Devine left the franchise in shambles, he'll always be remembered as one of the most unpopular coaches in team history.

54 Gale Gillingham

Imagine you're widely recognized as the best offensive guard in the National Football League, and perhaps the finest to ever play for the Green Bay Packers. Now imagine your head coach comes to you while you're still in your prime and tells you he's shifting you to defensive tackle.

Unfortunately for Gale Gillingham, this was his reality in 1972, when Packers coach Dan Devine felt the urge to have him switch sides of the ball.

"That was about as brilliant as it gets," Gillingham said during an interview before his death in 2011. "I almost laughed. But I was captain and stuck it out and went there. But that was about as dumb as it gets. I don't know how anybody in their right mind could have done that."

Devine, notorious for making one disastrous move after another, saw this one blow up in his face with a larger boom than most. Gillingham, who had gone to the Pro Bowl from 1969 to 1971, suffered a season-ending knee injury in just the second game of the year against Oakland when he was hit from the side.

According to Gillingham, though, Devine never admitted the move was a mistake.

"Dan never did anything wrong in his entire life," Gillingham said. "I could've played defensive tackle. That wasn't a problem. But with the career I was having at guard, why would you move me? That didn't make any sense."

Gillingham was having one of the better careers a Packers lineman has ever had. Chosen with the 13th overall pick in the 1966 draft out of the University of Minnesota, Gillingham quickly became a dominant player on the NFL's most dominant team. He started the final two regular-season games in 1966 and became a permanent starter in 1967 as the Packers won Super Bowls I and II.

"It was an incredible beginning, wasn't it?" Gillingham said. "And playing for Vince [Lombardi] was absolutely the best. He kept things very simple, and you knew exactly what you were supposed to do at all times. He put the pressure on you in practice so that you would find it easier in the game, and by God, the games were easier than practice. He knew how to win and he knew how to push you so you wouldn't get complacent. The guy was the greatest, by far."

Gillingham began making his mark as one of the greatest of his era, too. He was ahead of his time in that he worked out year-round and lifted weights before it became standard practice. In a day when the average guard played around 260 pounds, the 6'3" Gillingham played his entire career between 275 and 290 pounds. The extra weight never detracted from his quickness, though, and Gillingham became an absolutely punishing blocker.

"I never liked football until I got to Green Bay, and I absolutely fell in love with it there," he said. "I spent every minute of my time when I was with the Packers trying to be the best guard I could be. And I thought I was the best guard of the era. I don't want to sound conceited, but I worked awfully hard at it. I worked out all off-season, I turned the scales back, and I tried to be as big as I could be and as good as I could be."

Gillingham earned All-Pro honors from 1969 to 1971. But six days before the 1972 regular season began, Devine went to Gillingham with his grand plan.

"It was probably the dumbest thing I've ever seen," Gillingham said. "[Devine] was just out of place there. Maybe I think the absolute worst of him, but I was there and I had to live through it, and it wasn't good."

Gillingham's relationship with Devine certainly bottomed out after the defensive tackle fiasco. Devine did have the common sense to move Gillingham back to right guard, and in 1973 and 1974 he returned to the Pro Bowl. The Packers had bottomed out by then, though, going 11–15–2 in those two seasons before Devine bolted for Notre Dame. The future didn't look much better, either, as Devine traded away five draft picks for over-the-hill quarterback John Hadl.

Gillingham, a proud warrior who had tasted enormous success under Lombardi, didn't want to end his career with a loser and asked for a trade before the 1975 season. When coach and general manager Bart Starr refused, Gillingham retired.

"I could see we absolutely weren't going to win, and I had had a enough of losing and enough of the stupidity," said Gillingham, who was also fighting through chronic knee pain. "And when Bart started there, he brought in some assistants who were just godawful. They didn't know anything, and I thought, *Shit. With my body and the way my knee is, that's enough. I'll just quit.*"

The Packers talked Gillingham into returning in 1976, but by then, his knee was shot.

Gillingham will always be remembered as one of the finest guards in team history. But he'll also be remembered as a player directly affected by Devine's ineptitude.

"I just keep thinking how stupid that was to have me switch positions," he said. "Really stupid."

55 Donald Driver

Donald Driver's first NFL catch was unforgettable, for both him and anyone who witnessed the theatrics. It was December 12, 1999, and Driver was playing in his just his third game for the Green Bay Packers. Driver, who was supposed to play strictly special teams that day, was pressed into duty when Corey Bradford got hurt.

Midway through the third quarter of a home game with Carolina, Driver lined up wide right. He got a clean release, beat linebacker Donta Jones across the middle, and hauled in an eight-yard touchdown pass from Brett Favre. Driver paused momentarily, then took three long, awkward steps as if he were robot. He flapped his arms in a bird-like manner before teammates Antonio Freeman and Tyrone Davis arrived to join the celebration.

"I didn't know what to do," Driver said. "I was nervous, I guess you'd say. I didn't know what the dance was, but they told me it was the West Coast Shuffle. It worked out, and now everybody loves it."

It's extremely doubtful that the 60,000 people sitting inside Lambeau Field that day could have guessed they were witnessing the start of history. But that's exactly what transpired. To the amazement of many, Driver went on to become one of the finest wide receivers in Packers' history.

When Driver retired at the end of the 2012 season, he did so as the franchise's leader in receptions (743) and receiving yards (10,137). Driver's 61 receiving touchdowns were third in team history, and he ranked No. 1 with nine seasons of at least 50 catches.

"You know, even though I feel that I can still play the game, God has made the answer clear to me. Retirement is now. I have to retire as a Green Bay Packer," Driver said during his retirement speech. "I've always said that I never want to wear another uniform—but always the green and gold.

"Sometimes, I sit at home and think about the history of this great franchise and I think of the players and the great coaches that came before me like Vince Lombardi, Bart Starr, Ray Nitschke, Willie Davis, Jerry Kramer, the great Reggie White, Brett Favre, James Lofton, Sterling Sharpe, Ahman Green, Rob Davis, I mean this list goes on and on and on. So I felt that this is an opportunity to walk away from the game knowing that I've given it all that I can."

It's a remarkable story that Driver—a former seventh-round draft choice out of little-known Alcorn State—had the career he did and became one of the most beloved Packers along the way. That's because back in the summer of 1999, Driver's only goal was to make the Packers' roster.

"I would have never expected it," Driver said. "That wasn't my goal coming in. My goal coming in was just to make the team and just have a great career. Not saying I was going to break records, but once you get to that first year, you're like, *Okay, if I can make it three years.* Then it's like, *If I can play six years.* It goes on and on, and before you know it, time has gone by. You're looking at all the things you've accomplished. I would have never thought."

Who could have?

Driver was the 213th selection of the 1999 draft, a pick the Packers acquired when they traded return specialist Glyn Milburn the previous season. Driver had been a two-year starter and three-year letter-winner at tiny Alcorn State. But many thought Driver's greatest chances for athletic success would come in track and field, where he qualified for the 1996 Olympic Field Trials in the high

Packers wideout Donald Driver dashes toward the end zone on a 53-yard touchdown reception against the Minnesota Vikings at Lambeau Field on November 21, 2005.

jump. Instead, then–Packers general manager Ron Wolf took a flier on Driver, and it turned out to be one of the best picks of Wolf's career.

"Very definitely, we have hopes for him," Wolf said the day he drafted Driver. "He averaged over 20 yards a catch. He's an exceptional athlete in that conference. A track athlete, as well."

Today it's easy to forget, but it took Driver a long time to make his mark. Driver started just four games and had only 37 catches during his first three years in the league. Driver finally broke on the scene in 2002, when he caught 70 balls for 1,064 yards. Driver also went to the Pro Bowl that season, becoming the lowest drafted Packer since Larry McCarren (12th round) in 1983 to earn Pro Bowl honors.

"God has a plan for everyone," said Driver, who also overcame a rough upbringing to reach such lofty heights. "My plan was to sit for four years and not play. Play a little here and there, catch a few balls, but I didn't get myself beat up."

After emerging in 2002, Driver became a model of consistency. Driver and the Colts' Reggie Wayne were the only two receivers that eclipsed 1,000 receiving yards each year between 2004 and 2009. Driver also reached the Pro Bowl in both 2006 and 2007.

"To me, it's the way he's gone about it," former Packers defensive end Aaron Kampman said of Driver. "He's a great example for the guys in the locker room of how to do it the right way. The way he prepares, the way he practices, the way he plays. He's just always done it the right way."

Former teammate Greg Jennings agreed.

"Just his consistency," Jennings said, when asked what he admired about Driver. "He's been consistent every year. His ability to go across the middle and make plays continuously, knowing what to expect after catching the ball, is second to none."

Driver was never mentioned with the NFL's elite wide receivers. And, amazingly, he could always be called underrated, despite everything he accomplished.

"You never get [recognition] until you're dead and gone," Driver said. "So maybe when I'm dead and gone someone will say, 'You know something…that man was a great player.'"

Chances are, many people will say exactly that.

56 Favre/Oakland

His father, Irv, had died from a heart attack just 24 hours earlier. His streak of consecutive games—which stood at 204 at the time—seemed likely to end. And his team's late-season playoff push was sure to be immensely tougher if their leader couldn't go. But Brett Favre did what Brett Favre always did. He played.

Only on this magical night in Oakland, Favre played better than at any time in his Green Bay Packers career. On December 22, 2003, Favre threw for four touchdowns and 399 yards, and led the Packers to an unforgettable 41–7 win over Oakland on *Monday Night Football*. "I knew that my dad would have wanted me to play," Favre said afterward. "I love him so much, and I love this game. It's meant a great deal to me, to my dad, to my family, and I didn't expect this kind of performance. But I know he was watching tonight."

Favre played in 277 games during his 16 years with the Packers, including the playoffs. But his passer rating of 154.9 that night was the best of his Green Bay career and remains the best in team history.

"I've never seen a leader or a player like Brett in my career, and I'm pretty sure that nobody else in this locker room has," tight end Wesley Walls said. "I think we wanted to make him proud.... Just getting up in front of the team at such a horrible and difficult time in his life really showed he cared about us. That was something I'll never forget."

Few will ever forget this game, in which Favre was remarkable, and his receivers made one improbable catch after another. On just Green Bay's fourth play from scrimmage, wideout Robert Ferguson made a sensational 47-yard grab. One play later, Walls snared a

22-yard TD pass in the back of the end zone, a play that appeared to have little chance of success.

"He played an amazing game for us, and we all felt we had to do the same for him," Walls said. "Sometimes, in special circumstances, you make special plays. I think it's fair to say we were inspired by Irv."

Favre hummed a gorgeous 23-yard touchdown pass to Javon Walker later in the first quarter. Favre also lofted a 43-yard TD strike to Walker when the standout receiver outmuscled a pair of Raiders defensive backs for the ball. Favre later hit Walker with another 46-yard completion, then capped that drive with a six-yard TD pass to tight end David Martin shortly before halftime.

Favre completed his first nine passes and threw for a personal-best 311 yards and four TDs in the first half alone. He also finished the first half with a perfect passer rating of 158.3.

"What he had to deal with was unmeasurable," wideout Antonio Freeman said. "You can't put a price on what he did. I don't know how he did it, but he did it in fine fashion."

Green Bay stayed in contention for a playoff berth that night. And the Packers qualified for the postseason the following week when Arizona stunned Minnesota in the final seconds to give the Packers the NFC North Division title. If there is such a thing as divine intervention, Favre was becoming a believer.

"I've been around people who have lost a family member or lost someone close to them, and they say that that person's there watching, or angels, or whatever," Favre said. "And I would say that two weeks ago I didn't really believe in that. But I think we'd better start believing in something."

That night in Oakland, Favre gave plenty of people something to believe in.

57 Dave Hanner

There are people who give their lives to one single company. In the world of professional sports, though, that type of loyalty is fantastically rare. Then again, Dave "Hawg" Hanner was a rare bird.

A massive man with a big heart, Hanner played and coached for the Packers a total of 43 years. It's one of the longest tenures by one person in the franchise's long history.

"I think what it tells you is that's a great organization," Hanner said shortly before his death in 2008. "I enjoyed everything I did when I was there."

Drafted in the fifth round in 1952, Hanner spent the next 13 seasons—two of which earned him All-Pro honors—as one of the NFL's finest defensive tackles. After his retirement in 1964, Hanner joined Vince Lombardi's defensive staff and was retained by coaches Phil Bengtson, Dan Devine, and Bart Starr, serving as defensive coordinator for both Devine and Starr.

In 1983 Hanner moved into scouting and oversaw the Southeast. He spent 14 years as a Packers scout before his retirement in 1996.

"It was all about being what's best for the Packers," former Packers general manager Ron Wolf told the *Milwaukee Journal Sentinel* of Hanner. "That's a rare quality in people. He lived by that code."

Hanner played that way, too.

His Green Bay career began in 1952, when the Packers selected him out of the University of Arkansas. While 350-pound defensive tackles have become the norm today, Hanner was a behemoth in his day at 270 pounds.

"There just wasn't anybody as big as me," said the 6'2" Hanner.

And few as talented.

Hanner, who was named to two Pro Bowls (1953, 1954) and twice selected All-Pro (1957, 1959), teamed with Henry Jordan during the early years of the Lombardi era to give the Packers the NFL's premier tackle tandem. After years of losing under Gene Ronzani, Lisle Blackbourn, and Scooter McLean, Hanner was thrilled to have Lombardi come on board, even if it meant training like he'd never trained before. During Hanner's first camp under Lombardi, he arrived weighing 278 pounds. But after two days of Camp Lombardi, Hanner had lost 18 pounds, keeled over from sunstroke, and wound up at St. Vincent Hospital, where he had to take liquids intravenously.

"I think when Lombardi came in, everybody's jaws just kind of dropped," Hanner said. "After those first couple days, I'd drink water or eat, and I just couldn't get anything to stay down. It was tough."

But it was worth the grind. By the end of camp, Hanner was down to a svelte 250 pounds and was playing some of the best football of his life. Lombardi had a similar impact on several other Packers, and Green Bay's fortunes took off.

By the time Hanner retired following the 1964 season, he had been part of NFL championships in 1961 and 1962 and a Western Conference championship in 1960.

"Lombardi just knew how to handle people and get results out of people," said Hanner, who was inducted into the Packers Hall of Fame in 1974. "He was the type of guy who, if he told you something, you believed it."

Before the 1964 season, Hanner had an opportunity to take a job as an assistant coach with the Los Angeles Rams. Lombardi told Hanner if he was interested, there was a job waiting for him on the Packers staff after he retired. Hanner stuck around and worked as a defensive line coach for seven years, helping Green Bay to three straight NFL titles, from 1965 to 1967. Devine then named

Hanner the first defensive coordinator in team history in 1972. In Hanner's first year in that position, the Packers finished No. 1 in the NFC, and in 1974 Green Bay allowed just 14.7 points per game, a mark that only the 1996 Super Bowl champion Packers have bettered since.

Hanner stayed on as Starr's defensive coordinator, but after Green Bay went 5–11 in 1979 and allowed 316 points, Starr had to make some moves to save his own hide. He fired Hanner, who was then out of football in 1980 and 1981. Those would prove to be the only years Hanner wasn't in Green Bay between 1952 and 1996. The Packers brought him back in 1982, and he began work as a college scout, which he did until retiring in 1996.

Hanner's longevity was a testament both to his talents and passion for the game. But much of it was also due to the organization he loved deeply.

"I was just lucky as the devil and very proud to have been there so long," Hanner said. "The people treated me great. I couldn't have been treated any better. It was just a great organization to have been part of, and it gave me a lot of great memories."

58 Packers-Redskins

In 1983 Mark Moseley was the NFL's version of death and taxes. In a world of unknowns, Moseley—the Washington Redskins' place-kicker—was automatic.

The previous season (1982) Moseley missed just one field-goal attempt and became the only kicker in NFL history to win the league's MVP award. Moseley was enjoying another stellar season in 1983, when he appeared ready to become a hero once more. Moseley's Redskins trailed the Packers 48–47 with three seconds left in a *Monday Night Football* game that already was an instant classic. With Moseley preparing for a 39-yard attempt, it appeared Green Bay's hopes of upending the mighty Redskins were about to end.

"I walked over to [kicker] Jan [Stenerud], and I said, 'Do you believe this?'" Packers quarterback Lynn Dickey recalled. "We're going to lose this game. What a shame."

Not so fast. Moseley, who had made 82 percent of his career kicks from inside the 40-yard line and 84.2 percent of his attempts in 1983, missed this one as time expired. And, amazingly, the Packers and a sellout crowd celebrated on a chilly October 17 night.

"We kind of rushed it," Moseley said afterward. "Maybe we should have taken more time. I just missed the kick." That was one of the few times all night either offense malfunctioned. The two teams combined for 1,025 yards of total offense, 552 from the Redskins and 473 from Green Bay. Washington quarterback Joe Theismann threw for 398 yards and two touchdowns, while Dickey matched him with 387 yards and three touchdowns.

The game featured five lead changes and, to this day, remains the highest-scoring contest in the history of *Monday Night Football*. That's no small feat, considering the 43-year-old show has produced more than 700 games.

"Listening to people talk about that game today, you'd think about 250,000 people were there that night," Dickey said. "Almost everyone I talk to tells me they were there."

They wish.

The Redskins, who would go on to win the NFC title but lose to the Raiders in the Super Bowl that season, entered as five-point favorites. The Packers, on the other hand, were a mediocre team that would finish the year 8–8 in what would be Bart Starr's ninth and final season as head coach. Before the game, the mild-mannered Starr gathered his team, turned out the lights, and put on an overhead projector. Up came a quote from Redskins tight end Don Warren that read, "The game is going to be a rout."

"Bart showed us all the quote again," Dickey said. "But then he said something new. He said, '[Warren] thinks it's going to be a rout. But he never said which way. Now let's go kick some ass!' Now that was cool! Bart just never said stuff like that. I'll never forget that."

This night was unforgettable on many levels. Packers tight end Paul Coffman, who caught six passes for 124 yards in the game, had two first-half touchdowns as Green Bay raced to a 24–20 lead at halftime.

"I remember getting home after that game, and friends of mine from around the league had left messages like, 'You're going back to the Pro Bowl,'" Coffman recalled. "That was a great game."

The second half was a seesaw affair, and Washington took a 47–45 lead after Theismann threw a five-yard TD pass to running back Joe Washington. Back came the Packers, though, marching 56 yards to set up Stenerud for a 20-yard field goal with just 54 seconds left that gave Green Bay a 48–47 lead. That drive capped an unforgettable night for Green Bay's offense. Coordinator Bob Schnelker had a terrific game plan, the Packers' skill players were outstanding, and their offensive line stymied Redskins standout defensive end Dexter Manley.

"Dexter had kind of spouted off in the papers before that game that he was going to wreak havoc," Packers left tackle Karl Swanke said. "Well, there were no disruptions with Lynn. And that night was a culmination for Bob Schnelker and our offense. Everything he called worked to perfection. It was an incredible night."

The incredible night was almost ruined when Theismann drove his team deep into Packers territory in the closing seconds. Shockingly, though, Moseley failed to deliver for one of the few times in his terrific 16-year career.

"You almost get dizzy watching a game like that," said Redskins running back John Riggins, who had two TDs in the game. "You eat the bear, and sometimes the bear eats you."

On this memorable night, the Packers got the last bite.

59 Dave Robinson

No one, but *no one*, has ever hated losing more than Vince Lombardi. He despised the very thought of it. Loathed those who got the better of him. And Lombardi held on to losses for a long, long time.

So it's easy to see why Dave Robinson's beginnings with the Green Bay Packers ruffled a feather or two of Lombardi's. Back in 1963 the defending NFL champions still played a preseason game against the college all-stars. Robinson, a standout linebacker from Penn State, whom Green Bay had chosen with the 14th overall selection that year, was part of that college all-star team. For Robinson, that meant not only facing the powerful 1962 NFL champion Green Bay Packers, but also his future teammates.

"None of us thought we had any chance against those guys that day," Robinson said of his college teammates. "I mean, these were the Green Bay Packers."

But on this day, they didn't play like the Green Bay Packers. Lombardi's team took the game for granted, and when former University of Wisconsin stars Ron VanderKelen and Pat Richter hooked up for a long touchdown pass, the collegians led 20–10 on their way to a 20–17 victory.

Afterward, Lombardi was steamed. He snubbed Robinson and a few of the other college stars at a postgame party. When the

Packers All-Pro linebacker Dave Robinson (89) closes in on L.A. Rams QB Roman Gabriel (18) during a game on December 9, 1967, at Memorial Coliseum in Los Angeles.

Packers' practice began the following week, Lombardi threw in a game tape and went ballistic. On one play, in which Robinson had beat tight end Ron Kramer and dropped running back Tom Moore for a loss, Lombardi stopped the projector and embarked on a classic tirade.

"He was just screaming and yelling at Kramer," Robinson said. "He said, 'How can you let that rookie beat you? He's probably not even going to make the team!' Willie Wood just leaned over to me and said, 'I wouldn't buy a house if I were you.' I didn't know what would happen."

Here's what: try a 10-year Green Bay career that rivals almost any linebacker to ever don the green and gold. Robinson was named to the AP and UPI All-Pro team three times, earned a spot on Green Bay's 50th Anniversary All-Time Packers Team in 1969, and also won a berth on Green Bay's Modern Era All-Time Packers Team in 1976.

Finally, after a 40-year wait, Robinson was named to the Pro Football Hall of Fame in February 2013. Robinson had been nominated for the Hall by the senior committee and was down to his final chance.

"I wasn't surprised as much as I was just relieved," Robinson told the *Milwaukee Journal Sentinel* afterward. "If I didn't make it this time, I didn't know what I was going to do.

"You can't get back on as a senior candidate. I'm 71 years old. I would never be back. This would be my one last shot."

Robinson certainly made the most of his shot in Green Bay.

While Lombardi was initially angered by the loss to Robinson's college All-Stars, he was no fool. It was apparent to Lombardi from the get-go that Robinson could play, which is why Green Bay elected to get in a bidding war for him.

The AFL was just getting off the ground in 1963 and wanted to make a statement by stealing Green Bay's first-round draft choice. The San Diego Chargers made a huge push for Robinson. But when the bidding got to $38,000, San Diego was out of money. Robinson then accepted a two-year, $45,000 deal from Green Bay that included a $15,000 signing bonus. In those days, that was good money—and Robinson earned every nickel.

Robinson was a fantastic physical specimen in the 1960s. At a time when several linebackers played around 210 pounds, Robinson played between 236 and 242 and became a fixture at left linebacker. Not only was Robinson big, he was fast and tough as nails. And the Green Bay defense never missed a beat when he stepped into the starting lineup in 1964.

During Robinson's run, the Packers won three straight NFL championships from 1965 to 1967, including Super Bowls I and II.

"I really think I could have been a star in today's game, very easily," said Robinson, who was also inducted into the Packers Hall of Fame in 1982. "I think there's fewer top-notch players today per team. The only difference is, with the money, I'd have played 15 to 18 years instead of 10 or 12."

Players today probably don't know it, but Robinson is one of the guys they should thank for salaries being where they're at. In the spring of 1968 the NFL had exploded with rich new television contracts and the highest fan interest ever, and players felt they weren't getting their fair share of the pie. Robinson was Green Bay's player representative, which meant he took part in negotiations against, among others, Lombardi. As talks dragged on for three months, the management group wanted to bring in replacement players. But Lombardi would have no part of it.

"He said he had worked way too hard to make the Green Bay Packers a unit," Robinson said of Lombardi. "Instead, Pete Rozelle decided to lock out all the teams."

The lockout didn't last long, though. Eventually the two sides came to an agreement, and the players received a deal they were quite pleased with. In addition to having minimum salaries and exhibition-game pay boosted, they won substantial increases in pension benefits and medical insurance.

"It wasn't easy going up against Vince," said Robinson, who was traded to Washington by Dan Devine after the 1972 season. "My father died my freshman year of high school, and Vince was always like a father figure to me. But I think he respected us, fighting for what we got. And we ended up getting what we wanted."

Much like the Packers, who got everything they wanted out of Robinson.

60 Charles Woodson

Charles Woodson will never forget the day, the moment, the time, his football life changed forever. It was April 2006, and Woodson was driving around Houston, Texas, with a friend. Woodson, a free agent who spent his first eight years in Oakland, had been heavily courted by the Green Bay Packers. But Woodson's interest in moving to the NFL's smallest city was virtually nonexistent, and for the most part, he'd given Packers management the cold shoulder.

Just one problem: no other NFL team had any interest in Woodson. And driving around Houston that day, reality finally sunk in. Woodson's next football home was going to be tiny Green Bay—like it or not.

"I wasn't happy that day," said Woodson, who signed a seven-year, $52 million contract. "I wasn't happy whatsoever. I wasn't sold on coming here, but there were really no other options. It got to a point where I just had to accept what was going on. There just wasn't a lot of interest. I was talking to my agent every day, and he was making phone calls to different teams, but nobody was interested. And every time I called him, he'd say, 'Well, Green Bay called.' And I'd say, 'Anybody else?' Man, I tried damn near every other team, but it wasn't happening."

Instead, here's what happened. Woodson took the Packers' offer and surprisingly found happiness both on and off the field. Woodson resurrected his career and repaired an image that was largely tarnished across the league. And during Woodson's seven years in Green Bay, he became the second-best free agent signing in team history behind only Reggie White.

"What Wood gave us was unbelievable," Packers cornerback Tramon Williams said. "He was obviously a great player and made a lot of plays for us. But then you could learn so much just by being around him and watching him."

During Woodson's seven seasons in Green Bay, he had 38 of his 55 career interceptions and set the franchise record with 10 return touchdowns. Woodson went to the Pro Bowl each year between 2008 and 2011 and was named the NFL's Defensive Player of the Year in 2009.

Most importantly, Woodson won a Super Bowl during the 2010 season. That gave Woodson the ultimate in both personal and team success, and should land him in the Pro Football Hall of Fame someday.

"I don't know," Woodson said. "That's a tough deal to get into that place. That's up to you guys [sportswriters]. If it happens, it's a great deal."

To this day, Woodson is still more shocked what a great deal coming to Green Bay was.

Woodson a former Heisman Trophy winner with a little Hollywood in him, wasn't sure how he would fit into the NFL's smallest city. Interestingly, though, he came to love Green Bay's tranquility, and it helped him focus more time than ever on football.

"It could not have worked out any better," Woodson said. "I don't know what else I could have done anywhere else that I've been able to do here. This has been a great fit."

It wasn't always easy, though. In fact, a few months in, both the Packers and Woodson might have been hoping for a trip to divorce court. Woodson, while extremely bright and fantastically articulate when he chooses to be, can also be moody. He refuses to let many people into his inner circle. He's viewed by some as a loner. He's been called high-maintenance. And, early on, Woodson butted heads with Mike McCarthy, who was a first-time head coach back in 2006.

"Charles and I had some big-time growing pains in his initial stages here," McCarthy said. "We made it through that, and the benefits have definitely outweighed the negatives."

In a league packed with countless eye-popping athletes, Woodson's gifts stood out even more. They helped him win a Heisman Trophy at the University of Michigan in 1997, and they helped him stay ahead of the competition as he got longer in the tooth.

"He's a Hall of Fame player," said Packers cornerbacks coach Joe Whitt Jr. "I tell my other guys, 'Don't look at Woodson now. He has the ability to do some things other guys just can't do.'"

But Woodson's success extended well beyond pure physical gifts. Woodson had the soft hands typically found on Pro Bowl wide receivers or nifty running backs. That's why, if a ball was even in the vicinity of Woodson, he was a good bet to haul it in. Woodson's teammates also discovered he studied as much film as almost any defender on the roster. That's why, when Woodson gambled from time to time, he almost always won.

"He has the combination you look for," Packers defensive coordinator Dom Capers said of Woodson. "He has the size and physical tools to play the position. The thing I like is that he's a smart player.

"Not only does he have good football instincts, but he understands the game. He gives you the flexibility where you can move him around."

Capers was a master at that, playing Woodson at cornerback, safety, linebacker, and from the slot. Woodson even played on the line of scrimmage in a package the Packers call "Bear."

Woodson experienced a career resurgence after signing with the Packers in 2006. And many days, he chuckled that his renaissance came in tiny Green Bay, a place he was trying to avoid like the plague.

"I guess you never know until you give something a try," Woodson said.

The Packers are thrilled they did. Amazingly, so was Woodson.

61 Boyd Dowler

Bart Starr. Jerry Kramer. Chuck Mercein. When heroes of the Ice Bowl are discussed, these are usually the first names that come up. It's easy to forget, though, that the late-game heroics of those players wouldn't have mattered were it not for the exploits of the great Boyd Dowler.

Dowler, one of the finest Packers receivers ever, scored two early TDs to help stake Green Bay to a 14–0 lead. The Packers later rallied to win the game 21–17, when Starr scored the game-winning TD with 13 seconds left. Thanks to Dowler, though, Starr had a chance to play hero.

"I don't know about that," Dowler said. "There were a lot of heroes that day. There's no doubt that fast start really helped us out, but who's to say somebody else wouldn't have scored those touchdowns if it wasn't me?"

The thing is, it was Dowler—as he hauled in early TD receptions of eight and 46 yards. And Dowler's performance that day—when the temperature was minus-46 with the wind chill—was comparable to the rest of his terrific time in Green Bay.

"My time in Green Bay was perfect," said Dowler, who played 11 seasons in Green Bay. "I was absolutely blessed to be born when I was and come in at the same time [Vince] Lombardi did. It was perfect. It could not have been better."

Dowler arrived in Green Bay as a third-round draft choice out of Colorado in 1959, the same season Lombardi came to Titletown. Over the next 11 years, Dowler and the Packers won a pair of Super Bowls and ended up as NFL champions five times. Through it all, Dowler was integral to the Packers' success. He broke onto the scene with a team-high 32 receptions for 549 yards and four touchdowns in 1959, a performance that earned him Rookie of the Year honors. Dowler led the Packers in receptions six more times over the next 10 years, finishing his career with the Redskins in 1971 with 474 overall catches for 7,270 yards and 40 touchdowns.

Dowler still ranks fifth in career receptions for the Packers (448) and fifth in career yards (6,918). Those old enough can probably still remember Dowler getting knocked goofy by Dallas' Mike Gaechter while hauling in a 16-yard touchdown pass from Starr during the 1966 title game. The Packers won that day, as well, 34–27.

Dowler's greatest moment, though, undoubtedly came in the 1967 NFL Championship Game versus the Cowboys, known to most as the Ice Bowl. Not only did he score Green Bay's first two touchdowns, Dowler later had a clutch 13-yard reception on the Packers' game-winning drive.

"That game was the focal point of everything," said Dowler, whose team would defeat Oakland 33–14 in Super Bowl II two weeks later. "The Super Bowl was almost anticlimactic. And I think that game against Dallas and that season was kind of the climax to the whole period."

And what a period it was.

There was the 1961 season in which the Packers went 11–3, defeated the New York Giants 37–0 for the NFL championship, and began their dynasty. There was the 1962 team, which Dowler called Green Bay's best after it went 13–1 and again defeated New York for the NFL championship. Then there were championships from 1965 to 1967, as those Packers cemented themselves as one of the greatest teams of all-time.

"Anyone who was a part of that run feels blessed," Dowler said. "You just don't see anything like that anymore."

Dowler would certainly know. After his playing days ended, Dowler remained in the game he loved, working as an offensive coordinator, position coach, and later a scout for several teams.

"I've been very blessed," Dowler said. "Everything I've done I've really enjoyed. Nothing compares to playing the game. It's a very special thing, the best thing you can experience in the game is to be a player."

Especially when you have the type of success Dowler did.

62 Super Bowl XXXII

"We're a one-year wonder, just a fart in the wind."

Ron Wolf, Green Bay's extremely candid general manager, uttered one of the Super Bowl's most memorable lines at the time of his greatest frustration. Green Bay entered Super Bowl XXXII as an 11½-point favorite over Denver. Having won seven straight games and being the defending NFL champions, the Packers were looking to stretch the NFC's winning streak in Super Bowls to 14. Instead, the Packers left San Diego's Qualcomm Stadium with arguably the most frustrating loss in franchise history.

Green Bay had no answers for Broncos running back Terrell Davis, who ran for 157 yards and three TDs, despite missing a quarter with a migraine headache. The Packers' offense failed to take advantage of several terrific opportunities. And when it was over, Green Bay's 31–24 loss that night is one that will haunt them for years and years.

"That game still drives me nuts," former safety LeRoy Butler said. "It really does. Did the better team win? I don't believe so. But all that matters, I guess, is the final score."

"I've always said the toughest loss I've ever had here was to Denver in the Super Bowl," former team president Bob Harlan said. "I felt we were the better team, we were the heavy favorite. To get to that game is so difficult and then to lose it is a terrible loss. The Super Bowl loss to Denver will always be my toughest."

With good reason. The Packers of the mid-1990s were in position to be discussed with some of great dynasties in franchise history. They were poised to challenge Dallas as the "Team of the Decade." But when Green Bay's defensive linemen wilted in the heat, and Davis ran roughshod, such hopes vanished.

"We came in here and shocked the world," Broncos tight end Shannon Sharpe said. "We didn't really shock the Denver Broncos, though…. [The Packers] never faced a running game like ours."

Green Bay had allowed just 61.5 rushing yards per game in the playoffs that season. But Davis and Denver's offensive line dominated the Packers' front four, and the Broncos piled up 179 yards on 39 carries. Denver's offensive line, coached by the esteemed Alex Gibbs, was smallish, but extremely athletic. Davis was on his way to a Hall of Fame career before a brutal knee injury ended those hopes.

Green Bay's beefy front, which averaged 307 pounds per man, tired throughout the game. And Denver's quicker, faster parts in the run game ruled the day.

"Their ability to run the ball as effectively as they did surprised us," Packers coach Mike Holmgren said. "That affected the game and wasn't expected because for the last seven weeks, we've been playing the run pretty well. But give Denver credit, they did a nice job."

Denver scored 17 unanswered points to take a 17–7 lead with 12:21 left in the second quarter. But with Davis sitting the rest of the second quarter, the Packers were able to forge a 17–17 tie early in the third quarter. That momentum vanished when the Broncos marched 92 yards in 13 plays for the go-ahead TD. Davis capped the drive with a one-yard TD to make it 24–17 with just 34 seconds left in the third quarter.

"It really was unheard of what they were doing to us on the ground," nose tackle Gilbert Brown said years later. "That still bothers people."

Packers quarterback Brett Favre—who threw three touchdowns that day—responded with a 13-yard TD strike to Antonio Freeman that tied the game at 24. That capped a four-play drive, in which Favre and Freeman hooked up three times and connected for their second touchdown of the game.

After each team punted, Denver delivered the knockout blow. The Broncos drove from the Packers' 49 to the 1-yard line in just three plays. On second down, Holmgren ordered his team to allow Davis to score, so his offense would have enough time to answer. The problem is, Holmgren thought it was first down. Had he known which down it was, perhaps his strategy would have changed.

As it was, Denver took a 31–24 lead, and Green Bay had just 1:45 to pull even. Favre drove the Packers to Denver's 31, where on a fourth-and-6, the Broncos brought seven rushers. Favre tried forcing a ball into tight end Mark Chmura, but the pass was knocked away by linebacker John Mobley, and Denver prevailed.

"We knew they'd be tough," Holmgren said afterward. "We played a whale of a game tonight; it just wasn't good enough."

Years later, many Packers insisted they were off their game and outcoached that night. They believed if they'd played Denver 10 times, they'd have won the overwhelming majority. Others believe Denver was a team on the rise that was in the process of passing Green Bay—and the rest of the football world. The Broncos began the following season 13–0 and repeated as Super Bowl champs.

"We knew what those guys were capable of," former Packers wideout Terry Mickens said. "I just think Denver played the best possible game they could, and it happened to us at the worst time it could. And we didn't play bad, but we didn't play close to our best game. It's unfortunate in a season of highs and lows it worked out like it did. But if you don't play your best game in the Super Bowl, you're going to lose."

And end up a fart in the wind.

63 Lynn Dickey

All Lynn Dickey ever wanted was a chance. A chance to show off his powerful right arm to the rest of the National Football League. A chance to lead a football team. A chance to make his mark. Which is why Dickey will always be grateful to Bart Starr.

"Bart's the guy who gave me a chance," said the former Green Bay Packers quarterback, who was acquired from Houston in 1976. "Bart's one of the few guys out there who believed in me."

Turns out Starr's leap of faith was a pretty wise one. During Dickey's nine-year stint in Green Bay, he threw for 21,369 yards and 133 touchdowns.

He still ranks No. 2 in Packer history for most passing yards in a season (4,458 in 1983) and most passing yards in a game (418 against Tampa Bay in 1980). He's also No. 2 in most consecutive completions (18 vs. Houston in 1983) and most consecutive 300-yard passing games (three in 1984).

"Playing in Green Bay was a great experience for me," Dickey said. "I enjoyed it immensely. I wanted to get out of Houston and get the opportunity to play, and Bart had enough confidence in me to give me the chance. It was a wonderful time in my life."

Dickey led some of the most exciting offensive teams in the NFL during the early 1980s. With pass-catching targets such as James Lofton, John Jefferson, and Paul Coffman, Green Bay averaged 26.8 points per game in 1983, the most since the 1962 bunch averaged 29.6 on their way to an NFL championship. Between 1981 and 1985, when Dickey started 65 of 73 games, the Packers averaged 23.4 points per game, but they also allowed 22.4 points per outing. For the most part, that meant mediocrity was the rule as Green Bay went 8–8 in four of those seasons. The strike-shortened 1982 campaign, in which the Packers went 5–3–1 and reached the second round of the playoffs, was the lone exception and marked Dickey's only two playoff appearances.

"How many years in a row did we go 8–8?" Dickey asked, knowing the answer but electing to forget. "We had a decent team, but it was always one thing or another. One year, the offense would roll but the defense would give up a lot of points. Then the defense would play well, and the offense wouldn't. Year in and year out, if you have a defense that can stop the run and an offense that can run the football, you're going to be one of the better teams in the league. And we didn't do well in those things."

Which meant Dickey stayed plenty busy. With a leaky defense and without a 1,000-yard rusher, Dickey and his sensational receiving targets were often asked to carry the team. While Dickey embraced the opportunity, defensive players often embraced him. Through the years, the less-than-agile Dickey suffered great punishment and would eventually have 10 different surgeries—four on a broken leg, three on his knee, two on his right shoulder, and one on a dislocated hip.

Dickey had plenty of weapons at his disposal. Lofton and Jefferson were as dangerous as almost any receiving duo in football. And while Coffman didn't possess great speed, his moves were second to none.

"I had no problem with my weapons," Dickey said. "That was a fun offense to be part of."

After the 1983 campaign, Starr was replaced as head coach by Forrest Gregg. And following two more 8–8 seasons, Gregg had pretty much cleaned house. That meant Randy Wright was Gregg's quarterbacking choice in 1986, and Dickey was gone. Two seasons later, Gregg was gone himself.

"Bart and Forrest were like night and day," Dickey said. "Bart would work you extremely hard physically. I've never worked harder than I did under Bart. But he treated people with decency and treated you like a man."

Not so with Gregg, who yelled at and berated his men in an attempt to motivate, according to Dickey and others.

"[Players] were late for meetings, and Forrest would say, 'If that happens again, you'll be out of here,'" said Dickey. "Well by the 10th week of the year, it was the same idle threats. They knew they weren't going anywhere. It was a bad situation."

Dickey still watches the Packers, and the entire league for that matter, religiously. He's a member of the Packers Hall of Fame and still attends several Packers-related functions. And he'll always reflect on his days in a Green Bay uniform with a smile.

"The fans there are like no other," Dickey said. "I always said, if you're 14–0 or 0–14, the stands are going to be full, and the people will support you. And to be honest, while I was playing, I realized how lucky I was to be doing the thing that I wanted to do. How many people can say that? It was a great time."

64 Favre Trade

Bob Harlan was scrambling. Green Bay's president was getting ready to watch his Packers face the Atlanta Falcons on December 1, 1991. Before the game, Ron Wolf—who had just been named Green Bay's general manager—told his new boss he was going down to the field to scout Atlanta's back-up quarterback. Wolf said if he liked what he saw, he was going to trade for that player. Just one thing: Harlan wasn't sure who the Falcons' back-up quarterback was.

"Ron left, and I started looking at the roster to see who the backup quarterback is," Harlan chuckled. "And Ron came back shortly before kickoff and said, 'Bob, we're going to make a trade for Brett Favre. Are you okay with that?' And I told him, 'I promised you it was your team to run, there would be no interference, I'm fine with it.'"

Before long, the Packers' acquisition of Favre would rank among the greatest trades in league history.

On February 12, 1992, Wolf sent a first-round draft pick—the 17th overall selection—to the Atlanta Falcons for the highly unproven Favre. Considering Favre was a second-round pick in 1991, Wolf took enormous criticism throughout the state.

"That was fine," Wolf said of the signature move in his 10-year tenure. "There's one thing about this league that's pretty simple: if you don't have a quarterback, you don't have much of a chance. Well, we didn't have a quarterback, and we had to go and get one. Something had to be done."

The move was fantastically bold, considering Favre's career statistics read 0-for-4 with two interceptions. Favre had fallen out of favor with Falcons coach Jerry Glanville and plummeted to third string on the depth chart. But Wolf didn't care. He had fallen in love with Favre the previous year when he was running the New York Jets' scouting department. When Wolf watched Favre throw that day in Atlanta, he saw a player whose arm strength matched anyone in football. And Wolf knew it was time to play, "Let's Make a Deal."

"We came back, and at some point we had an executive committee meeting," Wolf said. "I told the people that we were going to make a commitment for this quarterback, told them all about this quarterback, Brett Favre, and how we were going to go work to get him. They had no idea who I was talking about. But they were all for it."

Wolf and Falcons' vice president of player personnel Ken Herock talked roughly every other day for approximately 10 weeks. Wolf offered a second-round pick. The Falcons demanded a No. 1. Wolf said if he'd give them a first-rounder, he had to get something back. The Falcons balked at that.

"Finally, the call came that said, 'It's got to be a first or we're not going to make the trade,'" Wolf said. "I knew that they wanted to get rid of him. It was just a matter of getting it done. I knew we were going to get this deal done because I didn't think anyone was going to pay what they were asking for other than me."

But Wolf didn't want to lose his chance to get Favre and decided not to play hardball any longer. He made the deal.

Favre, who would go on to win three MVPs and a Super Bowl in Green Bay, ranks among the greatest to ever play the quarterback position. And Wolf kicked off his days as GM with one of the most lopsided trades in league history.

"I looked at it like this: if I was going to be successful, I was going to be successful because of Brett Favre," Wolf said. "And if he wasn't good enough, then I wasn't going to be successful. So I put everything on him, and it worked out."

65 Packers-Bears NFC Championship

B.J. Raji and Sam Shields came from different ends of the football universe. Raji, the Green Bay Packers nose tackle, was the ninth overall pick in the 2009 NFL Draft, and was given $18 million in guaranteed money on his rookie contract.

Shields, a cornerback, went undrafted in 2010, then was given a paltry $7,500 in guaranteed money to sign with Green Bay as a free agent.

"It doesn't matter where you find guys," former Packers director of football operations Reggie McKenzie said. "Just so you find them."

The Packers did yeoman's work to find these two young stars. And even though their paths were remarkably different, Raji and Shields will always share this bond: they played the role of hero in the 2010 NFC Championship game.

Shields had a pair of interceptions, including one with 37 seconds left and Chicago driving for the potential game-tying score. Raji bailed out an inept Green Bay offense with an 18-yard interception return for a touchdown midway through the fourth quarter.

Those plays were immense in Green Bay's 21–14 win over archrival Chicago in the 2010 NFC Championship Game.

"It's an unbelievable feeling," said Shields, who entered the game with only two interceptions all year. "There's a lot of guys that wait a long, long time for this. Now, we're going to the Super Bowl."

Green Bay and Chicago have always formed one of the greatest rivalries in all of sports. The teams first met in 1921 and have had no use for each other in the 90 years since.

Back in the day, Chicago's George Halas and Green Bay's Curly Lambeau despised one another. It stayed that way for generations, as these two outfits continued an immense dislike for the other.

By the end of the 2010 regular season, the Packers and Bears had met 181 times with Chicago holding a narrow 92–83–6 advantage in the series. Amazingly, though, these bitter adversaries played just once in the postseason. That came in 1941, when Halas' Bears defeated Lambeau's Packers 33–14 in a Western Division playoff game played at Wrigley Field in Chicago.

So the anticipation was off the charts when these two foes met in Chicago for the right to play in .the 45th Super Bowl.

"We don't like their team and they don't like our team. I get all that," Packers coach Mike McCarthy said. "But I respect the way they play. They play the right way. We play the right way.

"But this is about winning championships. And we're going down there to play for the NFC Championship Game. And you have to beat teams like the Chicago Bears to achieve that goal. That's really what it comes down to. But there will be plenty of energy on that field."

Although Chicago was the No. 2 seed in the NFC and the Packers were seeded sixth, the red-hot Packers were installed as a three-point favorite.

"It's going to be backyard football," said Bears defensive end Israel Idonije. "Man on man. They throw a punch, we throw a punch. We're going to slug back and forth and the first one to flinch or drop is going to lose the game."

When Bears coach Lovie Smith was hired in 2004, he listed his goals in this order:

1. Beat the Packers.
2. Win the NFC North.
3. Win the Super Bowl.

Green Bay had always been the measuring stick for Smith's Bears. Now, there was more at stake than ever before.

"It just doesn't get any better as I see it, than for the NFC championship to come down to the Packers coming down to our turf this time," Smith said. "The Packers and Bears to finish it up. That's how it should be."

Green Bay's performance in the conference title game wasn't always pretty, especially on offense. There were plenty of tense moments down the stretch as the Bears rallied back from a 14–0 deficit.

But thanks in large part to Shields and Raji, the Packers were headed to the Super Bowl for the first time in 13 years.

"I'm numb. It's a great feeling," McCarthy said. "I'm just so proud of our football team. You know, it's always tough coming into Chicago to win a football game. I have tremendous respect for the organization and coach Lovie Smith. We felt we had them on the ropes there for a while. We just couldn't get the game to a three-score game."

The way the Packers started against the Bears, it looked like they'd breeze into the Super Bowl.

On Green Bay's first drive, quarterback Aaron Rodgers led a seven play, 84-yard march that he capped with a one-yard TD run. Rodgers was 4-for-4 on the drive for 76 yards and hit Greg Jennings twice for 48 yards.

"Frankly, the first drive was the way we anticipated coming into this game," McCarthy said. "I thought we were able to get into a tremendous rhythm."

Green Bay stayed in rhythm and went ahead 14–0 just four minutes into the second quarter.

The Packers needed only five plays to cover 44 yards on that drive. Running back Brandon Jackson (16 yards) and wideout Jordy Nelson (15) both had big catches on the march, and running back James Starks finished the deal with a four-yard TD run.

"The way we started out, I thought we were going to put up 40 points," Packers right guard Josh Sitton said. "We came out and were running good, throwing good, just rolling."

But Green Bay's offense hit the wall. After scoring twice in their first four possessions, the Packers' final 10 possessions resulted in six punts, two interceptions by Rodgers and two kneel-downs to end halves. It was an unexpected turnaround for a Green Bay offense that had been white hot.

"I don't know what happened," Sitton said. "We were just really out of sync and lost all of our momentum. Thankfully, our defense stepped up and made sure we're still playing."

No one stepped up more than Shields and Raji. With the Packers clinging to a 14–7 lead midway through the fourth quarter, Raji made a play that McCarthy called a "game-winner."

The Bears had a third-and-5 from their own 15. Raji lined up over center Olin Kreutz, showed rush, then dropped into the middle of the field. Chicago third-string quarterback Caleb Hanie—who had replaced an injured Jay Cutler and an ineffective Todd Collins—was trying to get the ball to running back Matt Forte.

Hanie never saw Raji, though, and threw the ball right into his enormous mitts. Raji caught the ball naturally, then waltzed to the right corner of the endzone to make it 21–7. Raji didn't have an interception in the NFL or college, so his timing was perfect for Packer Nation.

"It's just a great feeling," Raji said. "It was a great call. I was behind the back and obviously he wasn't expecting that. I just caught it and ran it back."

Shields then capped Green Bay's huge defensive effort with his second interception of the day and his biggest play as a Packer.

Hanie had rallied the Bears back to within 21–14. Chicago then drove to Green Bay's 29-yard line, where they faced a fourth-and-5 with 47 seconds left.

Hanie worked out of the shotgun, the Bears sent out four receivers and the Packers rushed five. Hanie took a shot down the middle for Johnny Knox, but Shields jumped the route knowing safety Nick Collins was providing help from behind.

With his coaches screaming, "Get down," Shields returned the interception 32 yards. When Shields rose up, he was mobbed by teammates that knew their next stop was the Super Bowl.

"We need to work on that last play, getting on the ground a little sooner," McCarthy said afterward. "Sam, for a rookie—and I told a couple other rookies this—you have no idea what you've accomplished here in your first year in the league. He is going to be a great player for the Green Bay Packers for a long time."

Green Bay's defense was the No. 1 reason these Packers were going to their first Super Bowl in 13 years. Green Bay forced three Chicago turnovers, held the Bears' three quarterbacks to a combined passer rating of 45.2, and allowed just 132 total yards through three quarters.

"It seems the defense has put these last three games away," linebacker Clay Matthews said. "We had our backs against the wall a little bit, but we made the play to win the game."

For years now, there were websites calling for the firing of general manager Ted Thompson. And just one month earlier, McCarthy's job security appeared tenuous, at best, when the Packers were 8–6.

Now, these two had led Green Bay back to the Super Bowl, highlighted by a win over their fiercest rival.

"Really, the way that our season went—the trials and tribulations that we encountered, to me, that was how we were shaped," McCarthy said. "I think it's made us a better football team. It's challenged our character. I think we've really grown through it.

"Our players truly believe that we will be successful in Dallas, just like how they truly believed that we were going to be successful here today. This was the path that was chosen for us, and I think it's really shaped a hell of a football team."

Which is something the 2010 Packers proved against the Bears.

66 **Paul Coffman**

The Lambeau Experience never ceases to amaze Paul Coffman. The most productive tight end in Green Bay Packers history loves combining the past with the present. So, when each of his four children turned 10, he took them back to Green Bay during Alumni Weekend. While it was a treat for the youngsters, Coffman himself may have gotten the biggest kick.

"My daughter and I were walking through the parking lot [in 2002] after a game," Coffman said of his youngest child, Cameron. "And people started recognizing me and yelling, 'Paul Coffman, you were the greatest!' Now, I was losing my hair and it was graying, and these people still don't forget you. They embrace their Packers with unconditional love. It's just incredible."

Most would describe Coffman's time in Green Bay as rather incredible. And even though Coffman hasn't donned a Packers uniform since 1985, it's easy to see why he's still remembered.

An undrafted free agent out of Kansas State, Coffman played in Green Bay from 1978 to 1985 and made three trips to the Pro Bowl. Coffman caught 322 passes and 39 touchdowns in a Packers uniform and teamed with quarterback Lynn Dickey and wideouts James Lofton and John Jefferson to form one of the NFL's deadliest passing attacks in the early '80s.

In the strike-shortened 1982 season, the Packers averaged 25.1 points per game, and all three pass-catchers were named to the Pro Bowl. The following year, Green Bay averaged 26.8 points per game, which was its fourth-highest total since it joined the NFL in 1921.

"Man, that offense was fun to be part of," said Coffman, who was inducted into the Packers Hall of Fame in 1994. "We had four guys catch over 50 passes one year [1983]. All three of us wound up in the Pro Bowl, and Lynn did a great job of getting us the ball. That was something else."

Coffman was something else himself. But few would have ever predicted it. He was so lightly regarded coming out of Kansas State in 1978 that he had to persuade former Packers assistant coach John Meyer to give him a tryout when Meyer visited the campus to work out a different Wildcats player. Coffman wasn't selected in the 12-round draft, but the Packers did sign him as a free agent.

Coffman played little his rookie year but burst onto the scene with a 56-catch season in 1979, which is the second-most receptions ever by a Packers tight end. But that was just the start. Year in and year out, Coffman was one of the NFL's most productive tight ends. Aside from the strike-shortened 1982 campaign, Coffman had at least 42 catches and 496 yards in every season following his rookie year and played in all but two games during his Green Bay career.

Coffman lacked great speed, and at 6'3" and 225 pounds, he was never going to be a physical presence. But he had a phenomenal football IQ, competed harder than most, and had sensational hands.

When his accomplishments are brought up, though, Coffman is a picture of modesty.

"Bob Schnelker paid so much attention to detail," Coffman said of his former offensive coordinator. "He didn't assume anything. He was one of the first people to utilize the tight end, and he was a big reason our offense produced as well as it did."

Coffman's production was never better than in 1983, when he caught 54 passes for 814 yards and 11 touchdowns. Those 11 touchdowns were the most by a Packers receiver since Bill Howton had 12 in 1956, and the only receivers in the NFL with more touchdowns that year were St. Louis' Roy Green (14), Philadelphia's Mike Quick (13), and the Raiders'

Todd Christensen (12). Included in that memorable season was Coffman's huge night in the Packers' 48–47 victory over Washington on *Monday Night Football*. In that game, Coffman caught six passes for 124 yards and two touchdowns.

Coffman added to his solid career, catching 43 balls with nine touchdowns in 1984 and 49 passes and six touchdowns in '85. Then, the inexplicable happened. During training camp in 1986, head coach Forrest Gregg determined the Packers needed a youth movement. So he cut the 30-year-old Coffman, along with Dickey. To this day, Coffman remains upset about how his Green Bay days ended.

"Forrest, he's someone I have nothing to say about," said Coffman, who played his final three seasons in Kansas City and Minnesota. "When James [Lofton] went into the Hall of Fame, he mentioned him. But I guess he's just got more class than I do."

Coffman has spent the last several years watching his two sons chase their football dreams. Chase Coffman has bounced around the NFL, while Carson Coffman is playing in the Arena Football League.

Both players have a long ways to go, though, to catch their old man. And if they don't believe it, all it might take is a return trip to Lambeau Field.

"Going back there and still getting recognized is really neat," said Coffman, who grew up in tiny Chase, Kansas. "Just playing there was unbelievable.

"From my perspective, I was living my dream. From the time I was a little kid, all I wanted to do was play in the NFL. And I was a small-town guy and I would have been lost in New York or L.A. So Green Bay was the perfect place for me."

Packers fans still feel the same way.

67 1962 Packers-Lions

The National Football League was formed in 1920. In the league's glorious 93-year existence, the 1972 Miami Dolphins are the only team that's gone undefeated and untied, going a perfect 17–0 that season, including winning Super Bowl VII.

To this day, many of the 1962 Green Bay Packers believe they should have accomplished perfection themselves. Green Bay went to Detroit for a Thanksgiving game that year with a 10–0 record and was trying to become the first team in league history not to lose or tie a game all season. Instead, the Packers left with a humbling 26–14 defeat. Green Bay wouldn't lose again that year and capped its 14–1 season with a 16–7 victory over the New York Giants in the NFL Championship Game. But the fact that those Lions prevented Green Bay from making history still eats at many of those Packers today.

"We'd always go to Detroit on Thanksgiving, and we'd almost always lose over there," said wide receiver Boyd Dowler. "But we thought that year was going to be different."

"That '62 team was probably the best one we had," former Packers tight end Ron Kramer said before his death in 2010. "That one still bugs me a little bit."

While several Packers who took part in that game look back with disappointment, Green Bay coach Vince Lombardi didn't seem the least bit bothered after the game. In fact, Lombardi almost seemed relieved.

"I think we'll be a better football team for having lost this one," Lombardi told the Associated Press after the game. "That business about an undefeated season was a lot of bunk. Nobody in his right mind could have expected it. The loss had to come sometime, but I honestly didn't think it would come today."

It did for several reasons. The Lions' defensive front dominated Green Bay's offensive line. And Packers quarterback Bart Starr was under siege all day.

"Detroit's defensive line blitzed and criss-crossed so well and so quickly, they were continually getting the jump on us," Lombardi said. "Every team blitzes, but Detroit made it work practically all the time. We couldn't find their defensive line long enough to block it. The ball was snapped, and they were gone. They were coming off the ball much quicker than we were. Detroit's defense played like guys who were on the needle."

Afterward, Starr called the Lions' blitz "the best—or maybe I should say the worst—I've seen this year. I didn't have time to find anybody most of the time. There were too many people chasing me."

Detroit was also far more physical than the Packers were. "The only way you can beat the Packers is to run over them," Detroit linebacker Wayne Walker said. "They expected it to be rough, and they like it that way. We didn't trick them. We just got the drop on them."

The Lions also had revenge on their minds. Just seven weeks earlier, Green Bay defeated Detroit 9–7 on a last-second field goal.

"My players have been building up for this ever since that game," Detroit coach George Wilson said. "The coaches didn't have to do a thing to get them up—just get out of their way. We didn't think the Packers should have won the first game. They were lucky. Then we'd been reading all those magazine stories about how great they were. Our kids were mad. I didn't have to say a word to them before the game. You could have heard a pin drop in our dressing room, and I didn't say anything at the half."

The setback proved to be the perfect wake-up call for Green Bay. The Packers won their final three games of the regular season, wound up winning the conference by two games over the Lions, then went on to defeat the Giants in the league title game. Still, years later Green Bay's players realized how close they were to history. And had Green Bay not played like turkeys during their Thanksgiving trip to Detroit, they'd have been the first team ever to enjoy a perfect season.

"I remember after that game Coach Lombardi wasn't all that mad," safety Willie Wood said. "But I look back now, and it's incredible how close we were to going unbeaten. Regardless, that was a great football team, probably the best of any we had there. But to win them all would have been great."

68 Coming of Age

Every great team has a breakthrough moment they always point to. That time they went from an up-and-comer to a legitimate contender. For the Green Bay Packers of the 1990s, that time was January 6, 1996.

The Packers went to San Francisco that day for an NFC Divisional Playoff Game. Green Bay was coming off an 11-win regular season, its most since 1966, but was still lightly regarded. The 49ers were the defending Super Bowl champions, the league's dominant franchise, and 10½-point favorite.

"No one gave us a chance," Packers safety LeRoy Butler said. "Everything we read said we didn't have a chance. If no one is going to give you respect, then you have nothing to lose."

The Packers certainly played that way. And when Green Bay exited with a 27–17 win, it marked the franchise's biggest win in nearly 30 years.

"This is the culmination of a lot of work by an entire team that completely believed in itself," Packers general manager Ron Wolf said afterward. "We had to show this, that we are indeed a real football team. By God, I think we've done that." On a gorgeous afternoon at 3Com Park, the Packers dominated the 49ers physically. League MVP Brett Favre threw for 299 yards and two TDs. And when the game ended, there had been a changing of the guard in the NFC.

"For some reason, they took us for granted," Green Bay linebacker George Koonce said. "We've got a quarterback that's hot, and we have a defense."

Both were on full display in this landmark win. On San Francisco's first offensive play, quarterback Steve Young threw a swing pass to fullback Adam Walker. Linebacker Wayne Simmons—who had one of the more memorable games by a Packers defender in years—forced a fumble, and cornerback Craig Newsome returned it 31 yards for a touchdown. And before the first quarter was over, Favre led a 62-yard TD drive in which he hit Keith Jackson for a three-yard score. Early in the second quarter, the capacity crowd was completely silenced after Favre's 13-yard TD to Mark Chmura made it 21–0.

"The way we started out playing, that set the tempo of the game," said Packers defensive end Reggie White. "This is the biggest game of my career. It's the farthest I've ever been."

Once the Packers got the lead, the 49ers became one-dimensional and had to throw. And that played right into the hands of Green Bay defensive coordinator Fritz Shurmur.

The Packers sacked Young three times and knocked him to the ground several others. Green Bay's cornerbacks—Doug Evans and Newsome—were terrific against San Francisco's star wideouts, Jerry Rice and John Taylor. But the defensive star undoubtedly was Simmons, who battered tight end Brent Jones throughout the game and set the physical tone the Packers wanted to play with.

"He was very physical, and he's an outstanding player," Jones said of Simmons. "You can take any couple of plays and make what you want out of it. I think they made it a point to be physical."

Green Bay, which played a 4-3 defense, also surprised the 49ers by switching to a 3-4 that day. The element of surprise confused the 49ers and their high-powered offense.

"We caught them off guard. I think it had to be the third quarter before they caught up and realized what we were doing," Butler said. "A lot of people would think it'd be hard to learn that defense in just a few days. But it wasn't. It was new, so we were so energetic."

The Packers would go on to lose the NFC Championship Game in Dallas the following week. But their destruction of the mighty 49ers laid the groundwork for big things to come. Green Bay won the NFC in both the 1996 and 1997 seasons, and won Super Bowl XXXI, as well. And the Packers could all agree it began with their surprising win in San Francisco.

"It's not like a regular-season game," Favre said. "It's a playoff game against the defending Super Bowl champions. It's hard to explain, it's hard to imagine what we've just done."

What they did was set the stage for future greatness.

69 Kabeer Gbaja-Biamila

It's great to have goals. Some, of course, seem realistic when established. Others are almost laughable. Back in 2000 you could have put Kabeer Gbaja-Biamila's aspirations in category No. 2.

"When I got to Green Bay, my goal was to break the sack record," said Gbaja-Biamila, better known by his easier-to-pronounce initials, KGB. "It wasn't going to make or break who I am. But I just had a goal. It didn't matter whose name was on it, but I wanted the record."

That all sounds well and good. But in all honesty, the odds of that happening seemed comparable to KGB winning Powerball. Gbaja-Biamila was taken in the fifth round of the 2000 draft and released during his first training camp in Green Bay. He was later reassigned to the practice squad and saw little action his rookie season. Amazingly, though, by the time Gbaja-Biamila's career ended in 2008, the Packers' all-time sack record was his. KGB finished his nine-year Packers career with 74.5 sacks, six more than previous record-holder Reggie White.

"Kabeer's a guy who I don't think people had a lot of expectations for coming out of college, but he worked his way up to become a prominent pass rusher," said linebacker Brady Poppinga, a teammate of KGB's from 2005 to 2008. "I think that's a great testament to his work ethic and his persistence. Kudos to him, man. Kudos."

What makes Gbaja-Biamila's story so surprising is he compiled those numbers despite being one of the smaller defensive ends in football. KGB was typically listed at 250 pounds, but admitted he usually played 10 pounds less than that. Still, he was lightning quick off the line of scrimmage, and left tackles everywhere struggled with his quickness.

"He's just amazing to watch," said defensive end Cullen Jenkins, a teammate of Gbaja-Biamila's from 2004 to 2008. "There aren't many guys that have that kind of speed off the edge. That's pretty rare."

That speed helped KGB make quite a living. Gbaja-Biamila broke out in 2001 when he had 13½ sacks, then moved into the starting lineup the following season. Between 2001 and 2004 KGB had 49 sacks and notched 10 multiple-sack games. Packers head coach and general manager Mike Sherman signed Gbaja-Biamila to a seven-year, $37.3 million contract after the 2002 season and felt compelled to play him virtually every down. While KGB often struggled against the run, he continued to develop into one of the premier pass rushers in football.

"I'm humbled," Gbaja-Biamila said after setting the sack record. "It took teamwork, it took coaching, it took other teammates, it took DBs. Like I said, I'm just grateful I have the opportunity to do it."

Through the years, KGB had several memorable games and moments. He posted four sacks against Chicago in 2004 and also had three sacks at Minnesota in 2007. The one sack that will always be most special to him, though, came on December 8, 2002.

Gbaja-Biamila's mother, Bola, had died one week earlier. KGB returned to his hometown of Los Angeles for the funeral, then came back to record a huge play in Green Bay's 26–22 win over Minnesota that week. On Minnesota's final drive of the night, KGB beat the Vikings' highly touted rookie left tackle Bryant McKinnie. Gbaja-Biamila sacked Daunte Culpepper and forced a fumble that sealed a huge Packers' win.

"That one was big," KGB said. "I bull-rushed [McKinnie]. He fell, and I jumped over him, got Culpepper, and knocked the ball out of his hands. That one meant a lot."

Gbaja-Biamila also was honored to pass a player like White. While the two never played together, Gbaja-Biamila said they developed a friendship before White died in 2004. At the heart of their relationship was religion, something extremely important to both men.

"That was big," Gbaja-Biamila said. "But then I would also call him if I had questions, or when he'd come to the game, sometimes he'd coach me up. So that was pretty cool. He was an inspiration."

While no one would ever claim that Gbaja-Biamila was a better defensive end than White, it's KGB who sits at No. 1 in the Packers record book for sacks. And now, the numbers KGB posted are being chased by today's defensive linemen.

"It means a lot because there's a lot more that goes into that than just the numbers," said Carl Hairston, Gbaja-Biamila's position coach from 2006 to 2008. "When you look at [KGB], you think he's more of a one-dimensional player. But that one dimension is something he did very well."

70 Chester Marcol

The Green Bay Packers have had some remarkable finishes in their long and glorious history. But the most improbable may have come in the 1980 season-opener.

The Packers, coming off a sorry 1979 season and a winless exhibition campaign, had taken the heavily favored Chicago Bears to overtime. Green Bay drove deep into Bears territory, and kicker Chester Marcol lined up for a 34-yard field goal. Marcol's kick was low and hit defensive tackle Alan Page in the facemask. Amazingly, though, the ball caromed straight back into Marcol's chest.

"I had no choice but to go left," Marcol said. "The left side was wide open because they overloaded the middle since they were going all out to block it. I just took off."

Marcol, a former soccer goalie with nifty hands, raced for the left corner of the end zone. Marcol picked up a key block from teammate Jim Gueno and scored one of the most memorable touchdowns in team history.

Packers 12, Bears 6.

"I played a lot in high school and college, and it gave me some football sense," Marcol said that day. "I've done these things before."

Dan Hampton, a defensive end for the Bears, wasn't nearly as complimentary.

"We bat the ball back, and that little weasel runs it in," Hampton said. "It was like bursting a balloon."

Marcol, who played nine seasons with the Packers, had several memorable performances in Green Bay. He kicked four field goals in the first game he ever played, the 1972 season-opener. He led the National Football League in scoring that year with 128 points and was named both Rookie of the Year and All-Pro. Marcol, a Polish immigrant who was taken in the second round, was quickly dubbed the "Polish Prince." There were Chester Marcol fan clubs popping up across the state, and he became an instant hero.

Marcol led the Packers in scoring six different seasons. And he holds the record for most field goals by a Packers rookie (33). But Marcol battled alcoholism much of his career. And shortly before that memorable win over the Bears, Marcol had become addicted to cocaine, as well.

"That was the straw that broke the camel's back," Marcol said. "When I started using cocaine, everything just crashed. Just crashed. I thought I could use it recreationally, but I'm the kind of person who, after a while, I wanted lots of it."

Just one month after Marcol's memorable TD against the Bears, the Packers released him. Green Bay said it was because Marcol's kickoffs were too short, but it had far more to do with his personal life.

"I believe today that everything happens the way it's supposed to happen," Marcol said. "But unfortunately, I induced several of these things. I believe I cheated myself, whatever you want to say, because I made those choices."

While Marcol's post-football years have been a struggle, he remains revered by much of Packer Nation—thanks in large part to his 1980 heroics against the Bears.

"I was just thankful I played other positions in high school and had some experience," Marcol said. "I knew what to do. It was a heads-up play."

One Packers fans will never forget.

71 Mike Sherman

They say nothing ages a man like becoming president of the United States. For proof, just check out Jimmy Carter's before and after pictures. But the aging process is certainly cranked to high when you're the coach of the Green Bay Packers. Just ask Mike Sherman.

Hired in 2000, the 45-year-old Sherman still looked his age and was in reasonable physical condition. When he was fired after the 2005 campaign, Sherman looked 15 years older and had gone up multiple pant sizes.

"It's an aging job. There's no doubt about it," then–Packers president Bob Harlan said. "It's a pressure business. It's a bottom-line business."

In the end, Sherman's bottom line wasn't good enough. Sherman had a modicum of success, going 57–39 in his six seasons as Green Bay's head coach. He also led the Packers to three straight NFC North titles between 2002 and 2004. But Sherman was just 2–4 in the postseason and never advanced past the divisional playoffs. Considering quarterback Brett Favre and running back Ahman Green were among the game's best players during this time, Sherman's playoff record was considered a monumental failure.

So following a 4–12 season in 2005, he was fired and replaced by Mike McCarthy.

"Decisions like this are never easy," Packers general manager Ted Thompson said the day he fired Sherman. "They require a lot of thought and consternation, but at the end of the day, I thought we needed to go in a different direction."

Green Bay's decision to go with Sherman was surprising in the first place. After nearly 20 years in the college ranks, Sherman was hired as Green Bay's tight ends and assistant offensive line coach for the 1997 and 1998 seasons. He then left to become Seattle's offensive coordinator in 1999. When the Packers were in the market for a head coach that off-season, they made the stunning move of hiring the largely obscure Sherman. And when general manager Ron Wolf walked away after the 2000 campaign, he didn't want to dramatically rock the boat. So he gave Sherman the dual role of head coach and GM, despite just one 9–7 season on Sherman's résumé.

"I do not assume to be Ron's equal in regard to personnel matters," Sherman said the day he was named general manager.

He wasn't. Sherman inherited a solid roster and lived off of Wolf's players for a few seasons. But Sherman struggled with the personnel side of things, missed badly in both free agency and the draft, and Green Bay eventually began to slip. After the Packers lost a home game to Minnesota in the 2004 playoffs, Harlan stripped Sherman of the general manager role and hired Thompson to replace him.

"I don't want the word *criticism* to be a part of this," Harlan said when announcing Thompson's hiring and Sherman's demotion. "I don't want us to falter. I want us to stay strong. And that's where this is coming from. To criticize [Sherman], I don't think is the right way to approach it. I told him, 'This is help. This is not criticism.'"

But others were more than willing to criticize Sherman. It was bad enough Sherman couldn't navigate the Packers through the playoffs. Sherman lost the first two home playoff games in team history and will always be remembered for being outcoached in a 2003 postseason loss to Philadelphia, better known as the "fourth-and-26" game. Sherman had also started to alienate many of those around him. During Sherman's time in Green Bay, he had gone from a humble man to one who was downright egomaniacal, and much of his coaching staff had grown tired of his act.

After the 2004 season, highly respected veteran coaches like Johnny Roland (running backs) and Ray Sherman (receivers) accepted lateral moves with losing teams.

"The head coach thought he was the only one with any brains," said Roland, who had 26 years of NFL experience. "There was a lot of collective knowledge in the people who have left. And that knowledge wasn't listened to. There were a lot of guys who have been around a long time. You think they should have a little bit of input into how this game should be played and things you should take advantage of. But that wasn't how it worked up there."

Finally, after the 2005 season—one in which Thompson gave Sherman a contract extension early in the season—the plug was pulled. And one of the more unfulfilling tenures in team history was over.

"We definitely should have won more than we did," former Packers guard Mike Wahle said. "We had the talent, and we had enough chances to get it done. We just never did."

Which not only aged Sherman dramatically—it also led to his eventual departure.

72 Don Majkowski

Don Majkowski showed up at Green Bay Packers training camp in 1987 a mystery to most. Majkowski's senior year at Virginia was wrecked by a separated shoulder. He couldn't participate in several drills that year at the NFL Combine. And he plummeted to the 10th round of the draft. Few expected anything from Majkowski, but Majkowski certainly wasn't one of them.

Packers quarterback Don Majkowski, the "Majik Man," works a little magic in the infamous "Instant Replay Game," November 5, 1989, in which Green Bay prevailed over the visiting Chicago Bears 14–13 on a last-second touchdown throw. Majkowski's heroics that day cemented his legacy, and his Pro Bowl season lifted the downtrodden Packers to a 10–6 record and hope for the future.

"I had a huge chip on my shoulder when I came into camp," Majkowski said. "But things worked out for the best. I think I got drafted by the absolute best team that was the best situation for me. We really didn't have a veteran quarterback that was very established, and I was able to come in immediately and compete and was thrown into the starting lineup the second game my rookie year. So it was a great situation."

Majkowski made it just that and quickly earned the nickname "Majik Man." During his six years in Green Bay, Majkowski produced several memorable moments—highlighted by the 1989 season in which he finished second in the MVP voting to San Francisco's Joe Montana. Majkowski also threw the winning pass in the Packers' memorable 14–13 win over Chicago in 1989 that was later dubbed the "Instant Replay Game."

While others might have had their doubts about Majkowski, he never questioned his own ability. In fact, after he was drafted, Majkowski was so confident in his skill set that he signed a one-year contract worth only $65,000 his rookie season. The move paid off, though, when Majkowski immediately proved he could be Green Bay's quarterback of the future. And heading into his second season, he and the Packers agreed on a one-year, $650,000 deal.

"I never had any doubts," he said. "What hurt me was the timing of my [shoulder] injury coming out of college."

During his first two seasons in the league, Majkowski and Randy Wright played virtually the same amount of snaps. But by year three, it had become Majkowski's team, and he had one of the greatest seasons in Packers history. In the 1989 campaign, Majkowski threw for 4,318 yards, the fifth-highest total in franchise history. His 599 passing attempts that season were a team record that has since been broken. He threw for 27 touchdowns and 20 interceptions and became the first Packers quarterback since Bart Starr in 1966 to make the Pro Bowl.

Green Bay also caught lightning in a bottle that season and finished 10–6. Four of those victories were by a single point, and seven were by four points or fewer. "That whole year was just awesome," Majkowski said. "We were in the playoff hunt for the first time in years. The whole community was so charged up. It was just a great time to be a Packer."

Majkowski's most memorable moment, of course, came during what will be forever known as the "Instant Replay Game." Green Bay trailed 13–7 late, when Majkowski threw a 14-yard touchdown pass to Sterling Sharpe in the game's final seconds. At question, though, was whether or not Majkowski had crossed the line of scrimmage. After a lengthy review, the Packers were awarded a touchdown and snapped their eight-game losing streak against Chicago.

"That's probably my defining moment as a Green Bay Packer," Majkowski said. "I'm proud to be remembered from that game.... To finally end the streak at home on the last play of the game in such dramatic fashion is pretty memorable."

Times weren't as sweet for Majkowski after that magical 1989 season. Shoulder and hamstring injuries limited his play the next two seasons. Then, Packers general manager Ron Wolf traded away a first-round draft choice for Brett Favre before the 1992 season. Majkowski opened that year as Green Bay's starter. But, when he suffered an ankle injury against Cincinnati in Week 3, Favre replaced him and didn't miss a start over the next 16 seasons.

Majkowski left for Indianapolis as an unrestricted free agent in 1993. He played two years with the Colts and two more with the Lions, yet still ranks sixth all-time in Packers history in career passing yards (10,870).

"In '92 it was really tough," Majkowski said of losing his job. "I was a six-year veteran, and Brett came in and did a nice job, but he was very green. But I understood the whole situation. I never held anything against Brett. We always remained best of friends. It was just a part of the profession. I don't blame Mike Holmgren or Ron Wolf. They traded a No. 1 pick away and they went with the future. So I understood everything professionally. I never caused any problems, I tried to be as professional as I could."

Which is one of several reasons the "Majik Man" is still remembered fondly around Green Bay.

73 Desmond Howard

Desmond Howard came *this* close to never playing for the Green Bay Packers. A flop in both Washington and Jacksonville, Howard was trying to resuscitate his career in Green Bay during the summer of 1996. The thing is, he was failing miserably. Then came the Packers' second preseason game that year, when Howard probably saved himself a trip to the unemployment line. Howard brought a punt back 77 yards for a touchdown against Pittsburgh that night and went from long shot to big shot.

"If we'd only played [one] preseason game, I don't know if he would have made the team," then–Packers general manager Ron Wolf said. "To be honest, he wasn't having much success in the NFL and was touted as overrated and all that. But I figured he was still an exceptional return guy."

Boy was he ever. And Howard spent the rest of the season proving exactly that.

Howard enjoyed a record-setting regular season, one in which he shattered the NFL record for punt-return yardage with 875. Then Howard had a memorable postseason, highlighted by his 244 all-purpose yards in Super Bowl XXXI, which earned him MVP honors.

Return specialist Desmond Howard runs a kickoff back 99 yards for a touchdown against the New England Patriots during the third quarter of Super Bowl XXXI, January 26, 1997, in New Orleans.

"I still think of the one year he had with us in 1996," Wolf said. "As that season went along, he became more and more a threat to take it all the way every time he touched the ball. He's the best return guy I've ever seen. He never really made it as a wide receiver, but he put it all together that year as a returner."

Howard won the Heisman Trophy at Michigan in 1991, then the Washington Redskins traded up to take him with the fourth overall pick in the 1992 draft. After three years, though, Howard had just 66 catches and five TDs, and Washington moved on.

Jacksonville selected Howard in the 1995 expansion draft, but he lasted just one season there. Wolf, who had targeted Howard when he was coming out of Michigan, thought he'd take a chance—and it paid off in a big way.

In that 1996 season, Howard led the NFL in punt-return yardage (875), punt-return average (15.1), and punt-return touchdowns (three). It was the postseason, though, where Howard really caught America's attention. First, on a muddy field in the NFC Divisional Playoff against San Francisco, Howard brought a punt back 71 yards for a touchdown to give the Packers a 7–0 lead. Later in the first quarter, Howard returned a punt 46 yards to the 49ers' 7-yard line to set up another TD in what would become a 35–14 Green Bay win.

"You could tell it broke their spirit," Packers running back Edgar Bennett said of Howard's returns.

That was nothing, though, compared to what Howard had waiting for the New England Patriots in the Super Bowl. Howard was in the middle of a solid night that immediately turned spectacular late in the third quarter. The upstart Patriots had just trimmed Green Bay's lead to 27–21 when Adam Vinatieri drove Howard back to his 1-yard line. Howard shot up the middle, got a handful of good blocks from the Packers' wedge, then juked Vinatieri for a 99-yard TD that was the longest return in Super Bowl history.

"We had a lot of momentum, and our defense was playing better," Patriots coach Bill Parcells said afterward. "But [Howard] made the big play. That return was the game right there. He's been great all year, and he was great again today."

Wolf and the Packers were surprised—albeit pleasantly—that New England even kicked the ball to Howard.

"My thought at the moment of his kickoff return was, *They just did.* And they paid for it," Wolf said.

Howard parlayed his remarkable year into a hefty free-agent contract with Oakland that off-season. He later played eight games in Green Bay during the 1999 season and three more years with Detroit. But Howard never came close to duplicating his remarkable 1996 season, in which he saved his career and helped the Packers break a 29-year title drought.

"He wasn't quite big enough or good enough to be a starter for us, not for our offense," Wolf said of Howard. "He was what he was: a great returner."

74 Attend the NFL Draft Party

Ted Thompson stood before several of his bosses in late April 2007. Green Bay's general manager told Packer Nation he had just used the 16th overall selection in the NFL Draft on Tennessee defensive tackle Justin Harrell.

Those fans had one common reaction. They booed. They booed loudly. And they booed for a long, long time.

"I think it's great because that's what the Green Bay Packers [are] all about…fans like that have passion and they care, and we are doing everything that we can to make this the best team possible," Thompson said later that day. "And if they disagree with our decisions, that's okay. It's just as long as we believe we're doing the right thing, we can take a few shots."

One of the recent traditions that's been established in Green Bay is the Packers Draft Party. And the reaction to Thompson's pick has become a highlight. Fans flock to the Lambeau Field Atrium for the first day of the NFL Draft. After Thompson makes his first-round selection, he comes and addresses those in attendance. The Packers have drawn nearly 2,000 fans for this event in recent years, and it's a terrific conclusion to "draft season," which has become an obsession for several fans when there are no games being played.

ESPN began televising the NFL Draft in 1980, and few paid attention. The network, in its infancy, showed just one and a half rounds back then. Even that took some fight, as NFL owners voted 28–0 the previous year against having the draft televised by ESPN.

"That's pretty funny," said Fred Gaudelli, who produced several of those early televised drafts. "Nobody knew what ESPN was about. Why would [the NFL want] to put its brand on their air? All anybody knew was ABC, NBC, and CBS."

Slowly, as ESPN became a heavy hitter, the draft's popularity began to rise. Mel Kiper became a household name, and fans everywhere became "draftniks." A key move came in 1988, when the draft was switched from a Tuesday to a Sunday and Monday. Then in 1994, the draft was given a Saturday-Sunday time slot. The event ballooned to three days in 2010, with the first round taking place on Thursday, and the final six rounds spread out over Friday and Saturday.

Today, both ESPN and NFL Network run wall-to-wall coverage on draft weekend, and hype surrounds the event for months beforehand. With countless websites and pre-draft publications available, fans have become more knowledgeable and excited about the draft itself.

So in recent years the Packers decided to turn the event into a giant party. Two large television screens show the event live, and there's wireless Internet available. Thompson, head coach Mike McCarthy, and some Packers players typically address the crowd, as well. The fans who booed Thompson mercilessly on that 2007 day wound up being right, as Harrell was an injury-prone player who busted. Thompson also got booed in 2008, when he traded out of the first round for wideout Jordy Nelson. Thompson has gotten the last laugh with that transaction.

"The more loyal fans stood up and clapped a little bit, but I had my share of heckling," Thompson said.

Things lightened up in 2009, when fans seemed to like the first-round selections of defensive tackle B.J. Raji and linebacker Clay Matthews. Of course, both players have since turned into pillars of the Packers' defense.

But the crowd's reaction is part of the fun of draft weekend in Green Bay. Everybody's got opinions, and many of the Packers' brass are front and center to listen.

75 Terrell Owens

"Owens! Owens! Owens! Owens! Owens! He caught it! He caught it! He caught it!"

Those were the words of San Francisco 49ers play-by-play man Joe Starkey. And to this day, that call from January 3, 1999, makes Green Bay Packers fans everywhere cringe. In one of the greatest wild-card games of all time, the Packers led the 49ers 27–23 with just eight seconds left. The 49ers had a third down at Green Bay's 25-yard line. Quarterback Steve Young dropped back and nearly fell to the ground when he tripped over a teammate's foot. Young regained his balance, then fired a dart down the seam that wideout Terrell Owens caught for a game-winning touchdown that immediately became known as The Catch II.

Not only did the 30–27 loss end the Packers' reign as two-time NFC champs, it was also the last game Mike Holmgren ever coached in Green Bay, as he took a job as Seattle's head coach, general manager, and executive vice president of football operations just five days later.

"I knew I was going to have to make a big play," Owens said afterward. "I started the game with a fumble and a couple of dropped passes. The guys stayed behind me." It was a remarkable ending for Owens, who dropped four passes and had a fumble that day. It was also a surreal conclusion for the Packers, who appeared poised to knock the 49ers out of the postseason for a fourth straight year.

On the fateful play, the Packers rushed just three and played zone with eight. Safety Darren Sharper was the primary culprit for the gaffe after dropping too deep in his portion of the zone. Linebacker Bernardo Harris also didn't drop deep enough, and safety Pat Terrell was late arriving. Owens took a lick when Sharper and Terrell drilled him a yard deep in the end zone. But when he held on, Green Bay's five-game winning streak over the 49ers had ended.

"The way this one ended was startling,'" Holmgren said. "When the ball goes down the middle like that, you don't think the ball's going to be caught, ever. I think it was a marvelous catch. It was the perfect throw, and he [Owens] made the play."

The Packers had made all the right plays to take the lead late in the game. Quarterback Brett Favre, who was sensational in throwing for 292 yards and two touchdowns, engineered an 89-yard scoring drive. The go-ahead touchdown came when the 49ers rushed eight. Favre audibled and hit Antonio Freeman for a 15-yard TD with 1:56 remaining.

On the 49ers' ensuing drive, Packers rookie safety Scott McGarrahan stripped wideout Jerry Rice of the ball, and Harris recovered. Officials ruled Rice down, though, and the drive continued. Replays proved the call incorrect, but because instant replay didn't begin until the following season, the 49ers kept the ball.

"That was clearly a fumble," Packers GM Ron Wolf told reporters afterward. "We clearly recovered. The game's over. It's tough to lose no matter how you do it. But when you make a play in a championship game and it's not awarded to you, there's something wrong with the whole system. It's something that has to be addressed."

Moments later the 49ers ran a play called "Three Jet Go," and Owens found the soft spot in Green Bay's coverage.

"When he made that catch, he almost lost [control of his emotions]," 49ers coach Steve Mariucci said. "He was frustrated because he dropped a couple passes. I told him to have a short memory, forget it."

The Packers—and their fans—certainly wish they could forget this ending.

76 Lindy Infante

Fans have short memories. They get giddy over the flavor of the day and are quick to forget the greatness of yesterday. Lindy Infante is certainly proof of that. After leading the Green Bay Packers to a 10–6 record in 1989—and falling short of the playoffs—Infante was voted as the best coach in team history, according to one poll. Better than Vince Lombardi. Better than Curly Lambeau. Better than them all.

Two years later Infante was out of work, having completed a 24–40 tenure in his four years as the Packers' head coach.

"The biggest thing is the fact the team could not win games," Packers general manager Ron Wolf said the day he fired Infante. "That's what I saw, an inability to win. I think the most important thing is that I have to feel comfortable in doing what I know how to do and who I can direct to do it with. I didn't particularly feel comfortable."

Back in February 1988 the Packers certainly felt comfortable with Infante. Green Bay had enjoyed just two winning seasons since 1972. And Infante—who had built a reputation as an offensive guru—was picked to reverse the Packers' dismal fortunes.

"I didn't take this job to be here two or three years and be a loser," said Infante, who signed a five-year contract when hired. "We'll work our tails off. We'll be a winner."

Aside from one memorable season, that never happened. The Packers were largely devoid of talent when Infante took over and went just 4–12 his first year. Green Bay was in position for the No. 1 overall draft pick late that season, but won its final two games. That meant Dallas moved up to No. 1 and took quarterback Troy Aikman, a future Hall of Fame player. The Packers picked No. 2 and made a colossal mistake in taking offensive tackle Tony Mandarich.

The following season, though, the Packers were the league's most improved outfit and finished 10–6. Much of it was done with smoke and mirrors, though, as six of those wins came by a total of nine points. Green Bay's signature win that season was a 14–13 victory over visiting Chicago that snapped an eight-game losing streak against the Bears. That contest, known to most as the "Instant Replay Game," saw the Packers rally back when Don Majkowski threw a 14-yard TD pass to Sterling Sharpe in the final seconds.

"I'm at a loss for words," Infante said after that game. "We may not be blessed with 10 or 15 Pro Bowlers at this point, but in 25 years of coaching I can't remember being more proud to be part of an organization and a group of guys as I was during that game.... [Beating the Bears] means a lot to me, but I think it means an awful lot more to our fans, who have suffered down through the years."

That off-season, the Packers gave Infante a contract extension through the 1994 season. And team president Bob Harlan later called it one of his greatest mistakes.

"We probably got a little bit too upbeat about things," Harlan said. "We had waited so long to win, and now we go 10–6, but four of those victories were by one point. So 10–6 could have easily been 6–10. So I probably got carried away, and I went to the executive committee and said, 'We've got to make sure we keep this guy. Let's extend him.' And then the next two years we went downhill. That was a big mistake."

The Packers slipped back to 6–10 in 1990 and 4–12 in 1991, in part because Majkowski was injured for large parts of both seasons. Late in that '91 campaign, Wolf was hired as Green Bay's general manager and realized quickly he wanted to go in a different direction. One day after the season ended, Wolf fired Infante and eventually replaced him with Mike Holmgren.

"It's not a pleasant thing to go through," said Infante, who later went 12–20 during a two-year stint as Indianapolis' head coach. "I gave my absolute best. I can live with that…. I'm not an excuse maker."

Nor was he a great coach—no matter what a certain poll may have said.

77 Tony Mandarich

Rich Campbell. Brent Fullwood. Vinnie Clark. Jamal Reynolds. Ahmad Carroll. Justin Harrell. These names will haunt Packer fans forever, all former No. 1 draft picks who busted like a bad blackjack player. But as awful as that collective group was, none can hold a candle to Tony Mandarich on the list of all-time flops.

Mandarich sits at the top of that list and ranks as one of the poorest draft picks in NFL history. The No. 2 overall pick in the 1989 draft, Mandarich played three forgettable seasons in Green Bay, then spent a fourth on the injured-reserve list before the Packers went in a different direction.

Tony Mandarich, shown backing off the line during a game against the L.A. Rams in his rookie season, was the Packers' top draft choice and No. 2 selection overall in that year's NFL Draft. Of the top five draft picks in 1989, he was not just the only player not to make the Pro Football Hall of Fame, but a complete bust in the NFL—after being the most hyped collegiate offensive lineman in history.

"When I'm called one of the biggest busts ever, I know it's the truth," Mandarich said. "The truth is the truth. It's nothing I don't already know."

Hype. Sizzle. Performance. Mandarich had it all when he left Michigan State with the promise of being a can't-miss left tackle for years to come.

"Tony was a product of his environment," said former Packers guard Ron Hallstrom. "He was the prototypical guy who knew how to sell a contract. It was the Brian Bosworth effect."

When Mandarich left MSU, many believed his combination of size and speed was something the NFL had never seen before. Widely regarded as the best offensive-line prospect ever, Mandarich measured 6'5", 315 pounds, and ran a 4.65-second 40-yard dash at the NFL scouting combine that year. Mandarich was roughly 25 pounds bigger than the average offensive lineman of his day. His speed was off the charts, and he bench-pressed more than 500 pounds. *Sports Illustrated* ran a cover story on Mandarich called "The Incredible Bulk."

After Dallas drafted future Hall of Fame QB Troy Aikman with the No. 1 overall pick that year, Green Bay took Mandarich at No. 2. The next three picks were running back Barry Sanders (Detroit), linebacker Derrick Thomas (Kansas City), and cornerback Deion Sanders (Atlanta). Those three players have all made the Hall of Fame, as well.

Mandarich, on the other hand, was a colossal flop.

"My problems had nothing at all to do with Green Bay," Mandarich said. "They had everything to do with me. I had a bad attitude. I was arrogant and extremely cocky. I look back at the situation, and I was lucky to go to a place like Green Bay with great fans and all that tradition. And I shot myself in the foot."

That wasn't the only place. In a 2008 interview with CBS Sports, Mandarich admitted that he was addicted to alcohol and painkillers the entire time he played for Green Bay. Mandarich also admitted that he used anabolic steroids at Michigan State, something that was largely suspected—but never proven—during his playing days.

"There's other factors that were involved that nobody knows about that were way more of an effect on why I had the huge downfall in Green Bay than steroids, [such as] drug and alcohol abuse," Mandarich said. "I was injecting a drug called Stadol…and it was euphoric. I went from doing one injection on that one day, and a week later I was doing between five to seven shots a day for the next three years. [I] was not the same person they drafted.... I got to the point where it was a struggle to work out three or four times a week because the priority of getting high was above the priority of working out."

That was apparent in Mandarich's on-field performance. Mandarich was a backup as a rookie and played just nine series. Then in 1990 he started all 16 games at right tackle and led the team in sacks allowed (12). Mandarich's play was slightly better in 1991, but he still allowed a team-high eight sacks. Mandarich suffered a severe concussion in the 1992 preseason, which left him with post-concussion syndrome and sidelined him the entire season.

By then, the Packers yelled, "No más!" and pulled the plug.

"To be candid, the Green Bay years were a bust," Mandarich said. "I think they were a disaster. I embarrassed the Green Bay Packer organization by my performance. I'm sorry for what I did in Green Bay."

Not as sorry as the Packers were for drafting him.

78 Ryan Longwell

Ryan Longwell could live to be 100, and every detail of September 7, 1997, will remain burned in his brain. Green Bay's then-rookie kicker had enjoyed a tremendous start to his professional career, making his first six kicks, including three that day at Philadelphia. With 15 seconds left that afternoon and the defending Super Bowl–champion Packers trailing 10–9, Longwell trotted out for what looked to be a chip-shot, 28-yard attempt.

Moments earlier, though, the football gods smiled on the host Eagles, and rain began pouring down. In a few short seconds, the turf at old Veterans Stadium became extremely slippery.

"I was running around to try the kick, and Brett [Favre] ran over to talk to me," Longwell said. "He said, 'Watch it. It's really slick out there.'"

Longwell quickly found out just how slick. As Longwell approached the ball, his plant foot slipped out from under him. That sent his body slightly out of whack, and he missed the kick wide right.

For an undrafted kicker who had made the team largely because third-round pick Brett Conway flopped, it was an extremely inauspicious beginning. And Longwell immediately wondered if he'd just kicked his last ball as a Green Bay Packer.

"There were only three rookies who made that team," Longwell recalled, "[Ross] Verba, [Darren] Sharper, and myself. It was a veteran-laden team, the defending world champs. There was talk of going 16–0 and repeating as Super Bowl champs, and as a rookie, we had to fit in. And when you miss that, certainly you didn't want to make a habit of it."

He didn't. While Longwell's flight home from Philadelphia was long that night, the rest of his Packers career was largely turbulence-free. Longwell led the Packers in scoring every year from 1997 to 2005, and he shattered the franchise's all-time scoring record with 1,054 points.

"I think he faced some adversity as a young player, which toughened his skin a little bit," said Rob Davis, who was Longwell's snapper for all but nine games. "He played with a certain amount of fear—not fear of an opponent, but fear to fail. And when you go out and approach your job like that, I don't care if it's flipping burgers or whatever, if a guy doesn't want to fail, most of the time he's not going to."

Longwell rarely did.

Despite kicking at Lambeau Field—one of football's toughest venues—Longwell was always one of the more accurate kickers in the NFL. He made 81.6 percent of his kicks as a Packer, which still stands as the best percentage in team history. Longwell also made 11 game-winning kicks, more than any Packer in history.

"He's so consistent that, if you watch him kick, whether it's an extra point or a 52-yard field goal, it's always the same swing," said John Bonamego, who was Longwell's special-teams coach from 2003 to 2005. "He has a really, really good understanding of how his ball's going to react to different situations, with wind and that type of thing. He knows what he has to do, and he's very, very accurate."

Much to the chagrin of Packer Nation, Longwell signed with the Minnesota Vikings in 2006 after Green Bay general manager Ted Thompson tried low-balling him. Still, Longwell gave the Packers nearly a decade of consistency and memorable moments. For example, he had an NFL-record four game-winning kicks in 2004, including a pair against Minnesota that helped the Packers steal the NFC North that season.

The 1997 NFC Championship Game in San Francisco was played in a driving rain and made kicking extremely difficult. But, on the final play of the first half, Longwell drilled a 43-yard field goal into a difficult wind to gave the Packers a 13–3 lead. Green Bay went on to win 23–10 to advance to Super Bowl XXXII, and Longwell still considers that the hardest kick he ever made as a Packer.

"I had to play a huge hook," Longwell said. "And it was at a point of the game right before halftime where it gave us a ton of momentum. That was a big kick."

But perhaps Longwell's biggest kicks came immediately after that 1997 miss in Philadelphia. The following week, Longwell went 3-for-3 against Miami, which put him back on track for a memorable ride in Green Bay.

"I think the key for me was always just staying as level-headed as possible," Longwell said. "There's a lot of guys who get real high and real low. I try not to get too excited after a long stretch of kicks or a game-winner, and I don't get too depressed over the misses, because you can't if you're going to be successful."

As the best kicker in Packers history, Longwell would know.

79 Mike Michalske

Mike Michalske never could make up his mind. One of the greatest performers in Green Bay Packers history, Michalske began his career wearing No. 19. Before his eight-year run in Titletown was over, Michalske also donned Nos. 4, 28, 30, 31, 33, 36, 40, and 63.

"He wore nine different numbers when he was here," Packers former historian Lee Remmel once quipped. "That's a record for most numbers in team history. The man liked change, I guess."

Those who could figure out who—and where—Michalske was saw one heck of a football player. Michalske, who played with the Packers from 1929 to 1935 and again in 1937, was one of the greatest two-way players in NFL history. First, he was a terrific offensive guard and became the first player from that position ever elected to the Hall of Fame. Although Michalske was just 6' and 210 pounds, he combined sensational speed and power to help clear the way for several standout Green Bay running backs.

The first three teams Michalske was part of—those from 1929 to 1931—all won NFL championships. And they did it thanks largely to a dynamic ground game. Michalske helped block for standout backs like Johnny "Blood" McNally and Bo Molenda.

And during the 41 games the Packers played in those three seasons, they outscored their foes 723–220.

In the other five seasons Michalske played for the Packers, they went 37–24–2, and he helped make running back Clarke Hinkle a star. That was only half the battle for Michalske, though. When Green Bay was on defense, Michalske would turn around and play defensive line. Michalske almost never left the field and was given the nickname "Iron Mike" for obvious reasons. Despite that heavy workload, Michalske missed just nine games during his Packers career.

Michalske was named All-Pro two times and received All-NFL honors after the 1931 and 1935 seasons. In 1964 Michalske received the ultimate honor when he was named to the Hall of Fame at one of the least glamorous positions on the field. Walt Kiesling and Dan Fortman were two-way performers from the pre-modern era who reached the Hall of Fame as guards. In football's modern era, there have been just eight offensive guards who reached the Hall. Clearly, Michalske was ahead of his time. And those who could figure out what number he was wearing witnessed one of the Packers' all-time greats.

80 Clay Matthews

Kevin Greene isn't ashamed to admit it.

He had a man crush. Immediately.

It was February, 2009, and Greene—the outside linebackers coach for the Green Bay Packers—was part of a group interviewing Clay Matthews at the NFL Scouting Combine. In many ways, Greene—one of the most dominant pass rushing linebackers of his time—felt he was looking in a mirror.

So when the meeting ended, Greene knew he'd do everything possible to convince his bosses to draft Matthews.

"When I spoke to him in Indy, I came away feeling that this man is on a mission to prove to everybody that he is a good athlete and a heck of a football player on his own," said Greene, who had 160 sacks during his 15-year career. "And I understand that hunger and that drive. That spoke volumes to me and that's what I loved.

"He was my No. 1 player at that spot, and I let it be known to all the powers that be. I said, 'This is the guy that I think you want.' Then they went and got him, which was even better."

Today, Greene and the entire Packer organization are reaping the benefits.

Matthews is off to one of the fastest starts in team history. Through four seasons, Matthews has compiled 42.5 sacks, which already has him in fifth place on the Packers' all-time list and second among linebackers behind only Tim Harris (55.0). Matthews has also gone to the Pro Bowl each of his first four seasons and has been a two-time All-Pro.

Matthews' career is off to a Hall of Fame start, and if he maintains his current pace, he'll certainly climb this list.

"Clay's got a combination of quickness and instincts," Packers defensive coordinator Dom Capers said of Matthews. "I think he's a very smart player. He has all the qualities that we look for in an outside linebacker because you can ask him to do many things."

Packers general manager Ted Thompson—one of the most conservative executives in the NFL—traded three draft picks to move into the first round and take Matthews with the 26th overall pick in 2009. That marked just the second time in Thompson's first five drafts that he moved up for a player.

After four seasons, Thompson's selection of Matthews rivals the drafting of quarterback Aaron Rodgers as his No. 1 move.

Matthews (6'3", 255) set a Packer rookie record with 10 sacks in 2009. He also became the first Green Bay rookie to reach the Pro Bowl since wide receiver James Lofton in 1978.

In 2010, Matthews had a career-best 13.5 sacks and finished second to Pittsburgh's Troy Polamalu in the Associated Press' Defensive Player of the Year voting. Matthews also had one of the biggest plays of Super Bowl XLV when he forced a fumble of Pittsburgh's Rashard Mendenhall that teammate Desmond Bishop recovered on the first play of the fourth quarter.

"I had a good feeling that play was going to come," Matthews said that night. "I told my defensive end to spin it for me and wrap it around the outside.... I got to make a play, and I did."

Matthews' sack total dipped to six in 2011. But he still finished with 38.5 quarterback knockdowns and hurries, which ranked fourth in football.

Then in 2012, Matthews posted 13 sacks in just 12 games. Matthews also had a whopping 48 pressures, and was rewarded with a five-year, $66 million contract extension in the offseason that made him football's highest-paid linebacker.

"Ted Thompson, when he hits the road during the regular season, he usually comes back on a Thursday or sometimes Friday morning and we have an opportunity to get together," Packers coach Mike McCarthy said. "When he returned from the USC workout that year, [Matthews] was the one player that he talked most about.

"He saw something in Clay. He was really excited about Clay Matthews. As the process went on leading up to the draft, it was no surprise where we had Clay Matthews ranked and when the opportunity presented itself that we stepped up and selected him."

Matthews certainly had genetics on his side. His father, Clay Jr., played 19 seasons with the Cleveland Browns and Atlanta Falcons. His uncle, Bruce, also played 19 years with the Houston Oilers/Tennessee Titans.

But that didn't lead to much early on.

Matthews was a walk-on at USC, earned a scholarship by his sophomore season, yet never started a game until his senior year. Matthews exploded in his final season, though, and scouts everywhere started taking notice.

Heart. Drive. Desire. Tenacity. Matthews had them all, and the Packers believed he could be an impact player, despite just one year of productivity.

"Hopefully what they saw was just how true I was and how passionate I am about wanting to be the best and wanting to be great," Matthews said. "I like to be that guy who makes plays, who's counted on, who the fans love, everything about this game. I want everything that this sport embodies."

Matthews has done all of that—and more—since arriving in Green Bay. Matthews has wowed teammates and foes with a motor that never dies, and he seems to get even more dangerous as games go along.

What makes Matthews so dynamic, though, is he isn't a one-trick pony. He can drop and cover tight ends. He's terrific in run support. And he almost never leaves the field.

Make no mistake, though, getting to quarterbacks is Matthews' calling card—and few do it better. What makes Matthews' success even more impressive is he's often beating double- and triple-teams on his way to opposing quarterbacks.

"I've been telling people since we drafted Clay that he's the perfect storm," Greene said. "He's the most complete outside linebacker I've ever seen. People are starting to believe me on that one.

"When we met with Clay, I was looking at more than 40-yard dash and all that. I was looking inside. I looked at his background. Being a former walk-on spoke to me...and I know what it takes to not have a scholarship, to work your way up to a starting role. You've got to have a lot of love in your heart and I put a lot of weight in that.

"I can relate to someone walking on, scratching and clawing for everything they can to finally seeing the field. So I can relate to where Clay has come from to get where he is now."

Greene holds the NFL's all-time record for sacks by a linebacker with 160. The way Matthews is going, though, that mark might not be safe.

"I haven't seen a lot of people come through like Clay," Greene said. "If anybody can do it, he can do it."

Matthews is just four seasons into his extremely promising career. But right now, there are no limits to what he's capable of.

"To think about 160 sacks is amazing, but it's something great to strive for," Matthews said. "I'm always striving for goals, whether it's getting to a Pro Bowl or chasing a sack record. Obviously, we're a little early...but as the same time I'm always trying to make my presence felt or etch my name in whatever history book there is.

"For Kevin to say that is a great compliment and he understands better than anyone that I'm pretty much a self-made man. I've had to fight and scratch and claw for everything I've gotten. You have to keep that same mindset like K.G. did his whole career. And I guess I'm off to a good start."

Good is a massive understatement. Packer Nation can't wait to see what's next.

81 Arnie Herber

Arnie Herber spent much of his youth around the Green Bay Packers. But the chances that he'd one day wear the green and gold certainly seemed remote. Amazingly, though, Herber bucked the odds and became one of the greatest Packers of all time—as well as the NFL's first-ever elite passer.

"Arnie Herber could throw the ball 80 yards," former teammate Harold Van Every said. "Greatest arm I've ever seen. The man was a terrific, terrific passer."

Herber, who played with the Packers from 1930 to 1940, was inducted into the Pro Football Hall of Fame in 1966 and became just the seventh quarterback in history to reach the Hall.

Herber always had a love affair with the Packers. He was born and raised in Green Bay and sold programs on game days during his youth. Herber was also a standout at Green Bay West High School, then played collegiately at the University of Wisconsin, and later Regis College.

When his playing days appeared over, Herber returned to Green Bay and became a handyman for the Packers. One day, Green Bay head coach Curly Lambeau offered Herber a tryout, and a star was born. Herber had extremely small hands, so instead of using the laces, he learned to palm the ball. That style certainly worked, and Herber became one of the league's more accurate and dynamic passers. Herber, who was technically a tailback, led the league in passing three times. He also helped the Packers win NFL titles in 1930, 1931, 1936, and 1939.

Herber was an All-Pro selection in 1932 after leading the NFL in touchdown passes (nine) and passing yards (639). He again led the league in those categories in 1934 (eight TDs, 799 yards). For the most part, though, the vertical passing game was a mystery back in the early 1930s, which limited Herber's attempts to throw the ball. But when the remarkable Don Hutson joined the strong-armed Herber in 1935, the league's first explosive quarterback-receiver duo had been formed.

Lambeau was miles ahead of his peers when it came to offensive formations and pass routes, and that allowed Herber and Hutson to enjoy terrific success. In Hutson's second game, he caught an

83-yard touchdown pass from Herber in a 7–0 Packers win. That game-winning pass traveled 66 yards in the air before Hutson caught it, according to Packers.com.

Another memorable game came later in that 1935 season, when Herber and the Packers rallied for a 17–14 win in Chicago. The Packers trailed 14–3 but battled back for a thrilling 17–14 win.

"The Bears kicked off after scoring, and Herber threw a long pass to Hutson for a touchdown," Chester Johnston, who played with Herber, told the *Milwaukee Journal Sentinel* during a 1996 interview. "We were still behind with about a minute to go, and the Bears fumbled [on the first play] after the kickoff.... Herber threw another pass [to Hutson], and we won the game. That was before television, and a lot of people had left when we were down by almost two touchdowns. We got back to the hotel, and people were saying they were sorry we had lost, and we said, 'What the hell are you talking about? We won the game!'"

Herber continued his winning ways, leading the Packers to the 1936 championship. That year, he again led the NFL with a career-high 1,239 passing yards and 11 TDs. Herber helped the Packers win the 1939 title, as well, when he threw for 1,107 yards and eight TDs. Among Herber's scoring strikes that year was a 92-yard TD pass to Hutson, which remains the fourth-longest TD pass in team history.

Herber still holds the Packers record for most years leading the NFL in passing (three). His 66 career touchdown passes also ranks fifth in team history. Not bad for a hometown hero who went from game-day employee to team handyman to star—and eventually the Hall of Fame.

82 Sterling Sharpe

Superstars are generally beloved figures. And there's no doubt Sterling Sharpe was a megastar, one of the best receivers the Green Bay Packers have ever had. But the last thing Sharpe and Packer Nation had was a love affair.

Part of it was because Sharpe chose to shut the fans out. He was aloof with autograph-seekers and stopped speaking to the local media after his rookie season. Part of it was that Sharpe threatened to skip the 1994 opener because he wanted a new contract. Although Sharpe was one of the most dynamic Packers on the field of the last generation, he was also one of the most enigmatic Packers off the field. So when his career ended prematurely due to a spinal injury during the 1994 season, few tears were shed internally or externally.

"I wish he had a better relationship with the folks in Green Bay, because Sterling should be beloved there," said ESPN's Mike Tirico, a close friend of Sharpe's and the host of *Monday Night Football.* "The guy was exceptional. He was willing to lay it on the line every game and every play. And I hope it's his productivity that's remembered there and not the other stuff."

In actuality, it will probably be a combination of both.

Sharpe, the Packers' first-round draft pick in 1988, was a five-time Pro Bowler and a five-time All-Pro selection. He led the NFL in receptions three times and led the league in touchdown catches twice. Sharpe led the Packers in receptions every year between 1988 and 1994 and ranks second on the team's all-time receiving list (595). Sharpe also has the top two seasons for receptions (112 in 1993 and 108 in 1992) in franchise history.

Those numbers were so gaudy that Sharpe was elected to the Packers Hall of Fame despite a somewhat short career.

"I'm extremely appreciative of the fact that all I had to do to achieve this honor was to play," Sharpe said the night he was inducted into the team's Hall. "I didn't have to kiss babies. I didn't have to campaign. All I had to do to achieve this honor was play. It's one of those things that you don't ask for, you don't wish for, you don't pray for, but it's really nice that people—however I got inducted into this—it's nice for people to appreciate the way you played, and this is one of the ways that they say they appreciated the way I played."

One reason that Sharpe wasn't fully beloved, though, was he never warmed to the fans who wanted to love him like a son. Stung by what he believed were unfair criticisms during his rookie year of

All-Pro receiver Sterling Sharpe scores on a 30-yard TD pass from Brett Favre in a game against the Buccaneers at Tampa Stadium on October 24, 1993. Sharpe had 10 catches for 147 yards and four touchdowns as the Packers won 37–14.

1988, Sharpe adopted a no-interview policy that he rarely strayed from. Was Sharpe overly sensitive? You be the judge.

Sharpe started all 16 games during his rookie season, set a Packers rookie record with 55 catches for 791 receiving yards. But his lone touchdown didn't come until Week 14, he made few impact plays and later admitted he played overweight.

"Sterling Sharpe has dropped way too many balls for a No. 1 draft choice," then–Green Bay general manager Tom Braatz said at midseason. "There isn't an excuse for Sharpe not to come in here and be an impact player."

That certainly was a far more stinging analysis of Sharpe's play than any newspaper account.

The *Milwaukee Journal* gave Sharpe a C grade and said, "Rarely made a big play and his drops were in double digits." The *Green Bay Press-Gazette* wrote, "Sharpe had one of the quietest 55-reception seasons imaginable. It took him 14 weeks to reach the end zone, one of the few times he did something exciting."

Still, Sharpe apparently felt those critiques were scathing enough to become mute. And those who know Sharpe say that's too bad.

"It's unfortunate because Sterling never showed his true personality with the fans and the media," said ESPN's Tom Jackson, a close friend of Sharpe's. "Everybody handles it the way they see fit. At that time and at that level, you can't guide someone like that where to go. But it's too bad because Sterling has a great sense of humor, is supremely confident, and is fun to be around, and the people in Green Bay probably never got to see that."

Instead, they saw a somewhat manipulative player in 1994. One day before the season-opener against Minnesota, Sharpe left the team, threatening not to play unless the Packers reworked his contract. The sides agreed to some adjustments in Sharpe's contract later that night, and Sharpe lined up and played the next day.

Still, the relationship with Sharpe, the Packers, and their fans was certainly strained.

"In all my years, I've never been through anything like that," said Bob Harlan, Green Bay's president at the time.

On the night Sharpe went into the Packers Hall of Fame, though, he insisted he had no regrets and wouldn't change a thing.

"When I came here, I wanted to be the best player that Tom Braatz and coach Lindy Infante spent their first-round draft pick on," Sharpe said. "Fans got a chance to see what I did on Sunday. They didn't know what kind of person I was. I'm not regrettable about that. I'm kind of happy about that because they got a chance to see a player, and they didn't get a chance to associate some of the things I may have done on or off the field, good or bad, whatever side of the fence you were on. I wanted to come here and play the best possible football I could. I think I did that. I can't answer if I cheated the fans. I was asked how I wanted to be remembered by fans. I honestly couldn't answer it."

83 Scooter McLean

Every poker game seems to have one. The guy who can't remember whether a full house beats a flush. The guy who knows he's in way over his head but just wants to be one of the fellas. Back in 1958 that guy in Green Bay was Ray "Scooter" McLean. The problem was that McLean was the Packers' head coach.

"Oh, man," Gary Knafelc, a receiver and tight end for the Packers, said of McLean. "Scooter would play poker with the players the night before the game. And what was worse is he wasn't even good at it. [Max] McGee would just take him to the cleaners."

McLean's players weren't the only ones. The rest of the NFL also took McLean—and the Packers—to the cleaners during his one miserable season as Green Bay's head coach. During that year, Green Bay went 1–10–1 before McLean resigned and was replaced by Vince Lombardi. McLean also went 0–2 in 1953 when he finished the year as the interim coach, and his 1–12–1 overall record is the worst in team history.

"He didn't exercise any authority, and we just had a disastrous season," Jim Temp, a Packers defensive end from 1957 to 1960, said of McLean. "The players just didn't have any respect for him." McLean was a standout two-way player for the Chicago Bears from 1940 to 1947. McLean scored 21 touchdowns on offense, intercepted 18 passed on defense, and had three punt returns for TDs. He became an assistant with the Packers in 1951 under Gene Ronzani. The Packers went just 11–22–1 over the next three seasons, though, as Ronzani was fired with two games left.

McLean and fellow assistant Hugh Devore finished the season as co–head coaches, and the Packers lost their final two games. McLean was hired as an assistant on Lisle Blackbourn's staff in 1954. But after four more bleak seasons that produced just a 17–31 mark, Blackbourn was fired.

On January 6, 1958, the 42-year-old McLean was named the fourth head coach in Packers history. It was a brief run, to say the least. McLean was trampled over by the team he was supposed to lead. He let the players decide how they should discipline themselves. He wanted to be their friend, not their boss. And, after starting the season 1–3–1, Green Bay finished the year on a seven-game losing streak.

"Scooter should not have been moved up," said Don McIlhenny, a Packers halfback from 1957 to 1959. "I remember in the last week of 1958, we were out on the West Coast, and we had just got our butts kicked. We had a team meeting, and one guy said, 'I got a problem.' Scooter started scratching his bald head and said, 'Take your problems to Jesus, son. Scooter's got problems of his own.'"

He sure did. At the end of the 1958 season, McLean resigned, and Lombardi was hired shortly thereafter.

Perhaps the only contribution of note that McLean made was moving the Packers to St. Norbert College during training camp. That tradition still exists today. Aside from that, though, McLean's résumé was far from stellar.

"There was always talent in Green Bay," said Tom Bettis, a Packers linebacker from 1955 to 1961. "Just not a lot of discipline."

Certainly not with McLean in charge.

84 Financial Woes

From a financial standpoint, these are salad days for the Green Bay Packers.

When the 2012 fiscal year ended, the Packers had $239 million in a reserve fund. The revenues during that fiscal year were $302 million and they had a net profit of $42.7 million.

And with the recent renovation of Lambeau Field, Green Bay is positioned to be one of the NFL's most prosperous franchises for years to come.

My, how times have changed. During the Packers' infancy, they had several financial scares.

Back in 1922 bad weather and poor attendance left the team in trouble. But local merchants raised $1,000 in the team's first stock offering, and Green Bay became a publicly owned corporation.

In 1934 a fan won a $5,000 verdict after falling from the stands and suing the Packers. After the insurance company went out of business, the Packers went into a receivership and appeared ready to fold. But more than $15,000 was raised in a stock drive, and Packers president Lee Joannes paid $6,000 to settle the case, then convinced the courts to end the receivership period.

When the 1949 season ended, Green Bay was in another financial crisis. A war between the NFL and the All-America Football Conference left the Packers so financially strapped they lost two of their three No. 1 draft picks to the AAFC between 1946 and 1948.

Stan Heath, the fifth overall selection in the 1949 NFL Draft, played one year in Green Bay for $15,000. Then that off-season, the Packers told Heath they could no longer afford him.

"It was just one of those deals where they weren't going to honor my contract," said Heath, who played running back. "They were having trouble financially and told me and some other players they couldn't honor the contract. There's no animosity on my part toward them. It was just one of those things. They were having a lot of problems, and they just couldn't pay everybody."

The Packers eventually worked their way out of financial ruin thanks to an old-timers' game on Thanksgiving Day in 1949 that raised $50,000. They also had a giant stock sale in 1950 that raised another $118,000.

"It was always a struggle early on," former Packers president Bob Harlan said. "For the most part, the team won a lot of games, but they had a really hard time staying afloat."

The Packers were like the Catholic church, though, and always found a way to get every nickel possible from their constituents. But what eventually allowed the organization to prosper financially was commissioner Bert Bell's push for a league-wide TV package.

By 1961 a deal was in place that allowed large-market and small-market teams to share revenue. And in 1966 commissioner Pete Rozelle signed the first NFL TV package with CBS and

NBC, which gave the Packers more than $1 million. Today the NFL's smallest city can prosper thanks to those enormous TV deals and revenue sharing.

The Packers also received a huge financial lift when Lambeau Field was renovated between 2001–03.

"With the stadium, we had to do it," said Harlan, who spearheaded a push for the stadium's renovation before leaving office at the end of 2007. "I really thought for a while, maybe we could delay it and maybe I wouldn't even have to be here when we got involved, that it would be after I was gone. But every time a team moved into a new stadium, we were falling further and further. We had to do something."

They always have—and have always been survivors.

85 Aaron Kampman

Marginal athlete. Limited ability. Lacks big-play capability. Aaron Kampman heard all the knocks during his early days in Green Bay. And all the Packers standout defensive end did was play winning football—play after play after play.

"You look at him, and you wouldn't think he'd be such a good football player," former teammate Grady Jackson said of Kampman. "But he is."

Between 2002 and 2009, Kampman had 54 sacks, which ranks fourth in team history. Kampman went to a pair of Pro Bowls in that time, led the NFC in sacks in 2006 (15.5), and was arguably the Packers' best defensive player of the decade.

"You can win a lot of games with a team full of Aaron Kampmans," Bob Sanders, who was Green Bay's defensive coordinator from 2006 to 2008, once said of Kampman. "He never quits. He's a tremendous worker, sets a great example for the rest of the team. Really, he's all you ask for as a coach."

Kampman was the poster boy for all of the NFL's underdogs. Despite a stellar career at the University of Iowa, NFL scouts were never sold on Kampman. He ran the 40-yard dash in a disappointing 4.87 seconds at the NFL Combine, making it questionable if he could succeed at defensive end. He also lacked ideal size (6'4", 284) to survive inside at defensive tackle. So it wasn't a great shock that Kampman was still on the board for the Packers to select in the fifth round of the 2002 draft.

"I was drafted and labeled the way I was labeled," Kampman said. "And that's just the way it goes. But I think I've proved to a lot of people that I definitely belong in this league and can play with anybody."

Kampman did that from the day he arrived in Green Bay.

Kampman got his chance to shine early when injuries sidelined players like Joe Johnson and Vonnie Holliday. By 2004 the Packers had committed to Kampman as a starting defensive end, and he made the organization look fantastically smart. Between 2006 and 2008, Kampman's 37 sacks were the third most in football. He sculpted his body and became a lean, yet powerful edge rusher. And he watched enough film to rival the late, great Roger Ebert.

"You can go down and down the list and find a lot of guys who are drafted late, then come here and want to prove to everybody that they can play," said wideout Donald Driver, a seventh-round draft pick himself. "And Kampman's one of those guys. I guess you can say he's hungry. He just goes out there and takes care of his business week in and week out."

Kampman, a man of great faith, became extremely involved in the Green Bay community. He also remained fantastically loyal to his roots and returned to Parkersburg, Iowa—the area where he grew up—and played a role in that town's cleanup after it was struck by an F5 tornado in 2008.

Through it all, Kampman played terrific football for the Packers. And even when the team moved him to outside linebacker in 2009, he was adjusting adequately before tearing his left ACL. Kampman went to Jacksonville the following offseason and was never the same player. But the Packers had no complaints about the eight seasons they got from Kampman.

"You know my mentality. I've always tried to work at things as hard as I possibly can," Kampman said. "You know my motivation. It can't be the external things. I mean, those are good things, but for me it comes down internally. That's what drives me, keeps me focused."

And what helped make him one of the top defenders in Packers history.

86 Ray Rhodes

The choice of Ray Rhodes to be the Green Bay Packers' 12th head coach stunned much of the NFL in 1999. Twelve months later, following an 8–8 season, Packers general manager Ron Wolf made an even bolder move and fired Rhodes just one year into a four-year contract. As a result, Rhodes joined Ray "Scooter" McLean (1958) as the only head coaches in Packers history to last just one season.

"Our players did not respond to this program," Wolf said the day he dismissed Rhodes. "It's not good enough with the team that we have. It's not acceptable."

The Packers had become one of the NFL's elite teams during Mike Holmgren's seven-year tenure (1992–1998). They won 67 percent of their games during that time, captured Super Bowl XXXI, and were runners up in Super Bowl XXXII.

When Holmgren left for Seattle after the 1998 season, Wolf made the surprising move of picking Rhodes. Rhodes had been Green Bay's defensive coordinator for two years under Holmgren, then was Philadelphia's head coach from 1995 to 1998. He went 29–34–1 with the Eagles and was fired following a 3–13 season in '98.

"The seat is going to be hot," said Rhodes, who became the first African American coach in Packers history. "The shoes are going to be big to fill. The key is to keep the machine running, keep the machine going. Make sure if you need a new tire here, or a new tire there, you put it on. But don't mess with the engine. Don't mess with it."

But the Packers often performed like a broken-down jalopy under Rhodes. Green Bay won three of its first four games that year, but needed dramatics from Brett Favre to do so each time. The Packers then dropped four of five and fell to 4–5 on the season. A three-game winning streak briefly restored hope before the Packers dropped three straight. That led to Green Bay missing the playoffs for the first time since 1992. The Packers' dominance of the 1990s was officially over, as they ended the decade with a miserable season.

"I make no excuses," Rhodes said after he was fired. "This is a business about getting things done, and I understand that. This was a tough year for a lot of our guys."

It wasn't just the win-loss record that prompted Wolf to make a coaching change. It was also a lack of discipline, fire, and intensity. After seven years of Holmgren's no-nonsense, dictatorial approach, Rhodes elected to loosen the reins with a veteran team. That approach blew up in his face. Many of the veterans still needed to be leaned on and took advantage of the softer standards. Several of the team's younger players also made serious mistakes, for which there didn't appear to be any repercussions.

Wolf also didn't sense any passion when he watched his team practice and later referred to the atmosphere as a "country club."

"You can get a pretty good pulse of the team at practice," Wolf said. "There was a different pulse in the latter part of the season. I think that [was] reflected in our play."

Rhodes, who had the reputation as a defensive guru, couldn't get that side of the ball fixed, and the Packers allowed their most points since 1990. In the end, it all added up to a fantastically frustrating year for all involved.

"With Holmgren, they would police you," former Packers safety LeRoy Butler said. "But with Ray Rhodes, you would police yourself. Every guy holds another guy accountable. So it's hard to tell a grown man to be in by 9:00 o'clock and guys took advantage of it. We were spoiled at the time and 8–8 wasn't good enough."

And neither was Rhodes.

87 Chuck Mercein

Packers fans never forget their own. Perhaps no one understands this better than Chuck Mercein. Mercein played in just 22 games for the Packers between 1967 and 1969. He had a paltry 105 rushing yards in that time. But as Mercein walks around Lambeau Field these days, you sense he could still run for mayor—and win handily.

Why? Because, during Green Bay's 21–17 win over Dallas in the 1967 NFL Championship Game—a game better known as the "Ice Bowl"—Mercein played an enormous role. While quarterback Bart Starr scored the game-winning touchdown, it was Mercein who put the Packers in position for victory.

Now, more than 40 years later, Packers fans remember it as if it were yesterday.

"People shouldn't forget what Chuck Mercein meant to us that day," Starr said. "We don't win that game, or we're certainly not in position to win that game, if it's not for Chuck Mercein."

Mercein, who was born in Milwaukee, joined the Packers midway through the 1967 season. But after posting just 56 rushing yards during the regular season, many fans had to grab a program to figure out just who Mercein was. By the end of the Ice Bowl, though, it was a different story.

On Green Bay's 12-play, 68-yard, game-winning drive, Mercein accounted for 34 of those yards and put the Packers in position for arguably the most memorable victory in franchise history. To this day, Mercein never has to break out his wallet when he's in the vicinity of Packers fans.

"It was just great to be placed in a position to make a contribution," Mercein said. "You always hope to be up to bat with the bases loaded and two outs. That's all I could have asked."

The only reason Mercein played that day was that starting fullback Jim Grabowski had reinjured his knee during pregame warm-ups. To this day, Mercein can't go more than a few days without being reminded of what transpired.

"The game has never gone far from my mind," Mercein said. "I still get fan mail nearly every week."

There's a good reason for that. Mercein and the offense took the field with 4:50 left on a day when the kickoff temperature was 13 below zero and the wind chill was minus-46. Their task? Try to erase a 17–14 deficit.

"I still remember [linebacker Ray] Nitschke walking off the field, yelling at the offense, 'Don't let me down,'" said Mercein, who was playing just his seventh game with the Packers that day. "Well, I sure wasn't going to be the one to let Nitschke down."

He didn't. Mercein got Green Bay's initial first down on the drive with a seven-yard run around right end. After the Packers drove to the Dallas 30-yard line with 1:35 remaining, Mercein made the biggest catch of his life. He had noticed during the drive that he was being uncovered in the left flat. Mercein then did something extremely rare, suggesting in the huddle that Starr look his way. Sure enough, Mercein was free. And on a day when throwing the ball was an adventure, Mercein made a terrific adjustment, hauled in the pass, and got out of bounds after a 19-yard gain to the Dallas 11.

"Nobody talked in that huddle except Bart," Mercein said of Starr, who called all the plays. "But I told him, 'I'm open in the left flat. Look for me if you need me.' It was a tough adjustment, but I had decent hands and made a big catch."

The Packers then ran a play called "Give 54" that looked like a variation of Green Bay's Power Sweep and was designed to take advantage of the aggressiveness of Cowboys Hall of Fame tackle Bob Lilly. Starr faked the sweep, and Lilly followed the guard, leaving a huge hole for Mercein, who rumbled to the 3-yard line.

"The 'Give' play was a great call by Bart," Mercein said. "Bob Lilly was sensing the sweep and ran down the line of scrimmage. [Left tackle] Bob Skoronski had a great block on the defensive end, and the play worked perfectly. I almost scored."

Mercein thought he'd get his chance to score after the Packers moved to the 1-yard line and took their final timeout with 16 seconds left. In the huddle, Starr called "35 Wedge," a play designed for Mercein to get the ball. But Starr worried that the icy conditions could lead to Mercein slipping. And without telling anyone, Starr decided to run a quarterback sneak. Mercein got a good start and didn't slip. And when Starr kept it, Mercein was momentarily stunned. But to this day, Mercein doesn't have a single regret with how the final play unfolded.

"It just goes to show you how smart Bart Starr is," said Mercein, who was on the cover of *Sports Illustrated* the following week. "The prudent thing to do was not take a chance that I would slip. He took all those potentially disastrous things out of the equation. There was no need to tell me I wasn't going to get the ball. I had chipped away some ice during the timeout, so I had pretty good footing. On the snap—hut one, hut two—I took off and, lo and behold, I'm not going to get the ball."

But Mercein didn't mind. He was just thrilled to be playing on the eventual Super Bowl champions, something that Packers fans have never forgotten. "Every minute, every second of that final drive, I can still remember it," said Mercein, who was out of football by 1970. "I remember it like it was yesterday. Going there and playing well was such a validation of my ability. I did what I was capable of doing and helped them win a world championship. It was one of the greatest experiences of my life. Those are moments that will never be forgotten."

88 Don Beebe

Don Beebe certainly wasn't expecting October 14, 1996, to be the greatest night of his professional life. As the Green Bay Packers' No. 3 receiver, Beebe came to Lambeau Field expecting to see the field on passing downs, have a few balls thrown his way, and possibly help the Packers topple the San Francisco 49ers on *Monday Night Football*. Beebe did all that—and a whole lot more.

"It was just one of those nights where I was touched by an angel," Beebe said.

It sure was. On the game's first play, starting split end Robert Books suffered a season-ending knee injury, and Beebe stepped into the spotlight. The diminutive speedster caught 11 passes for 220 yards and guided the Packers to a dramatic 23–20 overtime win over the 49ers. Beebe's 220 receiving yards still ranks third in Packers history, while his 11 catches are tied for fifth.

Considering what was at stake that night, Beebe's performance was even more impressive. Had Green Bay lost, the 49ers would have finished with the NFC's best record and earned home-field advantage throughout the playoffs. Instead, the Packers finished one game ahead of San Francisco, had the NFC's top record, and rode their home-field advantage all the way to a Super Bowl XXXI championship.

"When a guy goes down, you have somebody else who has to come in and play," said Beebe, who had been on the losing side of four Super Bowls with the Buffalo Bills earlier in his career. "And I had a lot of experience in the playoffs and big games with Buffalo, and it certainly helped me."

Nobody could ever have predicted how much Beebe would help the Packers on that critical night against the 49ers. Midway through the third quarter, Beebe dove and hauled in a 28-yard pass from quarterback Brett Favre. San Francisco cornerback Marquez Pope also went to the ground and presumably touched Beebe's knee when both players were down. The referees, though, didn't see the contact, and Beebe wasn't sure if he was touched or not. So when Beebe didn't hear a whistle, he sprang up and went the final 31 yards for a 59-yard touchdown. The play stood because there wasn't instant replay in the NFL yet.

"I was always taught to go until I heard the whistle, and I didn't hear a whistle," Beebe said. "It was a big play, but there were a lot of big plays in that game."

Beebe had his share of them, catching two passes as the Packers drove for a tying field goal late in regulation. Then in overtime,

Beebe had a huge 13-yard reception to set up the eventual game-winning field goal.

"This is a game that, honestly, I thought we had lost, and then I thought we had won it, and then I thought we had lost it again," Favre said. "The Bills gave up on [Beebe], I guess, but right away we could see that he still had great speed and an uncanny ability to get open and get the ball."

Beebe, who played collegiately at tiny Chadron State, always had blinding speed. In the six times he was timed in the 40-yard dash, he was clocked between 4.21 and 4.31 seconds. Beebe still had a lot left in the tank when he arrived in Green Bay. He finished the 1996 season with 39 catches for 699 yards and four TDs.

But his performance on that Monday night against the 49ers will be remembered by Packer Nation for generations. Beebe's monster night was a big reason the Packers later became Super Bowl champs for the first time in 29 years.

"Having been part of four Super Bowl losses, then getting a chance to win one, I think I'll always cherish that victory more than anybody else," Beebe said. "I think what I'll remember most is the camaraderie and the leadership we had that year. It was just a fantastic time."

89 Packers-Bengals

Kitrick Taylor played in 47 NFL games over six seasons. In that time, he had just one receiving touchdown. It's a pretty safe bet that the overwhelming majority of Green Bay Packers fans will never forget that touchdown. And, because of it, Taylor's name will always hold a special place in Packers lore.

It was September 20, 1992, and the Packers appeared dead in the water. Green Bay trailed visiting Cincinnati 23–17 in the closing moments and still was 35 yards from the end zone. With 19 seconds left in the game, reserve quarterback Brett Favre—in the game only because starter Don Majkowski was injured—called "All Go." It was a play where the three receivers all ran to the end zone.

The Packers lined up with Robert Brooks in the slot on the left, Sanjay Beach wide left, and Taylor wide right. Favre pump-faked in Taylor's direction and got cornerback Rod Jones to bite. Taylor streaked by Jones and had a good three yards of separation. Favre then fired a laser beam to Taylor that didn't get more than 12 feet off the ground. It was a good thing, too. Safety Fernandus Vinson was closing fast, and had their been more air under the ball, the Bengals safety would have likely broken up the pass.

Instead, Favre's bullet threaded the needle between the two Cincinnati defenders and landed right on Taylor's hands with 13 seconds showing. It was the only receiving TD of Taylor's career, and it gave the Packers a 24–23 win.

"When I got past the cornerback and saw the safety moving toward the middle to cover the tight end, I knew Brett would be coming my way," Taylor said. "I just told myself to make sure I caught the ball. After scoring, I just remember putting my arms up in the air in the end zone, and then people were all over me after that."

It's easy to see why. The win was the first in Mike Holmgren's tenure as Green Bay's coach. It also marked the start of Favre's magical run in Green Bay. Beginning the following week against Pittsburgh, Favre would make 253 straight regular-season starts as a Packer.

Taylor, who was no better than No. 4 on Green Bay's receiving depth chart, was in the game only because Sterling Sharpe suffered a rib injury earlier on the drive. "Kitrick made a very tough catch,"

Holmgren said of Taylor. "The pressure was on that young man to make that play. Kitrick has not had a lot of practice time and a lot of reps, but he made the big play."

Taylor was a Plan B free agent when he joined the Packers before the 1992 season. Despite his heroics that gorgeous September day, Taylor's stay in Green Bay didn't last long. He played in 10 games for the Packers that year and finished with just two catches for 63 yards. Late that year Taylor was released, then played briefly in Denver the next season before calling it a career.

"I'm just really proud to say I was part of that game," said Vince Workman, who was Green Bay's leading rusher that day. "That play really gave us an extra boost of confidence. It was our first victory, and it helped us start to believe in ourselves."

90 Fun Things to Do

There are certain absolute musts for Green Bay Packers fans everywhere. Here's a sampling of some of those:

Eat at Kroll's

Before Vince Lombardi, Bart Starr, and Brett Favre, there were Harry and Caroline Kroll. Who, you ask?

Back in 1931 the Krolls began serving food in a family hotel, food that became fantastically popular. By 1936 the Krolls had opened their first restaurant marketed around the wildly popular "Kroll's Hamburger." Today, Kroll's West remains a family-owned restaurant located right across the street from Lambeau Field. And no trip to Green Bay—or a Packers game—is complete without a visit to this local landmark.

"It's like Mardi Gras on football games," said Mike Wier, the owner of the popular restaurant. Kroll's will entertain roughly 2,500 people before an average home game. Wier said that number can climb to as many as 6,000 for a playoff game or a highly anticipated regular-season contest.

On a Packers Sunday, live bands kick off as early as 9:00 AM, and many tailgaters and partiers will then linger throughout the day.

"It's just a huge game-day party," Wier said. "We think it's a big part of the Packer experience."

Getting to this point wasn't easy, though. The Krolls opened their first restaurant on Main Street in Green Bay back in 1936. Shortly before World War II, Kroll's moved to a basement under the Labor Temple Auditorium. When customers kept coming to this remote location, though, the Krolls knew they had something big. Kroll's Downtown became a hotbed after the war. Then, with business booming, Kroll's moved to its current location in 1974 and has only grown in popularity since.

Interestingly, though, Caroline Kroll used to shut the restaurant down on game days because she didn't want the floors to get dirty. Instead, their only revenue those days came from parking cars in their lot. Wier, who married Kroll's granddaughter, Bobbie Van Der Perren, talked Kroll into opening the bar in 1975. Later they began selling sandwiches for $1 each. Eventually, Kroll's opened its restaurant, brought in bands, and grew one of the area's biggest spots for game-day parties.

"It's kind of funny, but for years and years, all we did was park cars," Wier said. "Caroline didn't think the restaurant could make a lot of money, but we put a band out front in the early '90s, started putting food out, too, and built our own bars and own food wagon. It's really evolved into a good time."

That it has.

Among the famous visitors have been Brett Favre, Reggie White, Santana Dotson, Don Hutson, Bart Starr, Larry McCarren,

John Madden, Lynn Dickey, Boyd Dowler, Fuzzy Thurston, Lee Remmel, Willie Wood, Herb Kohl, Al Gore, Rick Majerus, Lex Luger, Dick Schaap, Ray Nitschke, Johnnie Gray, George Karl, Mike Sherman, Max McGee, Paul Coffman, Jim Taylor, Tony Canadeo, and Gilbert Brown.

The original Kroll's hamburger remains a favorite today, as do several other menu items. But the greatest appeal is the fun and frivolity before all Packers home games.

"It's a great place to be," Wier said. "The people love it."

See a Game at Lambeau

The passion is unparalleled. The sightlines are sublime. The experience is unforgettable. And now there are 80,000 seats. If the Green Bay Packers are important to you, attending a game at Lambeau Field is one of those "bucket list" moments that will stay with you forever. Granted, tickets are tough to come by. But, like anything in life, if there's a will…

Tailgate with the Masses

There is some evidence that Packers fans began tailgating as early as 1923, when the team played at Bellevue Park. The practice took off when the Packers moved to City Stadium's larger parking lots in 1957 and is a way of life for most fans today.

Take a stroll through the Lambeau Field parking lots today, and you'll see old-school tailgating at its best. Brats. Burgers. Beers. Fans begin tailgating several hours before the game and continue well past the final gun. Healthy, they are not. Happy they most certainly are.

Get on the Season-Ticket Waiting List

Green Bay's waiting list for season tickets was roughly 105,000 at the start of the 2013 season. Those awarded tickets had put their names on the waiting list in the mid-1970s. Granted, if you put

Two Navy F-18 Hornets fly over the capacity crowd at Lambeau Field prior to a game against the New Orleans Saints on September 17, 2006.

your name on the list today, odds are you'll be long gone when your time for tickets arrives. But that doesn't take away from the excitement of moving up the list each year.

And if you don't eventually receive tickets, perhaps your children will. Or your children's children. Or your children's, children's, children. You get the idea.

Visit Fuzzy's

One of the more enjoyable places for Packers fans to eat and drink is Fuzzy's #63 Bar and Grill, owned by former Packers great Fred "Fuzzy" Thurston and located just a few miles west of Lambeau Field.

The bar includes pictures of countless former and current Packers. There are also themed license plates from the majority of the 50 states. Thurston and several other Packers are in the bar on home-game weekends. And Thurston often grabs the microphone at the end of the night to pay tribute to the Packers and their fans.

Go to the Broke Spoke

Sure, there are several Packers fans who have soured on legendary quarterback Brett Favre since his decision to suit up for Minnesota. But a trip to The Broke Spoke, a bar in Favre's hometown of Kiln, Mississippi, remains a thrill for those not bitter over Favre's departure.

The parking lot is mud. Fans carve their names into a plywood bar. And, at the entrance, there's a huge Confederate flag with the bar's name on it. Pretty it is not. But inside there's plenty of Packers paraphernalia to entertain and keep Green Bay fans coming back for more.

91 Tim Harris

Tim Harris didn't look the part of a sack machine. The 6'5" Harris weighed just 235 pounds. And his 40-yard dash time was a somewhat pedestrian 4.80 seconds. But Harris had a unique ability to get to quarterbacks, something he did time and time again during his five seasons as an outside linebacker in Green Bay.

Harris had 55 sacks in that stretch, which ranks third in team history. And his 19.5 sacks in 1989 remain a Packers single-season record.

"I take a lot of pride in that," Harris said in the same raspy voice he became known for. "Every time I got a sack, that was a good moment."

Harris had plenty of good moments in a Packers uniform.

Green Bay swapped first-round draft picks with Buffalo in 1985 so it could move up and grab tackle Ken Ruettgers with the seventh overall pick. To do so, the Packers gave up their second-round draft choice in '85, but got a fourth-rounder back in '86. They used that choice on Harris, a player many scouts were torn over. Harris didn't have the speed scouts wanted from outside linebackers, and he was too small to play defensive end.

For Green Bay, though, Harris was just what the doctor ordered. Harris fit perfectly at outside linebacker in coach Forrest Gregg's 3-4 defense. And Harris had a rare ability to get to the quarterback, so the Packers could turn him loose on passing downs.

"I wasn't that fast," Harris said. "But I played a lot faster than I timed. You get out of bed at 9:00 am and have to run a 40? That's hard to do. But I fit right into what Green Bay wanted to do on defense."

Harris led the Packers with eight sacks as a rookie and led the team his other four seasons, as well. Harris was downright dominant in the late 1980s, notching 13.5 sacks and a team-high 111 tackles in 1988. Then in 1989 he posted a franchise record 19.5 sacks and was named to the Pro Bowl. "They taught me how to play football in Green Bay," Harris said. "I liked it there. We didn't win enough, but I liked it."

Harris was also as vocal and demonstrative as any Packer player during his era.

He told offensive players he was coming for them, then delivered. He celebrated big plays by turning his hands into imaginary guns. He played with the youthful exuberance that escapes many players when they reach the sport's highest level.

"I wasn't a hot dog at all," Harris said. "But it was also my time to express myself and have a little fun when things went well. That probably didn't always sit the best with some of the teams we played against. But there was never any disrespect. I was just having fun."

Unfortunately for the Packers, Harris' fun in Green Bay was short-lived.

After the 1990 season, Harris' contract was up, and he and general manager Tom Braatz couldn't come to an agreement. Harris was asking for $900,000 per season, while Braatz wouldn't budge from $600,000.

"He was paying all these offensive linemen that much, the same guys I was whipping in practice every day," Harris said. "I thought I deserved that much." So Harris held out at the start of the 1991 campaign. Finally, after four games, Braatz had enough and dealt Harris to San Francisco for a pair of second-round picks. Ironically, one of those second-rounders was later dealt back to the 49ers for future coach Mike Holmgren. The other was used to move up and draft George Teague in 1993.

"Tom Braatz and I never could get along," Harris said. "I really didn't want to leave. But San Francisco wasn't a bad place. There wasn't any snow, and I got my Super Bowl ring."

That he did. Harris played the 1991 and 1992 seasons with San Francisco, then one year in Philadelphia before returning to the 49ers for two more years. That final trip back west proved a wise one, as San Francisco captured Super Bowl XXIX with a 49–26 rout of San Diego.

While Harris was thrilled how his career ended, he also knows his best—and most memorable—days came in Green Bay.

"Those were good days, man," Harris said. "I liked Green Bay, I really did. I just had to move on if I was going to get what I thought was fair money."

92 Ron Kramer

Ron Kramer doesn't regret his decision for one second. But, oh, how he wishes circumstances could have been different. The former Green Bay Packers standout tight end had the decision of a lifetime to make before the 1965 season. His son, Kurt, had lost an eye while playing with a pair of scissors. His daughter, Cassie, was terribly sick with allergies. And Kramer's family wouldn't come to Green Bay. So the former Packers great did what he believes any family man should do—return to his.

"I would love to have stayed my whole career in Green Bay," Kramer said before his death in 2010. "I loved all of my teammates…but I look at my children today, and I'm so proud of the decision I made.

"If I could have played in Green Bay all those years, I would have. But I made the decision that had to be made.

"It's not noble when it comes to your family. I had to make sure the kids would be okay. And even though the marriage didn't make it, the kids and I did."

Kramer, who played out his option after the 1964 campaign, returned to Detroit to be with his family and succeeded in getting traded to Detroit to be closer to home. Under the old Pete Rozelle Rule, the Packers were awarded a No. 1 draft choice, which they used to select fullback Jim Grabowski in 1966.

"Every time I see Grabowski, he kisses me and thanks me for letting him become part of two more championship teams," said Kramer, who played in Detroit from 1965 to 1967. "It was tough because my years in Detroit were awful. The head coach [Harry Gilmer] was the dumbest guy I ever met. People didn't come on time, and people didn't care. It was polar opposite of where

I came from. But I did what I had to, and Coach Lombardi was great. He said, 'I understand that you have to do what you feel is right. I can't replace you, but I'll understand whatever decision you make.'"

Kramer, who was inducted into the Packers Hall of Fame in 1975, was in the midst of a brilliant career with Green Bay at the time. The fourth overall pick of the 1957 draft out of Michigan, Kramer possessed a frightening combination of size, strength, and agility. He tore up his knee as a rookie, then spent the 1958 season as an officer in the Air Force. When he returned in 1959, though, his play skyrocketed at the same time Green Bay's did.

Between 1961 and 1964, Kramer caught 138 passes for 2,202 yards and 15 touchdowns. He was named All-Pro in both 1961 and 1962 and was named to the Pro Bowl in 1962.

In the 1961 NFL Championship Game, Kramer caught four passes for 80 yards and two touchdowns. That marked the first of five titles Green Bay would win under Lombardi between 1961 and 1967.

"He was the best coach ever, and I think few would question or argue that," Kramer said. "He always had you ready to go, mentally and physically. All you had to do was watch him and emulate him, and you'd be ready to play. Plus, he was just a tremendous teacher, very thorough. It was an honor to play for him."

Green Bay won titles in 1961, 1962, 1965, 1966, and 1967 under Lombardi, although most agree the 1962 team Kramer was part of was the best of them all. That group went 20–1 (including exhibition games) and again defeated the New York Giants for the NFL championship, 16–7.

"That team was incredible," said Kramer, who finished his career with 299 receptions for 3,272 yards and 16 touchdowns. "Everybody was in their prime, everybody had a great year."

About the only thing Kramer believes could have been better is if he'd have been able to finish his career in Green Bay, and instead of having two rings, he'd have five. But the choice Kramer made is one he's never looked back on.

"I'd go back and do it all over again," said Kramer, who had been living with Paul Hornung and Max McGee prior to leaving Green Bay. "I loved Green Bay, and nothing compares to the Green Bay experience anywhere. I would have loved to spend a little more time there, but I never regret what I did for a minute."

93 Packers-Seahawks

"We want the ball, and we're going to score."

These were the bold words of Seattle quarterback Matt Hasselbeck. His Seahawks had just won the coin toss to start overtime in a 2003 NFC wild-card playoff game in Green Bay. And Hasselbeck called his shot, one that was picked up by the referee's microphone and heard on the public-address system.

"I still can't believe he did that," Packers running back Ahman Green said during a 2009 interview.

Hasselbeck proceeded to throw the game-winning touchdown, all right. He just did so to Packers' cornerback Al Harris. Early in the overtime, Harris jumped in front of a Hasselbeck pass intended for wideout Alex Bannister. Fifty-two yards later, Harris was in the end zone, and Green Bay was celebrating a 33–27 victory that still qualifies as one of its most dramatic postseason wins ever.

"We hadn't pretty much got any work all day over there," said Harris, who had been obtained in a trade from the Philadelphia Eagles before the season. "I jumped a lot of routes. [Hasselbeck] made a lot of good reads because I jumped a lot of routes today, and he would look it off and go to the guy that was open. I was just praying that he would throw the ball, because I knew I was going to gamble on that play. As a DB, you pray that they will run that route—a hitch or a slant—something you can jump quick and get to where you have to go."

The two offenses had controlled this football game, which is one reason Hasselbeck felt so confident of victory when his team won the coin toss. With the game tied at 27, Seattle's red-hot offense faced a third-and-11 from its own 45. Green Bay defensive coordinator Ed Donatell, who had watched his unit get picked apart the entire second half, wanted a lot of pressure—and fast— to force Hasselbeck into a short throw. Donatell called for a blitz package titled "Thriller," and a record-setting crowd at Lambeau Field and Packers fans everywhere couldn't have picked a more perfect name.

Defensive linemen Kabeer Gbaja-Biamila, Cletidus Hunt, and Jamal Reynolds, along with linebackers Nick Barnett and Hannibal Navies, all rushed up the middle. Safety Darren Sharper blitzed off the left edge and safety Marques Anderson came off the right side, leaving only Mike McKenzie, Michael Hawthorne, Bhawoh Jue, and Harris in the back half. Seattle lined up with four wide receivers, and Hasselbeck took a three-step drop. He never took his eyes off of Bannister and let go of the ball in 1.09 seconds.

Green Bay anticipated Hasselbeck would have to throw something short and quick in the face of intense pressure, so Harris squatted on Bannister's route, then jumped it beautifully at the Green Bay 48-yard line. By the time Harris hit the Seahawks' 45-yard line, he had a hand in the air, knowing full well that the slow-footed Bannister wasn't going to catch him. Hasselbeck still had a shot and lunged for Harris at the 9-yard-line, but he just missed Harris' right foot, and the Packers were soon celebrating.

"That's what we spend a lot of time upstairs waiting for, these times," Donatell said of dialing up the all-out blitz. "And when the critical time comes for a player or a coach to step up and make a play or know that it's time to call that play, then it's time. It's that time. And our players delivered under pressure. They did what they were supposed to do when they were supposed to do it in a playoff environment. I think it's a big thing to build on."

Before the dramatic ending, Green Bay called timeout when it saw Seattle come out with a five-wide-receiver package—a look that had too many pass catchers for the "Thriller" defense to defend. When the Seahawks returned, they went to four receivers, and Green Bay stayed with its intended blitz scheme. Then Hasselbeck came to the line and audibled.

"It was a play that I thought was pretty safe," Seattle coach Mike Holmgren said. "Either Al Harris made a wonderful play or we did something just a little bit wrong, the depth of the route or something like that."

To this day, a giant picture of Harris' interception return hangs in the hallway outside the Packers' locker room, along with photos of other great moments in the team's history.

"I'm not exactly sure how it all went down," Hasselbeck, a one-time Packer, said afterward. "But knowing Al Harris, knowing the kind of player he is, he is a smart player. He takes chances sometimes."

This one paid off. Hasselbeck's bold prediction did not.

94 Gene Ronzani

It's been said that timing is everything. Gene Ronzani found that out the hard way. Ronzani became the second head coach in Green Bay Packers history in 1950, replacing Curly Lambeau, who had held the gig the previous 29 years. When Ronzani took over, the

Packers were devoid of talent. The team was barely staying afloat financially. Even Lambeau realized how bleak things were and bolted to become the head coach and vice president of the Chicago Cardinals.

"I loved Gene," said Babe Parilli, Green Bay's quarterback from 1952 to 1953 and again from 1957 to 1958. "I think Gene would have been great in today's game because the players loved him. We just didn't have any talent."

And it showed.

After consecutive 3–9 campaigns, Ronzani's Packers went 6–6 in 1952. But when the Packers opened the 1953 season at 2–7–1, Ronzani stepped down with two games left. His four-year mark of 14–31–1 yielded the second-worst winning percentage in team history (.311).

"He was pretty good," John Martinkovic, a defensive end from 1951 to 1956, said of Ronzani. "Most of us liked him. We just didn't have the talent other teams did."

Not all of his players felt that way.

"Ronzani was kind of a weird guy," said Billy Grimes, a Packers running back from 1950 to 1952. "One day you were his fair-haired boy, and the next day you were dirt. You never knew what to expect. He was difficult to understand."

Ronzani's former players described him as one of the most suspicious men you'd find—particularly when it came to the Chicago Bears. Ronzani had spent eight years playing under Bears coach George "Papa Bear" Halas from 1933 to 1938 and 1944 to 1945. So, when he came to Green Bay, Ronzani invented offensive formations such as the double-wing and the shotgun, as well as the umbrella defense to confuse Halas and the Bears.

"He was a nice fellow," fullback/kicker Fred Cone said of Ronzani. "But there was a lot of player movement back then, and he was highly suspicious that guys would take our offense back to Halas. So, during meetings, he'd hold up the plays on a big cardboard sheet.

And he'd only hold it up long enough for you to write down what your job was. His way of presenting things wasn't real good."

Martinkovic tells a similar story: "We would always practice at a baseball park [Joannes] near City Stadium," he recalled. "And Ronzani would always walk around that stadium and look to see if anyone was peeking and trying to watch our practice. It was pretty funny."

Ronzani had several major accomplishments of note during his time in Green Bay. First, he made green the primary color of the Packers' uniforms, discarding Lambeau's blue-and-gold color scheme.

"We are the 'Green' Bay Packers," Ronzani said at the time.

Second, he hired Jack Vainisi as a full-time talent scout. Vainisi later stocked the roster with six Hall of Fame players and countless other standouts that helped the Packers win five championships in the 1960s. Third, he signed Robert Mann, who became the first African American to play for the Packers. The move was widely criticized at the time.

The Packers never did enjoy much success against the hated Bears, or the rest of the NFL, under Ronzani. He went just 2–5–1 against Chicago before stepping away late in the 1953 season.

"We were kind of like a farm team of the Bears back then. Still, that was always the game," Grimes said. "[Halas] would send spies to Green Bay to watch us practice, so we'd set up trick stuff, then never use it in the games. We'd set up crazy things just to try and fool them. But that strategy never really worked."

Unfortunately, neither did the Ronzani regime.

95 Lisle Blackbourn

Lisle Blackbourn was Wisconsin through and through. Blackbourn grew up in tiny Lancaster and played collegiately at Lawrence University in Appleton, where he was an all-state player three times. He worked on the coaching staff at the University of Wisconsin, and he was the head coach at Marquette University.

So when Blackbourn was named the third coach in Green Bay Packers history in 1954, it was the ultimate "local boy makes good" story. Not so fast. Blackbourn lasted four seasons, compiled a bleak 17–31 record (.354), and never had a winning season.

"He was a good coach. His personality was a little peculiar," former Packers defensive end Jim Temp said of Blackbourn. "He was a little man and had trouble communicating with the players. He certainly didn't put the fear of God in you."

Green Bay's best season under Blackbourn came in 1955, when it went 6–6. He was around in 1957, when the Packers opened City Stadium with a 21–17 win over the Chicago Bears. But the Packers were just 3–9 that year, and Blackbourn resigned afterward.

"He was a very good coach who didn't get along with the executive committee," said Gary Knafelc, an end from 1954 to 1962. "I think he would have won if they would have allowed him to go along."

Not all former Packers players spoke as glowingly about Blackbourn as Knafelc. Some said Blackbourn was never true to his word and couldn't be trusted. Others knocked him for an inability to communicate. "The Lizard," is how former defensive end John Martinkovic described Blackbourn. "He was slimy. He talked with a forked tongue. He'd tell you something, then a half-hour later he'd say, 'Why'd you do it that way?' He was not well-liked.

Consequently, if you told him off, he'd get rid of you. And I told him off a few times."

Don McIlhenny, a Packers running back under Blackbourn, agreed with Martinkovic. "Blackbourn was a real impersonal guy," McIlhenny said. "There was no zip or anything."

There wasn't a lot of zip to Packers football at that time, either. There was still a lack of talent from issues earlier in the decade. And many never bought into what Blackbourn was selling.

Following Blackbourn's resignation, he remained a Packers scout and helped draft future standouts Bart Starr, Paul Hornung, and Ray Nitschke. Blackbourn also coached at Carroll College in 1958, and later returned to Marquette to coach the final two seasons that school had. Blackbourn even went the high school route, posting a 141–30–6 record during 22 years at Milwaukee Washington. Still, the Packers' job is the one Blackbourn would have loved to conquer. Instead, he's just another coach in the 1950s who tried—and failed—to reverse Green Bay's fortunes.

"He was a real sound fundamental coach," former fullback and kicker Fred Cone said of Blackbourn. "It's just that, when you don't have a lot of talent, there's not much you can do. That was our biggest problem."

96 2007 NFC Championship Game

In theory, Green Bay Packers fans don't have much to complain about. The Packers' 13 world championships are more than any team in football. And, of the three major sports, only the New York Yankees (27), Boston Celtics (17), and Minneapolis–Los Angeles Lakers (16) have more titles than the Packers.

A cold Brett Favre eyes the scoreboard during the 2007 NFC Championship Game against Michael Strahan (92) and the New York Giants. After a subpar second half, Favre threw a key interception on the second play of overtime to set the Giants up for a game-winning field goal. It would turn out to be Favre's last pass as a Packer.

Perhaps that's why some of the losses are so hard to forget. Take the 2007 NFC Championship Game, for instance. Green Bay entered the game a 7½-point favorite against the New York Giants, a team the Packers had already drilled 35–13 back in Week 2. But on the second-coldest night in Lambeau Field history and the third-coldest in NFL history, the visiting Giants handled the elements better than the hosts. And much to the chagrin of the record-setting 72,740 fans who shivered and shook through the night, the Giants toppled the Packers 23–20 in overtime.

"It's horrible. Just horrible," said Packers defensive tackle Ryan Pickett, who also had been a member of the St. Louis Rams when they lost Super Bowl XXXVI. "I've been through this before, and it's hard. Everybody's hurting. And it's a feeling you don't want to have again. It's brutal, just brutal."

Everything about the night was rough on Packer Nation, starting with the cold. Temperature at kickoff was –1 with a wind chill of –23. During the legendary Ice Bowl played on December 31, 1967, it was –13 at kickoff with a wind chill of –46. "It was cold," Giants quarterback Eli Manning said. "Me and Amani [Toomer] and Plaxico [Burress] came out about two hours before the game to do our warm-up, and we only got through about a quarter of it, and we said, 'Hey, we've got to go in.' My left hand was numb. My receivers, they didn't have any hand-warmers, they were done."

But the Giants handled the conditions far better than the Packers did. New York outgained Green Bay 380–264 and held the ball for 18 minutes longer than the Packers. Burress was one of the Giants' stars, abusing Packers cornerback Al Harris throughout. Burress finished with 11 catches for 154 yards and did almost all of his damage against the overmatched Harris.

"We watched film all week, and just watching everything that he did…we just pretty much played to his weaknesses tonight," Burress said of Harris. "[He] played a bump-and-run, and we took advantage of it."

The Packers' 38-year-old quarterback Brett Favre also struggled immensely in the miserable conditions. After posting a 104.6 passer rating in the first half and leading the Packers to a 10–6 advantage, the cold seemed to have a huge effect on Favre. His passer rating was an anemic 52.9 after halftime. But it's the final pass Favre threw that Packers fans will never forget.

Green Bay won the toss in overtime, but on just its second play, Favre's pass for Donald Driver was intercepted by Giants cornerback Corey Webster. Driver ran a 15-yard out pattern, and Favre's throw needed to be to the outside, but he missed badly and floated a ball to the inside, where Webster was able to make an easy interception. That wound up being the last pass Favre ever threw for the Packers.

"I just didn't throw it outside enough," Favre said of the final pass. "It was what we call a shake route. Donald had slipped him more like an out route, which was fine. I just didn't get it out far enough. It's too bad."

Four plays later, Giants kicker Lawrence Tynes—who had missed two kicks earlier, including a 36-yarder to end regulation—drilled a game-winning 47-yard field goal.

Two weeks later, the Giants stunned the previously undefeated New England Patriots and won Super Bowl XLII. And the Packers were left wondering, *What if?*

"We did not take advantage of the opportunities that we had," Packers coach Mike McCarthy said. "When you don't execute at the level that you're capable of executing with the things that you practice every day, that's what is disappointing. We did not play our best football in a time when we needed to play our best football."

And they suffered a loss that will haunt their fans for years to come.

97 2009 Playoffs

This was Aaron Rodgers' chance to play hero. A chance to put some of the Brett Favre talk to rest for good. Making his first-ever postseason start, Rodgers was terrific in helping the Packers erase a 21-point deficit and force overtime at Arizona. But on what became the final play of Green Bay's 2009 season, Rodgers fumbled, and the Cardinals' Karlos Dansby returned the loose ball 17 yards for a 51–45 Arizona win.

To say this NFC wild-card game was wild would be a gigantic understatement.

"That's probably one of the best games ever played in the play-offs," Cardinals coach Ken Whisenhunt said afterward. Certainly one of the most entertaining. The teams combined for 1,024 yards of total offense, including 531 from the Cardinals. Arizona quarterback Kurt Warner threw for more touchdowns (five) than incompletions (four), hitting on 29 of 33 passes for 379 yards. Rodgers threw for a Packers playoff record 423 yards, completing 28 of 42 balls and hurling four touchdowns. So having the game end with a defensive score was certainly unexpected, considering it was the highest-scoring postseason contest in league history.

"I should have held on to the ball," Rodgers said. "I was looking at the front side for [Donald Driver]. It looked like he was getting grabbed a bit. Then I was looking for James [Jones], and they were driving in on him as he was running a little in cut, so I kind of pulled the ball back, and someone hit my arm."

That someone was 5'8" cornerback Michael Adams, who had been picked on by Rodgers and the Packers throughout the game. But on the final play of Green Bay's 2009 campaign, Rodgers had 3.5 seconds to throw before the blitzing Adams got home. Adams knocked the ball loose; it went off of Rodgers' foot and caromed to Dansby, who raced home with the winning score. Adams clearly grabbed Rodgers' face mask on the play, but no call was made.

"The way the game ended, you don't want it to come down to an officiating call," Packers coach Mike McCarthy said. "Nobody wants that. You want it to be about player productivity. There was a lot of productivity in that football game, especially from an offensive standpoint." That's for sure, as the two teams provided fans everywhere with one of the more entertaining playoff games of all-time.

Warner worked his magic throughout and helped stake the Cardinals to a 31–10 lead. Green Bay, which entered the game ranked No. 2 in total defense, was gashed by both Warner and the Cardinals' ground game (156 yards).

But the Packers, thanks to a gutsy onside-kick call by McCarthy in the third quarter, worked their way back into the game. Rodgers threw four second-half touchdown passes and led the Packers on seven straight scoring drives—six of them for touchdowns. Finally, when he hit tight end Spencer Havner for an 11-yard TD with 1:52 left, Green Bay had pulled even at 45.

"It was a little uncharacteristic the way we started the game," McCarthy said. "That is disappointing, but I had no doubt in my mind that we'd fight back and win the football game."

Green Bay dodged a bullet when Arizona's Neil Rackers missed a 34-yard field goal to end regulation. And the Packers seemed to be in great shape when they won the coin toss to start overtime. But Rodgers' fatal flaw throughout his career has been holding onto the ball too long. This time, it was extremely costly.

"This is just going to make myself and these guys want it that much more," Rodgers said after the loss to Arizona. "It might not look like we came that close, but we still feel like we were close to achieving all the goals we set forth at the beginning of the season."

98 Willie Buchanon

The 1970s were a bleak time in the NFL's smallest city. The Green Bay Packers had just two winning seasons. They played in just one playoff game. And the Packers had a miserable .413 winning percentage.

One bright light, though, was Willie Buchanon. The Packers drafted Buchanon with the seventh overall pick in 1972. And he was arguably the organization's best cornerback between that time and Charles Woodson's arrival in 2006.

"Unbelievable football player," said Johnnie Gray, Buchanon's former teammate. "Willie had amazing football gifts. There wasn't anything he couldn't do."

It didn't take long for Buchanon to start displaying that, either. Buchanon (6', 180 pounds) won the starting left cornerback job in his first training camp and tied for the team lead with four interceptions that year. Buchanon was named NFL Defensive Rookie of the Year by the Associated Press and NFC Defensive Rookie of the Year by Newspaper Enterprise Association that year.

But more important, the Packers were winning.

Little did Buchanon know Green Bay's NFC Central Division championship that year would be the last the Packers would see until 1995. And the playoff appearance—which ended in a 16–3 loss to Washington—would be the Packers' last until 1982.

"That was the year," Buchanon said of 1972. "We had a good combination of players who came in, and we really shored up the secondary. It was also a year where I learned a lot about football. [Running back] MacArthur Lane was my mentor, and he taught me a lot about the politics of football, how to adjust, and always be ready that someone could be waiting to take your job."

Buchanon didn't have to worry about that much. Although the Packers went in the tank under Dan Devine and later Bart Starr, Buchanon continued to play at a high level. He had a terrific combination of size and speed. And if Buchanon ever got his hands on a ball, odds are he was catching it.

Buchanon fought through injuries in the 1973 and 1975 seasons. But when he was on the field, Buchanon and the Green Bay secondary were excelling. The group of Buchanon, Mike P. McCoy, Steve Luke, and Gray—which started together in 1977 and 1978—nicknamed themselves "SWAT." Luke was the *S*, Buchanon the *W*, Gray the *A* for his nickname "Abdul," and McCoy the *T* for his nickname "Tasmanian Devil."

"Steve Luke came up with the acronym, and we had fun with it," Buchanon said. "Our safeties were big hitters, and we were pretty good corners. And anytime we needed a big play or to make something happen, we'd yell, 'SWAT!'"

Buchanon made plenty happen in 1978, which would be his last season in Green Bay. Buchanon and the Packers couldn't agree on contract terms, so he was in the process of playing out his option and auditioning himself around the league. And what an audition it was.

Buchanon finished the year with nine interceptions, which remains tied for second on Green Bay's single-season list, and he was voted to his third Pro Bowl as a Packer. Buchanon's signature game came in Week 4 that season, when he intercepted four passes in a 24–3 win over his hometown San Diego Chargers. The four picks in a game remain a Green Bay record, and ironically, they came against the team Buchanon would eventually be traded to.

"I didn't want to leave Green Bay," Buchanon said. "I just wanted them to pay me the salary I deserved. And it was too bad, because the difference ended up being $25,000."

Instead of paying Buchanon, the Packers traded him to the Chargers that off-season for a first-round draft choice that became George Cumby, and a seventh-rounder they used on Rich Wingo. Buchanon, meanwhile, joined one of the most prolific offensive teams in league history, one that featured Dan Fouts, Charlie Joiner, and Kellen Winslow. Buchanon stayed with the Chargers four seasons and participated in what many consider the greatest game ever played.

In the 1981 AFC divisional playoffs, the Chargers defeated Miami 41–38 in overtime when the Dolphins rallied from a 24–0 deficit. The Chargers scored late to force overtime, then won it in the extra session.

"That was the greatest football game ever played," said Buchanon, whose team lost the following week in Cincinnati in the AFC Championship Game. "I've never been more tired in my life. After the game, everybody sat there for at least a half an hour. No one showered, no one moved. We couldn't. The humidity and the intensity of that game were unbelievable. I still think about that game all the time."

Much like he thinks about his years in Green Bay.

"My time in Green Bay was a lot of fun," said Buchanon, who was inducted into the Packers Hall of Fame in 1993. "Seven great years and a lot of great friends. I'll always be loyal to that organization."

99 Merry Christmas!

It's doubtful many of the Green Bay Packers can remember what they got for Christmas in 1995. Maybe another tie from their kids. Perhaps an account for that crazy new invention sweeping the country called the Internet. Or if they were really good, possibly a trip, jewelry, or even a new vehicle. It's just as certain, though, that no Packer will ever forget the gift they received at Lambeau Field that Christmas Eve.

With Pittsburgh's Yancey Thigpen playing Santa, the Steelers receiver delivered Green Bay its first NFC Central championship in 23 years. Thigpen dropped a certain touchdown pass from Neil O'Donnell on fourth-and-goal with just 11 seconds left. Thigpen's gaffe allowed the Packers to escape with a thrilling 24–19 victory and capture their first division title since 1972 with an 11–5 record.

To this day, the Packers should still be sending Christmas cards Thigpen's way.

"I dropped it," Thigpen said afterward. "I had it, but my knee came up and knocked it out. It's not something I can dwell on. Merry Christmas to Green Bay. That's my present."

One the Packers were thrilled to receive.

Pittsburgh faced a fourth-and-goal from the Green Bay 6-yard line with 16 seconds left. After calling their last timeout, the Steelers lined up five wide receivers. Green Bay rushed four and dropped seven..Thigpen, who caught 85 balls that year and was named to the Pro Bowl, left Green Bay dime cornerback Lenny McGill five yards in his tracks on a slant route in the left corner of the north end zone. O'Donnell's pass was thrown perfectly, and after holding it for a split second, the ball slipped from Thigpen's fingers, went off his right thigh pad, and fell to the ground.

Merry Christmas.

"When a play like that happens, you don't try to figure it out," Packers coach Mike Holmgren said afterward. "You just go, 'Thank you.'"

Several Packers were trying to figure out their good fortune, though, and could only attribute it to one thing: divine intervention. And they don't mean Dan Devine.

"I think God had something to do with it," McGill said. "It was a catchable ball."

Added cornerback Doug Evans, "The guy upstairs did it for us. And we'll take it any way we can."

Reggie White, Green Bay's most outspoken member when it came to spiritual topics, had a surprisingly different opinion. "He just dropped it," said White, who had credited God in two other instances that season when he made it back from injury. "I can't say God knocked it out of his hands."

The thrilling finish capped a wild contest in which the Packers won for the sixth time in seven games and snapped the Steelers' eight-game winning streak. Behind a pair of Brett Favre touchdown passes and a nine-yard Edgar Bennett touchdown run, Green Bay

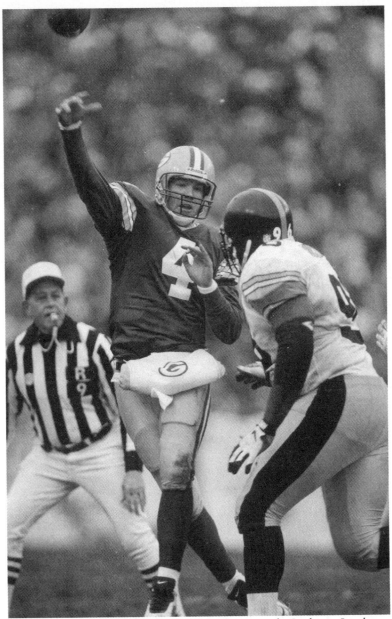

Brett Favre fires a pass during the season finale against the Steelers at Lambeau Field on Christmas Eve 1995. The Packers needed a win for an NFC Central title, and thanks to Pittsburgh's generosity, Green Bay held on for a 24–19 win.

built a 24–13 lead just 90 seconds into the fourth quarter. It was far from easy, though, as Favre was suffering a beating in which Kevin Greene knocked him woozy, and another hit near the goal line left him spitting up blood. "Never in my life have I spit up blood that bad," Favre said.

The scintillating finish eased his pain, though. Pittsburgh, playing without its top three running backs, drove 67 yards and got a two-yard TD from Tim Lester to make it 24–19 with 5:11 left. Then, after a Green Bay drive died on the Steelers' 40, Pittsburgh had one final chance. O'Donnell engineered a 19-play, 79-yard march in which the Steelers converted a pair of fourth downs.

The second fourth-down conversion gave the Steelers a first-and-goal at the Green Bay 5 with 28 ticks left.

"Your back literally is against the wall," Holmgren said. "You have to make four plays in a row." Which is just what the Packers did, with a little help from the Steelers. After O'Donnell spiked the ball on first down, he overthrew an open Thigpen on second down.

The Steelers ran a quarterback draw with Kordell Stewart on third down, but LeRoy Butler sniffed it out and dumped Stewart for a one-yard loss. That set the stage for one of the most memorable plays in Packers history, and one of the biggest gifts the Green Bay organization was ever given.

"I know the people here have been waiting a lot longer than I have, but it seems like an eternity," Favre said of winning the division. "I think we earned it. It's a great feeling."

Incredibly, the two teams almost met again that same season. Pittsburgh rolled through the American Football Conference playoffs and reached the Super Bowl for the fifth time in franchise history. Green Bay would go on to defeat Atlanta and San Francisco in the postseason, before losing to Dallas in the NFC Championship Game.

But the Christmas Eve Miracle was undoubtedly a springboard for many of Green Bay's future successes, which included a Super Bowl championship the following season.

"To have come so close…" general manager Ron Wolf said afterward, shaking his head. "But we didn't lose. Eleven wins, it's a huge number. A lot of things were said at the beginning of the year about how lousy we'd be. Well, everybody will have a Merry Christmas."

They did, thanks to Thigpen's generosity.

100 Bob Skoronski

The Marx Brothers had Zeppo. The Fab Five had Ray Jackson. Led Zeppelin had John Paul Jones.

Every great group always seems to have an anonymous member. And the fantastic Green Bay Packers' offensive lines of the 1960s were no different. While players such as Jerry Kramer, Forrest Gregg, Jim Ringo, Fuzzy Thurston, and Ken Bowman received much of the attention, steady, reliable, and durable left tackle Bob Skoronski was about as dependable as they came. And even though he didn't get the glory, Skoronski was as vital as any other member of the line.

"The coaches used to grade out every performance we had, and I'll tell you what, I slept pretty well at night," said Skoronski, who was named to the Modern Era All-Time Packers Team. "The line didn't operate with four guys, and we used to run important plays everywhere, not just to one side or the other. I don't think any player ever thought anyone was better than anyone else. And in my own way, I'm very satisfied with my career."

Football is something Skoronski most certainly loved, and doing it for one of the most storied teams of all-time was even more special. The Packers drafted Skoronski in the fifth round out of Indiana in 1956, and after starting most of that year, he had to fill a two-year ROTC commitment. When he returned for the 1959 season, new coach Vince Lombardi was waiting. And it took Skoronski about three seconds to realize that things would never be the same again. "If I could put one word on it, it would be *discipline*," he said. "Discipline in our study. Discipline in the execution. Discipline in how we prepared. There was a chain around us all the time. Plus, [Lombardi] got us in the kind of physical shape that, when the game was decided in the fourth quarter, we were in shape to do it. He brought an attitude about winning and a professionalism that we lacked, and if you weren't prepared for every play, it was a calamity."

What began to happen was a complete reversal of fortune that saw Green Bay win five NFL championships between 1961 and 1967. And Skoronski was in the middle of it throughout. It took Skoronski just a few games to replace Norm Masters at left tackle after he returned in 1959, and he remained there throughout the 1963 season. When the Packers sent Ringo to Philadelphia in 1964, Skoronski was shifted to center for a time before Bowman was ready. "They called me down and asked me to snap the ball," Skoronski recalled. "I did it maybe eight or 10 times, and they said, 'Okay. We've seen enough.' Well, the next thing I know, they trade Ringo, and I'm the center. I had no idea what they had been up to."

Skoronski certainly knew what was happening on the field, though. After Bowman was ready to take the reins at center, Skoronski moved back to left tackle, where he started through the 1968 season—his final one in the league. He was a punishing run blocker and received some recognition when he was voted to the Pro Bowl by the coaches in 1966. He was also named to the Packers Hall of Fame in 1976. Like many of his linemates, Skoronski will